Mixed Fortunes

'In *Mixed Fortunes* Vladimir Popov has provided a remarkably original and provocative analysis of economic growth and institutional change across the world but particularly in China, Russia, and the West. While most conventional interpretations have seen this process as a consequence of either enhancing or stifling the power of market forces, Popov stresses the differing roles of the state in building institutional capacity as the major explanatory variable. This book can be read profitably by both specialists and laymen interested in the past, present, and future of the world economy.'

Ronald Findlay, Ragnar Nurkse Professor of Economics Emeritus, Columbia University

'Filled with fresh thinking on the factors behind economic development, Popov's analysis cuts through old orthodoxies and offers a host of new insights. This is the best study yet of why the last two decades have been marked by stunning economic success in China, and frustrating failures in Russia. Blending attention to institutions and capital accumulation with analyses of the social order as shown in murder rates and income inequality, Popov demonstrates how promoting economic growth requires custom fitting of policies to a country's stage of development, political institutions, and historical legacies. This book, in non-technical terms, points the way to a new and more productive approach to economic development.'

Jack A. Goldstone, Hazel Professor of Public Policy, George Mason University

'In a wide historical sweep, Vladimir Popov charts the rise of the West after the first Industrial Revolution, the apparently successful but ultimately failed development challenge launched by the Soviet model, and the current rise of China. He emphasizes the role of indigenous institutions in fostering economic growth and the failure of imported models. It is a powerful indictment of development economics as practiced during the last couple of decades. There are few economists better equipped than Popov to handle these large issues of rise and fall of economic powers.'

Branko Milanovic, author of *The Haves and the Have-Nots:*
A Brief and Idiosyncratic History of Global Inequality, Basic Books

'A big, bold book that provides a unified framework for explaining why some countries and regions get ahead economically while others fall behind. Popov shows how inequality, institutions, saving rates all matter – but sometimes in surprising and unexpected ways.'

Dani Rodrik, Institute for Advanced Study

'Challenging conventional wisdom, Vladimir Popov offers a rare perspective on the economic development challenges of our times by bringing together his profound understanding of economic history, development theory, and 'post-communist' transition. Offering a nuanced statist developmental view of capitalist transformation and accumulation, he provides rich comparative insights into the interaction and sequencing of various key elements accelerating or retarding and sustaining growth and economic transformation.'

Jomo Kwame Sundaram, FAO Assistant Director General for Economic and Social Development; UN Assistant Secretary General for Economic Development, 2005–2012.

Mixed Fortunes

An Economic History of China, Russia, and the West

Vladimir Popov

OXFORD
UNIVERSITY PRESS

OXFORD
UNIVERSITY PRESS

Great Clarendon Street, Oxford, OX2 6DP,
United Kingdom

Oxford University Press is a department of the University of Oxford.
It furthers the University's objective of excellence in research, scholarship,
and education by publishing worldwide. Oxford is a registered trade mark of
Oxford University Press in the UK and in certain other countries

First Edition published in 2014

Impression: 1

Published in the United States of America by Oxford University Press
198 Madison Avenue, New York, NY 10016, United States of America

British Library Cataloguing in Publication Data

Data available

Library of Congress Control Number: 2013947871

ISBN 978–0–19–870363–1

As printed and bound by
CPI Group (UK) Ltd, Croydon, CR0 4YY

Table of Contents

List of Figures

List of Schemes

List of Tables

Introduction*

Among many puzzles in economic history, the most crucial and intriguing is the 'Great Divergence', the gap in productivity and per capita income between Western and developing countries that started to emerge from the sixteenth century and widened until at least the mid twentieth century. The USSR in the 1920s–60s was the first major non-Western country to experience successful catch-up development and to narrow the gap with the West, although afterwards (1970–1980s) the gap stopped narrowing, and later (1990s) widened. Japan, South Korea, Taiwan, Hong Kong, and Singapore in the 1950–1980s were the only developing states that successfully caught up with the West and became developed. In recent decades, a similar process has been underway in Southeast Asia and China. Together with the recent acceleration of growth of India and some other developing countries, this could mean that we have reached a tipping point in the Great Divergence and that from now on the world will gradually experience global convergence in the level of income.

The goal of this book is to provide a non-technical interpretation of the 'Great Divergence' and 'Great Convergence' stories—the widening of the gap in 1500–1950 and the narrowing of this gap afterwards. The usual explanation is that countries that we now call developed, or the West, acquired in the sixteenth century and beyond some features that were absent in more traditional societies. The list of these features ranges from abolition of serfdom and protestant ethics to protection of property rights and free universities. The problem with this reasoning is that it is assumed that these features emerged initially only in Northwestern Europe and only in the sixteenth–eighteenth centuries. However, in fact, there were many countries before the sixteenth century with social structures that possessed, or were conducive to, many of these same features, but they never experienced productivity growth comparable to that which started in Britain and the Netherlands in the sixteenth century, and later in the rest of Europe (0.2–0.3% a year in 1500–1800 and 1% and more a year afterwards).

* The opinions expressed herein are strictly personal and do not necessarily reflect the position of organizations with which the author is associated.

After reviewing the existing explanations in the literature, I present a different interpretation. Western countries exited the Malthusian trap by dismantling traditional collectivist institutions: this was associated with increased income inequality and even decreased life expectancy, but allowed the redistribution of income in favour of savings and investment at the expense of consumption. The elimination of collectivist (community) institutions was a risky experiment that put masses of population below the subsistence minimum and caused a reduction or slowdown of growth of the population, the foundation of the military might (number of people—number of soldiers) in the Malthusian growth regime.

'A great civilization is not conquered from without until it has destroyed itself within'—said Will Durant about the Roman Empire (Durant, 1980), but apparently this diagnosis could explain the collapse of many ambitious civilizations. Early attempts to ensure the priority of the rights of individual over the rights of the community at the expense of collective interests and low inequality (Greece, Rome, Byzantium) led to the impoverishment of the masses, higher mortality, and foreign conquest. Only in Northwest Europe in the sixteenth to eighteenth centuries did this policy somehow succeed for the first time in history.

It is not the abundance of competition or entrepreneurship or ideas for technological innovations that allowed the West to accelerate the growth rates of productivity by an order of magnitude; it is first and foremost the abundance of savings and investment that resulted from growing income inequalities and allowed an increase in the capital/labour ratio and the casting in metal of ideas for new products and technologies. To put it differently, the West became rich not due to its inventiveness and entrepreneurial spirit, but due to the cruel and merciless dismantling of community that previously provided social guarantees to the poorest.

When the same pattern was applied to developing countries (colonialism—Latin America—LA, Sub-Saharan Africa—SSA, or voluntary Westernization in an attempt to catch up—Russian Empire), it resulted in the destruction of traditional institutions, an increase in income inequality, and the worsening of starting positions for catch-up development. This group of countries replicated the Western exit from the Malthusian trap—they experienced an immediate increase in income differentiation, and a rise in savings and investment and in the growth of productivity, but at a price of rising social inequality and deterioration of institutional capacities.[1]

---

[1] The notion of state institutional capacity is discussed later in the book. It is understood as the ability of the state to enforce rules and regulations and is measured by such objective indicators as crime rate, murder rate, and the share of shadow economy. The weakening of the institutional capacity during the dismantling of collectivist institutions and increase in income inequalities

Other developing countries (East Asia, South Asia, and Middle East and North Africa—MENA) were less affected by colonialism and managed to retain their traditional institutions. This delayed their transition to modern economic growth (Kuznets, 1966) until the mid twentieth century, but allowed them to preserve a good starting position for economic growth—low inequality and strong institutions. Eventually, slow technical progress allowed them to find another (and less painful) exit from the Malthusian trap—increased income permitted a rise in the share of savings and investment in GDP without a major increase in income inequality, without worsening of institutional capacity, and without a decrease in life expectancy.

More Westernized countries of the global South (LA and the Russian Empire) raised their savings–investment rate and exited the Malthusian trap earlier than the rest, in the eighteenth century, but at a price of undermining necessary conditions for future growth—low inequalities and strong institutions. So LA and Russian growth subsequently was not enough to catch up with the West. Colonization of SSA (except for South Africa), unlike colonization of LA and Westernization of Russia, did not result in any considerable transfer of technology and human capital, but only increased inequalities and undermined institutions. So SSA countries were disadvantaged on all counts and had the worst growth record in the world. On the contrary, most of the less Westernized countries of East and South Asia and MENA managed to preserve low inequality and efficient collectivist institutions. Their savings–investment ratios stayed at a level below 10% until the mid twentieth century, so they did not grow before that, but once saving increased it turned out that they had all the preconditions for fast growth. Some of them became economic miracles, rapidly catching up with the West (East Asia), others have sped up their development in recent decades (South Asia), while others (MENA countries) could probably become economic miracles in the future.

To have a closer look at the two trajectories of catch-up development of non-Western countries, I examine in greater detail the differences in institutional and economic development of China and Russia in the long term—the period of socialism and before—and in the short term (since market-type reforms). The roots of the impressive long-term performance of China lie in the exceptional continuity of the Chinese civilization—the oldest in the world, which managed to preserve its uniqueness and traditions without major interruptions. It is argued that institutional continuity (East Asia, South Asia, and MENA) is more conducive to growth than attempts to replace existing institutions with allegedly more advanced institutions imported from abroad (Latin America, Russian Empire, and SSA). Like Russia in 1917,

---

results from the polarization of the society which is not contained by the community already and is not yet contained by the state.

China re-established collectivist institutions in 1949 as a response to the failure of Westernization. Unlike Russia after 1991, China in 1979–2013 managed to preserve 'Asian values' institutions that are based on the priority of community interests over the interests of the individual. However, the rapid increase in income inequality since 1985 could be a factor leading to a weakening of collectivist institutions, which is the single most important threat to the continuation of fast economic growth.

Socialism in Russia and in China contributed to the restoration of the collectivist institutions—income inequalities decreased and the institutional capacity of the state improved. But, as argued in this book, the centrally planned economy (CPE) could be viable only for 25–30 years because CPEs can make new investment, but cannot replace retiring fixed capital stock efficiently; and because without democracy the leadership lacks control from below. Once physical capital and human capital start to retire, problems emerge and dynamism is lost. In China, 30 years of socialism were allegedly enough to return the country to the trajectory of strong collectivist institutions. In Russia, the CPE and bureaucratic apparatus started to malfunction in the 1960s, but even another three decades of socialism proved to be not enough to return the country to a strong institutional trajectory: once market reforms were carried out in the 1990s, inequalities increased greatly, as did corruption, crime, and the shadow economy.

Whether we try to explain differences in Chinese and Russian economic performance under central planning (China in 1949–79 and Russia in 1917/29–91) or more recently, since the start of market reforms in China (1979) and Russia (1989), various trajectories of institutional development turn out to be the crucial factor. This is not to say that these trajectories totally pre-determine all economic outcomes; other factors, including good and bad policies, certainly do play a role. But, as the saying goes, there is nothing more endogenous than the government policy—it is not easy to have good policies with bad institutions. In practice, there are only so many historical junctions where there is a chance to change policies and to move to a different trajectory of institutional development.

This analysis allows the formulation of the main arguments about the implications of China's rise for the world. Usually these implications are seen in terms of forthcoming geopolitical shifts (China as a new rising superpower, together with, or instead of, the USA), in emerging shortage of resources leading to a new increase of raw material prices, and so on. But there may be less-expected and more far-reaching consequences as well.

First, the rise of China, if it continues, may become the turning point for the world economy because, for the first time in history, a successful economic development on a major scale is based on an indigenous, not Western-type, economic model. Because the Chinese growth model was so successful in ensuring catch-up development, it is no surprise that it is extremely appealing to the developing world. The attractiveness of the Chinese model of economic growth today could be compared with the popularity of the Soviet model of catch-up development in the 'third world' in the 1960s. Even though the Soviet model collapsed, the Chinese model became the logical and natural heir of the Soviet model—it is no longer a centrally planned economy, but it is by no means the model of a liberalized market economy that is recommended by the advocates of Washington and even post-Washington consensus.

Second, the rise of China could lead to the profound reform of world economic order and international relations. Trade protectionism, industrial policy, undervaluation of the exchange rate via accumulation of foreign exchange reserves (also, as argued later, a variety of export-oriented industrial policy), control over the international capital flows (not only short-term, but FDI as well) can become legitimate tools of catch-up development. There may be new regimes of protection of intellectual property rights and technology transfers, new regulations for international trade in energy and resources, new rules for international migration, new agreements about cutting emissions of pollutants (reconsideration of Kyoto protocol), and so on (Montes and Popov, 2011).

In addition, the principles of international relations could change radically as well. The 'Beijing consensus' may not yet be a rigorous term (Ramo, 2004), but it is clear that the Chinese approach to international politics (no interference in domestic affairs, no military interventions, no trade embargoes) provides the developing world with a real alternative of building relations with other countries. China rejects the use of force, embargoes, and sanctions in international politics nearly as a matter of principle. Even in its relations with Taiwan, China always pushed for wider economic and cultural exchanges, while Taiwan authorities resisted. The new rules of the international relations may (1) explicitly limit the use of force to cases of severe violations of non-political rights (i.e. mass repressions, hunger, ethnic violence, etc.) and prohibit the use of force against liberal authoritarian regimes (just for the sake of 'establishing democracy') and (2) prohibit unilateral military interventions (without the consent of the UN).

These 'less-expected' consequences of China's rise are probably already creating more favourable conditions for catch-up development in the South. The result may be the bridging of the gap between the world rich and the world poor, the West and developing countries. Overall, this gap was expanding between 1500–1900, reaching 6:1 ratio in terms of per capita GDP, and it was not closing in the twentieth century—in 2000 the ratio of per capita GDP in the West and in the developing world was still 6:1. Even in the last two decades of the twentieth century this gap was in fact widening for all developing countries as a group, if China is excluded (Wade, 2004). Now, in the twenty-first century, the rise of China could make the dirigisme-based model of catch-up development not only attractive, but also legitimate, and might create a new international economic climate favouring such a catch up. We may well witness 'the triumphal march' of the Chinese model in the South. Not all developing countries have the same institutional capacity as China—the necessary component of the successful non-Western growth model—but many do and those who do not will eventually be compelled to move in the direction of limiting inequality and strengthening institutional capacity.

There could be far-reaching implications for development economics as well. Development thinking of the second half of the twentieth century can hardly be credited for 'manufacturing' development success stories. It is difficult, if not impossible, to claim that either the early structuralist models of the Big Push, the financing gap and basic needs, or the later neo-liberal ideas of the Washington consensus that dominated the field from the 1980s, have provided crucial inputs to economic miracles in East Asia or elsewhere. On the contrary, it appears that development ideas, either misinterpreted or not, contributed to a number of development failures. The USSR and Latin America of the 1960s–1980s demonstrated the inadequacy of the import-substitution model (the debt crisis of the 1980s in Latin America and dead end of the Soviet-type economic model in the 1970s–1980s). Later, every region of the developing world that became the experimental ground for Washington consensus-type theories, from Latin America to Sub-Saharan Africa, to the former Soviet Union and Eastern Europe, revealed the flaws of the neo-liberal doctrine by experiencing a slowdown, a recession, or even a severe depression in the 1980s–1990s.

The policy of multilateral institutions—GATT/WTO, IMF, WB—might have been coherent in its own way: in different periods it was based on a relatively coherent, even though not necessarily the same, set of economic theories (Toye, 2009). But this policy, as well as development theories, cannot be held responsible for engineering development successes, let alone economic miracles. Japan, Hong Kong and Taiwan, Singapore and South Korea, Southeast Asia and China achieved high growth rates without much advice and credit from IMF and the WB (and in case of Hong Kong, Taiwan, and China—without being members of GATT/WTO for a long time).

Economic miracles were manufactured in East Asia without much reliance on development thinking and theoretical background—just by experimentation of strong-hand politicians. The 1993 World Development Report 'East Asian Miracle' admitted that non-selective industrial policy aimed at providing a better business environment (education, infrastructure, coordination, etc.) can promote growth, but the issue is still controversial. Structuralists claim that industrial policy in East Asia was about much more than creating a better business environment (that it was actually picking up the winners), whereas neo-liberals believe that liberalization and deregulation should be largely credited for the success.

It is said that failure is always an orphan, whereas success has many parents. No wonder both neo-classical and structuralist economists claim that the East Asian success stories prove what they were saying all along; but it is obvious that both schools of thought cannot be right at the same time.

Why did there emerge a gap between development thinking and development practice? Why were development successes engineered without development theories, whereas development theoreticians failed to learn from real successes and failures in the global South? It appears that development thinking in the postwar period went through a full evolutionary cycle—from the dirigiste theories of Big Push, financing gap, and import-substitution industrialization (ISI) of the 1950–1970s, to the neo-liberal deregulation wisdom of the 'Washington consensus' (1980–1990s), to the understanding that catch-up development does not happen by itself in a free market environment—but with a lack of understanding about what particular kind of government intervention is needed for manufacturing fast growth (2000 onwards).

The confusion in the development thinking of the past decade may be a starting point for the formation of new paradigm. There is an emerging understanding that without mobilization of domestic savings and industrial policies there may be no successful catch-up development. National Development Strategies (NDS, 2008) for countries at a lower level of development should not copy economic policies used by developed countries; in fact, it has been shown more than once that Western countries themselves did not use the liberal policies that they advocate today for less-developed countries when they were at similar stages of development (Chang, 2002; Reinert, 2007; Findlay and O'Rourke, 2007).

This general principle—that good policies are context dependent and there is no universal set of policy prescriptions for all countries at all stages of development—is definitely shared by most development economists. But when it comes to particular policies, there is no consensus. The future of development economics may be a theory, explaining why at particular stages of development (depending on per capita GDP, institutional capacity, human capital, resource abundance, etc.) one set of policies (tariff protectionism, accumulation of reserves, control over capital flows, nationalization of resource enterprises—to name a few areas) is superior to another (Polterovich and Popov, 2006). The art of policymakers, then, is to switch the gears at the appropriate time to avoid getting into the development trap. The art of the development theoretician is to fill the cells of 'periodic table of economic policies', prescribing particular policies at different stages of development.

The emerging theory of stages of development will hopefully put the pieces of our knowledge together and reveal the interaction and subordination of growth ingredients. The successful export-oriented growth model à la East Asian tigers seems to include, but is not limited to:

- Building strong state institutions capable of delivering public goods (law and order, education, infrastructure, health care) needed for development.
- Mobilization of domestic savings for increased investment.
- Gradual market-type reforms if the starting point was a non-market economy.
- Export-oriented industrial policy, including such tools as tariff protectionism and subsidies.
- Appropriate macroeconomic policy—not only in the traditional sense (prudent, but not excessively restrictive fiscal and monetary policy), but also a growth oriented exchange rate policy: undervaluation of the exchange rate via rapid accumulation of foreign exchange reserves.

If this interpretation of development experience is correct, the next large regions of successful catch-up development will be the MENA Islamic countries and South Asia—these regions seem to be most prepared to accept the Chinese model. But, eventually, Latin America, Sub-Saharan Africa and Russia will catch up as well. If so, it will also become obvious in the process of successful catch-up development that the previous policies that the West recommended and prescribed to the South (deregulation, downsizing the state, privatization, free trade, and capital movements) were in fact hindering, rather than promoting, their development.

1

How the West Became Rich: Stylized Facts and Literature Review

Before 1500, countries that are now called 'the West' were no more developed than the rest. All countries had roughly the same GDP per capita (about $500 in 1990 prices) and similar life expectancy, consumption, and literacy levels (Mel'yantsev, 2006; Maddison, 2008). Even more so, during the Tang dynasty (seventh–tenth century), Chinese per capita income was probably 20–30% higher than the European; this kind of 'paradox' is known in the literature as the Needham puzzle—from the name of Joseph Needham, the author of a multivolume study of science and civilization in China since ancient times (Needham, 1954–2004).

From the sixteenth century, the West started to grow faster than 'the rest' by one or even two orders of magnitude, so that by 1900 the gap between the groups of countries that are now called developed and developing increased to 6:1. In 2000, the gap was roughly the same. Although in the second half of the twentieth century several developing countries/territories (Japan, South Korea, Taiwan, Singapore, and Hong Kong) managed to join the 'rich club', while others (Southeast Asia, China, and, more recently, India) succeeded in considerably bridging the gap with rich countries, other regions (Sub-Saharan Africa, Latin America, Eastern Europe, and FSU) fell behind or failed to reduce the gap with the West (Fig. 1.1).

Productivity growth in Western Europe in the first millennium was not only absent, but was in fact negative. In most countries, according to Maddison (2008), there was no increase in per capita GDP, whereas in Italy it actually fell by about 50%—from $809 in the 1 AD to 450 in 1000 AD. The next 500 years saw a slow recovery to the income levels achieved in the Roman Empire—per capita GDP grew by 0.13% a year and nearly doubled. Since 1500, however, in the Netherlands and then in Britain, growth of per capita income accelerated to 0.25–0.6% a year and in the nineteenth–twentieth century growth in Western Europe and the USA increased to 1–2% a year (Table 1.1).

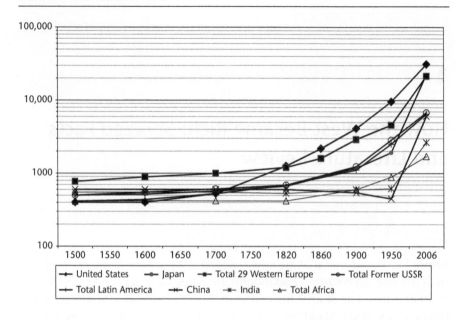

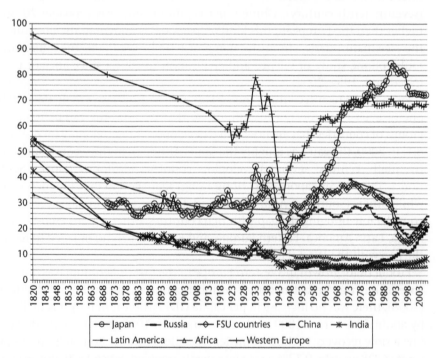

Figure 1.1. PPP GDP per capita in major countries and regions since 1500, international Geary–Khamis dollars of 1990

Source: Maddison, 2008.

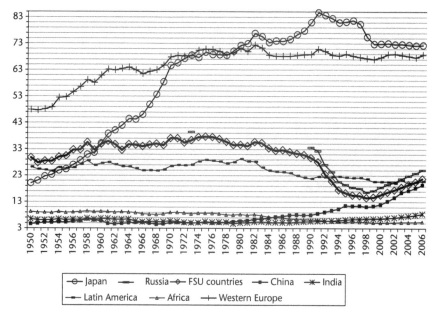

Figure 1.1. Continued

Table 1.1. Per capita GDP growth rates, percent

Countries/ periods	1–1000	1000–1500	1500–1600	1600–1700	1700–1820	1820–1900	1900–2000
The Netherlands	0	0.12	0.60	0.43	−0.12	0.78	1.89
United Kingdom	0	0.12	0.31	0.25	0.26	1.22	1.52
Italy	−0.06	0.18	0	0	0.01	0.59	2.38
Total 12 Western Europe	−0.03	0.13	0.13	0.13	0.16	1.14	1.89
USA	0	0	0	0.28	0.73	1.49	1.96

Source: Maddison, 2008.

This transition to modern economic growth after millennia of stagnation and centuries of slowly creeping forward productivity was a truly ground-breaking event in human history. To understand the magnitude of change: with 0.1% annual growth it takes nearly 700 years to double the initial level, with 0.5% annual growth it takes nearly 140 years, with 1% annual growth— 70 years, with 2%—35 years.

Due to this rapid growth of Western Europe and its 'offshoots' (Australia, Canada, New Zealand, USA) there soon emerged a gap between the two worlds—the developed and developing countries. Latin America, MENA

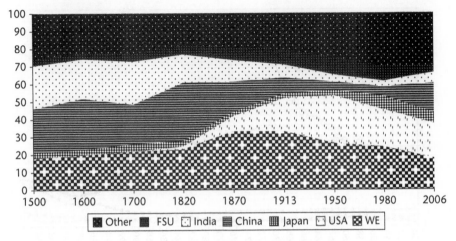

Figure 1.2. Share of major countries in world PPP GDP, 1500–2006
Source: Maddison, 2008.

countries, Japan, Eastern Europe, and former Soviet Union countries did not really start to grow until the beginning of the nineteenth century, whereas East and South Asia and Sub-Saharan Africa entered the growth race only after the Second World War (Fig. 1.1, 1.2).

These estimates are based on rather primitive sets of data on incomes and prices from various historical periods and in various countries. Even today, the purchasing power parity ratios computed within the framework of International Comparisons Program are being revised in such a way that per capita income changes not by 20–30%, but sometimes by more than twice,[1] not to speak of estimates for earlier historical periods.

Nevertheless, the most general trends can hardly be questioned. First, for several thousand years before 1500, space (geographical) and time (historical) differences in per capita incomes were not large—20–30% between continents

[1] In 1996 per capita GDP in China amounted to 79% of Russian level ($3330 and $4190) according to PPPs of 1993 (World Bank, 1997). But, according to PPPs of 2005, the same Chinese GDP per capita of 1996 amounted to 30% of the Russian level ($1667 and $5529 respectively). The PPPs of 2005 are considered most reliable—they are based on the information on prices in many cities of China. Some Chinese specialists, however, believe that regional offices of National Bureau of Statistics were intentionally choosing the most expensive Chinese goods for comparison (so that PPP of yuan is understated and China remains a 'poor developing country'). Low estimates of the Chinese per capita GDP do not conform well with the very high growth rates—if today's per capita GDP is interpolated into the 1950s by dividing it by accumulated growth figures, it would turn out that over half of the Chinese population in the 1950s was below subsistence minimum and should have died out. Estimates of PPP per capita income in China in 2006 by A. Maddison are two times higher than that of the World Bank. See for details: Karamurzov and Friedman, 2011a, 2011b; Maddison, 2005. A. Subramanian, who previously worked in the IMF research department, believes that IMF understated total Chinese GDP by 40%, which most probably means that China surpassed the USA in terms of total GDP back in 2010 (Subramanian, 2011).

and about 50% between countries in extreme cases. Second, from 1500, the West started to grow faster than the South and the gap in per capita income constantly increased until 1950, when it almost reached the level of 10:1. Third, from 1950, many developing countries—mostly in East Asia and later in South Asia—started to grow faster than the West, so that even though other developing countries did not experience accelerated development, the gap in per capita incomes between the West and all Southern countries started to narrow. One could safely claim that most economists and statisticians would agree with such a description of the stylized facts. How to interpret these trends?

Two conventional explanations

The oldest and most crucial question in economic history about the nature and causes of the wealth of nations—why particular countries grow faster and become wealthier than others—remains largely controversial. There were and are at least two traditions in dealing with this question.[2] One emphasizes the evolutionary nature of historical progress and the logic of social development, whereas the other focuses primarily on the mere coincidence of events and the play of fortune, attributing successes and failures of development to existing geographical conditions or historical accidents.

According to the first, evolutionary, school of thought (Landes, 1998; Mokyr, 2002—to name just a couple of contemporary authors), the growth of Western countries in 1500–1900 that allowed them to become the wealthiest in the world was the inevitable result of social changes introduced during this period. Many interlinked social changes are found to be crucial: abolition of serfdom and guarantees of human rights, the Reformation and the protestant ethic, the *Magna Carta*, and the European Enlightenment are said to have caused the openness and flow of ideas and technological innovations that finally led to the Industrial Revolution and acceleration of growth.

The conventional wisdom, endorsed by many economic historians, most notably by Douglass North, points to a connected set of legal, economic, and social institutions that are thought to be necessary for or at least specially conducive to sustained economic growth. The most important are the rule of law itself, secure property rights, relatively untrammeled markets, and a degree of social mobility. They function by reducing the uncertainty surrounding saving, investment, and entrepreneurial activity, and by sharpening the incentives for able people to devote themselves to economic activity instead of violence and prayer. The Industrial Revolution happened when it did because these background conditions were

---

[2] The debate is summarized with appropriate references in Bryant, 2006.

met as they had not been met before; and England is where they were met soonest and most fully (Solow, 2007).

The point of view, that freedom and democracy are responsible for long-term economic success, was defended recently by Acemoglu and Robinson (2012), who claimed that countries 'such as Great Britain and the United States became rich because their citizens overthrew the elites who controlled power and created a society where political rights were much more broadly distributed'.

On the other hand, another school questions the logic of evolution triggered by social forces themselves (Diamond, 1997; Pomeranz, 2000; Wong, 1997—once again, just to give several contemporary examples) and pays special attention to seemingly minor historical events—fortunate and unfortunate, but mostly accidental—that pre-determined the development of countries and continents for centuries to come. 'In this view'—explain the editors of the book that examines important unrealized counterfactuals in human history—'Western dominance was the by-product of natural forces that reflect no credit on Western civilization: geographical accidents such as location of mountains and coastlines, geological accidents such as the ready availability of coal or gold or arable land, climatological accidents such as the timing of the ice ages or the direction of the ocean currents, and biological accidents (not always so accidental) that affect the susceptibility of various population groups to lethal diseases' (Tetlock, Lebow, and Parker, 2009: 9).

In recent decades, the rise of Asia has given additional credibility to theories that reject the superiority of Western economic model and the inevitability of the Western success. 'As Japan, the Asian Tigers and China developed into major economic powers'—writes Ian Morris—'more and more scholars concluded that theories explaining West's success through long-term cultural, environmental, or racial causes simply could not be right. The big story in the world history, they began suggesting, was not the long-term inexorable rise of the West; it was the tale of multipolar world, which the West had only recently, temporarily, and perhaps even accidently come to dominate' (Morris, 2013: 2).

Diamond (1997), for instance, argues that the lack of wild animals suited to domestication in Pre-Columbian America, Africa, and Australia and the abundance of these animals in Eurasia gave the latter a huge advantage. Or perhaps the origins of comparative development can be traced to climatic and environmental conditions on the Eurasian continent that allowed sufficiently high agricultural productivity to support a high density of population—a necessary pre-condition for the spread of technological innovations and rapid economic growth.

Findlay and O'Rourke (2009) conclude that the British navy was no less instrumental for the Industrial Revolution than the technical inventions of the seventeenth–eighteenth century—the chance to turn inventions into innovations emerged due to the availability of the new markets for British textiles that in turn was made possible by the expansion of the frontiers of the empire.[3] They do not explain though, why previous famous empires (Rome, Byzantine, China under Tang and Song, Mongols, and Caliphate) did not achieve such a breakthrough.

Pomeranz (2000) argues that, even in the eighteenth century, China was not inferior to Europe in terms of technology, social structures that could support technological innovation, large pools of accumulated capital, and so on. Literacy rates in China (close to 30% in the eighteenth century) were not much lower than in Europe, whereas numeracy rates, as measured by the degree of age-heaping, were noticeably higher (Gupta and Ma, 2010). According to Pomeranz, the reason that Europe 'succeeded' and China did not was largely determined by pure chance—a lack of large deposits of coal and iron ore close to each other and the absence of large outward migration (after Zheng He, the greatest world traveller before Columbus, reached Saudi Arabia, the African Horn, and Madagascar in the early fifteenth century, the emperors of the Ming Dynasty prohibited the construction of big ships, and the Middle Kingdom experienced self-imposed isolation for four centuries). Pomeranz's argument is that mass emigration from Europe played a crucial role in the transition to a modern growth regime from a Malthusian regime.[4] When technological progress accelerated in the nineteenth century, and population growth rates still remained high and growing (0.6% in 1820–70) because the demographic transition had not yet occurred, mass migration to North America helped to alleviate pressure on a scarce resource, land, and to avoid diminishing returns.[5]

---

[3] 'As pointed out long ago by Jacob Viner, the twin objectives of Mercantilist policy, 'power' and 'plenty', were not in conflict with each other. The naval power of the state sustained its trade, while economic success enhanced military prowess. Great Britain proved herself to be the most formidable contender in this global competition, with victories over the Dutch in the second half of the seventeenth century and over the French in the eighteenth, finally crowned by the defeat of Napoleon in 1815. By this date the Industrial Revolution was already underway, but the technological innovations associated with this crucial transition had a much greater economic impact as a result of the global trading empire that the Royal Navy had secured through the defeats of its Dutch and French rivals...The elasticities of both raw material supply and final product demand were much higher as a result of Britannia ruling the waves after the Age of Mercantilism, permitting the expansion of output and exports to occur without being choked off by too steep a rise in input costs and fall in final product prices.' (Findlay and O'Rourke, 2009).

[4] The latter was characterized by the growth of population that was 'eating up' all the potential increases in income per capita resulting from technological change (Galor and Weil, 2000).

[5] The other, more traditional, evolutionary explanation of the economic success of the West (criticized in Pomeranz, 2000) also assigns a non-trivial role to emigration: early elimination of serfdom in Europe made free labour more expensive, which in turn stimulated the development of

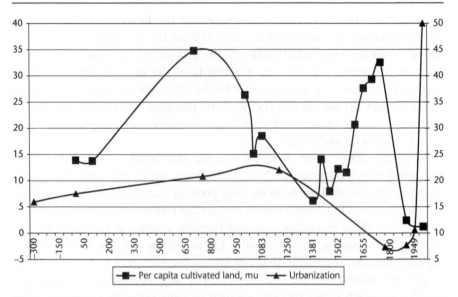

Figure 1.3. Per capita cultivated land (mu, left scale) and the level of urbanization (percent, right scale) in China
Source: Maddison, 1998; Wen, 2008.

In a similar vein, land scarcity is seen as a factor that stimulates urbanization and industrialization. It is argued that

> during the Song Dynasty, despite the fact that China lost a significant amount of arable land to invading nomads as its population peaked, China witnessed a higher urbanization level, more prosperous commerce and international trade, and an explosion of technical inventions and institutional innovations. However, after China significantly improved its man-to-land ratio in the period after the Song only to find itself induced deeper into the agrarian trap, resulting in reduced urbanization, withering foreign trade, a declining division of labor, and stagnation in technology (Wen, 2008).

Strictly speaking, raw data (without controlling for other factors) does not seem to provide very persuasive support (Fig. 1.3), but could be interpreted as giving some ground to believers.

It is even more difficult to apply this theory to international comparisons: arable land per capita was not that scarce in Europe, not to mention Australia and North America (Fig. 1.4) where levels of urbanization surpassed those of Japan, China, and India at least several hundred years ago.

---

labour-saving technologies. Without mass emigration to America and other offshoots, labour in the Old World could have remained less expensive.

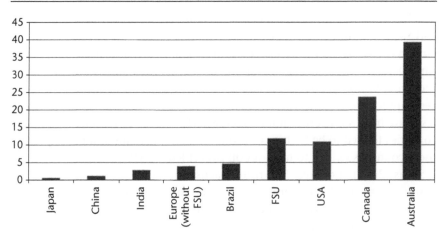

Figure 1.4. Per capita cultivated land, mu (1/15 of a hectare), in 1993
Source: Maddison, 1998; Wen, 2008.

Several explanations concentrate on demographic developments. Gregory Clark (2007) claims that differential fertility (higher numbers of surviving children in rich families) was more pronounced in medieval England than elsewhere, so the educated classes spread their knowledge across society faster. Turchin (2005) presents a model of the rise and fall of empires that is based on expansion (and overexpansion) of the elite population.

New data that have appeared in recent years, especially indices of the quality of institutions, have triggered new debate not only among economic historians but also among general macro and growth economists. In an important paper (Acemoglu, Johnson, and Robinson, 2001) entitled 'Colonial Origins of Comparative Development', the authors used an astute indicator as an instrument for the institutions variable—the mortality rate among settlers in the colonies of major European states in the nineteenth century. Their argument was that, if these settlers' mortality rates were very high (Gambia, Mali, and Nigeria had mortality rates hundreds of times higher than Australia, Bahamas, Canada, Hong Kong, New Zealand, and the USA), the settlers did not bother to set up good institutions in those countries. It was also claimed that the local population largely had immunity to diseases that were fatal to newcomers, so the settlers' mortality rate did not affect economic growth directly, but only via its impact on institutions. That is why this indicator can be used to resolve the endogeneity problem (institutions = > growth = > institutions) and to properly estimate the impact of institutions on growth. The authors concluded that, after controlling for the impact of institutions, the geographical location does not really have an impact on growth.

Other authors, however, have insisted that geography has not only had indirect impact but also an important direct impact on growth and development. In a series of papers, Sachs and Warner (1995, 1997a, b, 1999) and Sachs (1996) argued that resource abundance has an adverse effect on growth via different mechanisms—overvaluation of the real exchange rate (the 'Dutch disease') and its corrupting impact on the quality of institutions. Sachs and Warner (2001) show that 'there is little direct evidence that omitted geographical or climate variables explain the curse, or that there is a bias resulting from some other unobserved growth deterrent. Resource-abundant countries tended to be high-price economies and, perhaps as a consequence, these countries tended to miss out on export-led growth.'

Sachs (2003) and Faye, McArthur, Sachs, and Snow (2004) also attribute many variations in performance to the direct impact of geographical location—through access to the sea that land-locked countries do not have, transportation costs, climate, and diseases. Arguing with Acemoglu, Johnson, and Robinson (2001), Sachs (2003) points to the fact that high correlation between the mortality rates of British soldiers around 1820 in various parts of the world and GNP per capita levels in 1990 is explained by the direct pernicious effects of malaria in blocking long-term economic development.

> Acemoglu, Johnson, and Robinson completely neglect the fact that disease dramatically lowers the returns on foreign investments and raises the transaction costs of international trade, migration, and tourism in malarial regions. This is like claiming that the effects of the recent SARS (severe acute respiratory syndrome) outbreak in Hong Kong SAR can be measured by the number of deaths so far attributable to the disease rather than by the severe disruption in travel to and from Asia (Sachs, 2003).

He argues that during the last two decades there have essentially been three groups of developing countries: (1) those where institutions, policies, and geography were all reasonably favourable (the coastal regions of East Asia, coastal China, and essentially all of Korea, Taiwan Province of China, Hong Kong SAR, Singapore, Thailand, Malaysia, and Indonesia); (2) those that were relatively well endowed geographically but, for historical reasons, have had poor governance and institutions (Central European states, whose proximity to Western Europe brought them little benefit during the socialist regime); and (3) impoverished regions with unfavourable geography, such as most of Sub-Saharan Africa, Central Asia, large parts of the Andean region, and the highlands of Central America, that have experienced the severest economic failures in the recent past and that have all been characterized by initial low levels of income and small populations (and hence small internal markets), that live far from the coasts, and that are burdened by disease, especially AIDS, tuberculosis, and malaria. This latter group of countries, Sachs (2003) insists, has 'essentially been trapped in poverty because of their inability to meet the market test for attracting private capital inflows'.

An opposite view is advocated by Rodrik, Subramanian, and Trebbi (2002) in an article with the self-explanatory title 'Institutions Rule'. The authors examine the impact of three basic factors on growth: geography (proxied by the distance to the equator and regional dummies), trade openness (the share of trade in GDP), and institutions. The difficulty, of course, is that all three factors are interlinked and that institutions and trade openness not only influence growth but also depend on growth themselves. To properly estimate the contribution of each factor, they instrument institutions using the settlers' mortality rate, like Acemoglu, Johnson, and Robinson (2001), and instrument the share of trade in GDP with the predicted share of trade (from gravity models). Then, after giving a 'fair chance' to geographical variables to compete with the instrumented variables of institutions and trade openness, they conclude that 'institutions rule', that is, it is the impact of institutions that is most crucial. Institutions are largely, but not totally, determined by geography, and in turn they determine trade openness and growth. The direct impact of geography on growth (apart from the impact through institutions) turns out to be insignificant. In short, it turns out that that institutions trump geography and that institutional capacity is not always determined by geography.

The difference from the straightforward geographical determinism approach is thus obvious, but there is an important difference from the Acemoglu, Johnson, and Robinson (2001) approach as well. Rodrik, Subramanian, and Trebbi (2002) believe that geography, particularly settlers' mortality rates, is a good predictor of institutional quality, but not the major cause of it. The genesis of institutions is a complex process with many determinants, and finding an appropriate econometric instrument is not the same as finding the proper explanation. Rodrik (2004b) explains the difference using the following example: the variation in GDP per capita in countries that were never colonies is no less substantial than among colonized countries; here, Ethiopia and Afghanistan are at one end of the spectrum and Japan is at the other end, with Turkey and Thailand lying somewhere in between. What accounts for the different quality of institutions in this non-colonized part of the world?

What is wrong with the two dominant explanations

The traditional view on how the West got rich stresses the demise of traditional collectivist institutions as a starting point, but assumes that the impact of this demise was to spur technical progress through unleashing individual entrepreneurship. It is often taken for granted that without rewarding the inventor (via strict intellectual property rights) and innovator (via private property) there is no entrepreneurial spirit or rapid innovation. Acemoglu, Robinson and Verdier (2012), for instance, take as a natural assumption in their modelling exercise that cut-throat competition with no social limits on the size of rewards to the inventor, and with greater income inequality (the USA as opposed to welfare states in Scandinavian countries), will also lead to faster technical progress.

Other authors stress the importance of various institutions that encourage private entrepreneurship and completion, even though there is a disagreement on what exactly these institutions are:

> The institutions that the Washington Consensus has stressed—private property, deregulation, low taxes, stable currencies (a somewhat idealized version of late 18th/ early 19th century laissez-faire U.S. and British institutions)—are clearly not the crucial ingredients of rapid growth that were promised; the examples of China, India, Brazil, and Turkey are proof of that. Rather, the institutions that do matter are those that support investment in human capital, encourage formation of new businesses, and promote competitiveness in the global economy (Goldstone, 2007).

Why is there a need for a new explanation? Isn't the conventional explanation good enough? It is not because it has its limits: 'How could the enormous variation in customs, social structures, institutions, languages, geography, husbandry, and much else produce no variation in long-term economic growth?... Why was this pattern suddenly disrupted or transformed so that growth rates that had been stable for at least ten thousand years suddenly shifted by two orders of magnitude within a century?' (Goldstone, 2007). Indeed, if the demise of traditional institutions results in such an acceleration of economic growth, why haven't we seen this happening before? In Greece, Rome, Byzantium, or China? Conventional theory does not explain, for instance, why ancient Greece—with personal freedoms, free flow of ideas, and entrepreneurship—did not have its own Industrial Revolution and did not escape from the Malthusian growth trap.

And why, after the West made a successful transition to modern economic growth, was this not successfully replicated elsewhere? On the contrary, all cases of successful catch-up development (mainly East Asia since mid 1900) occurred in countries that obviously did not dismantle traditional institutions.

Conventional theory does not explain why the USSR (until the 1970s) and China under central planning (1950s to 1970s) and beyond were and are catching up with the West. If it is not private property that is a necessary pre-condition for the successful growth, but institutions that encourage investment in human capital and the formation of new businesses, then perhaps a central planning board performed the role of such institutions in the USSR and China? The Soviet economic model was quite successful in the catch-up development until the 1970s, but later lost its dynamism.[6] However, China was bridging the gap with the West both in 1949–78, under central planning (yes, despite all the 'great leaps' and 'cultural revolutions'), and after 1979 under the market system. Even though the Soviet model collapsed, the Chinese model became the logical and natural heir of the Soviet model—it is no longer a centrally planned economy, but it is by no means a model of the liberalized market economy that is recommended by the advocates of the Washington and even post-Washington consensus. Can we really say that the rapid East Asian growth became possible due to the demise of traditional collectivist institutions?

The traditional view stressing the importance of clearly defined and strictly enforced property rights for successful economic development does not actually have that much empirical support. Township and village enterprises (TVE) in China—business entities with the most murky and unclear property rights—are usually credited for the success of Chinese reforms in 1979–1996 (later TVEs were reorganized and some went bankrupt). And historically there is solid evidence that property rights were respected in pre-industrial Europe, which nevertheless did not lead to the acceleration of growth (Angeles, 2011). Private enterprises, especially in developing countries and in resource industries, where the institutions and ability to enforce complicated contracts are often lacking, turn out to be less efficient than state enterprises (Chang, 2007).

And the view that strong protection of intellectual property rights is needed to stimulate inventions and innovations has been challenged more than once on both theoretical and empirical grounds. On the one hand, research and scientific progress did not proceed more slowly in countries that did not protect adamantly intellectual property rights (Boldrine and Levine, 2007; Popov, 2011a). On the other hand, innovations and dissemination of new products and technologies are actually hindered by the establishment of intellectual monopolies and appear to proceed faster in countries with loose protection of property rights (Popov, 2011a).

---

[6] In the 1950s, Soviet economic growth was as successful as that of Asian tigers, and the reasons for the subsequent slowdown of growth have nothing to do with a lack of entrepreneurship (Popov, 2007c). The issue is discussed later, in Chapter 4.

2

Why Did the West Become Rich First? Why Are Some Developing Countries Catching Up, But Others Are Not?

A different interpretation of the genesis of institutions in colonized and non-colonized countries is the continuity perspective. In the past, all countries had traditional community structures; everywhere before the Reformation, under the Malthusian growth regime, the law of the land was what we now call 'Asian values'— the superiority of the interests of the community over the interests of the individual. The institutions that maintained 'Asian values' were the agricultural community and the state—they ensured a high degree of equality in income and wealth distribution, which was a prerequisite for the survival of the poor and for the preservation and increase of the population. In the words of Confucius: 'equality brings wealth; harmony brings large population; contented people brings survival of the governance' (Confucius, *ca.* 500 BC). Promoting individual rights at the expense of collective interests was like a Faustian deal with the devil, to borrow the expression from Ron Findlay (2009) used in a different, but somewhat similar, context.[1]

On the one hand, individual rights led to increased productivity—not because private property stimulated inventiveness and innovations (as it is usually stated), but because elimination of collectivist institutions was giving rise to income inequalities, which in turn boosted savings and investment and the capital/labour ratio. On the other hand, destruction of the commune and rising inequalities led to impoverishment of the masses, social conflict, weakening of the state institutions, increased mortality, and reduction of

---

[1] 'As we now know all too well, however, the cost of this reliance on fossil fuels in terms of the ongoing and seemingly irreversible damage to the global climate and environment has made this a crucial aspect of the trade–development nexus, marking more sharply than anything else the advent of "modernity", perhaps the ultimate Faustian bargain that the human race will ever engage in' (Findlay, 2009).

population, all of which increased the danger of foreign conquest. Many countries and civilizations were attempting to make this Faustian bargain, but only Western Europe, in the fifteenth–eighteenth centuries, succeeded.

Developing countries, after becoming 'developing', that is after the West got rich before the rest, followed two major different routes: (1) Latin America (LA), Sub-Saharan Africa (SSA), and Russia replicated the road of the West by dismantling collectivist institutions, allowing inequalities to rise, pushing up saving and investment, but this at the price of growing social tension and weakening institutions; (2) East Asia, Middle East and North Africa (MENA), and South Asia tried to preserve collectivist institutions to a different degree, holding back inequalities and savings and investment, but also preserving institutional capacity and social order.

Exit from the Malthusian trap in Western countries

The Malthusian growth trap emerged due to the inability to mobilize savings from low-income populations. Lack of savings/investment did not allow the capital/labour ratio ($K/L = k$) to increase: because population growth rates were high and all investment went into creating jobs for new entrants into the labour force, nothing was left to increase k. Moreover, population growth rates depended on y, productivity (output per employee), so when y increased due to technical progress, A, the population growth rate, n, grew as well, eating up all increases in y achieved due to increases in A.

In the Solow growth model, labour productivity can increase due to technical progress A and due to the increase in the capital/labour ratio, $k=K/L$:

$$y = A{*}k^a$$

The required investment per employee (I_n) to create jobs for new entrants into the labour force and to replace retiring elements of capital stock (d—the share of capital stock that retires annually) is equal to:

$$I_n = k(n + d)$$

Actual investment per employee, I_a, is equal to the savings rate, s, multiplied by output per employee, y:

$$I_a = s{*}y = s{*}A{*}k^a$$

Equilibrium emerges at point E, where needed investment, I_n, is equal to actual investment, I_a (see Scheme 2.1).

However, if population growth rates are not constant, but change with increases in productivity (and GDP per capita)—first rising with acceleration, then slowing down—we get two equilibriums: one stable at a low level of

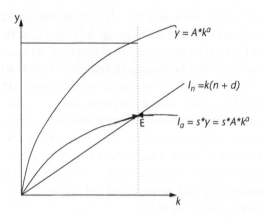

Scheme 2.1. Equilibrium in the Solow model with fixed growth rates of the population

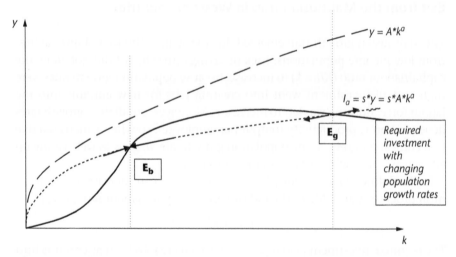

Scheme 2.2. Malthusian trap in the Solow model with changing population growth rates

income (bad equilibrium, E_b, growth trap) and the other unstable at a high level of income (good equilibrium, E_g, Scheme 2.2).

In a Malthusian growth regime, before the transition to modern economic growth, all countries were in bad equilibrium, E_b, so that increases in productivity and per capita GDP, wherever they came from, were quickly absorbed by rising population growth rates, and per capita income declined. Countries had roughly the same productivity and competed on the basis of population: the might of a country was determined by the number of people within its borders and the number of soldiers that the country was able to mobilize in case of a war. Success in technical progress led to growth of the population (like in China before the Opium Wars), not to the growth of per capita income.

The savings rate is determined by many factors (Norman, Schmidt-Hebbel, and Servén, 2000), but at a low level of income the crucial factor is income inequality. At a very low level of income (subsistence minimum) people are not making any savings and all income is used for consumption. Increase in inequality resulting from redistribution of income will lead to the reduction of consumption by the poor (they will not make any savings, and may possibly even die out), but the rich will make some savings as they are not able to consume all the increased income.

Micro studies consistently show that rich households and individuals save more than the poor, but the national savings rate is not necessarily higher in countries with high inequalities. Redistribution and an increase in inequalities will lead to higher savings of those who get rich, but to lower savings of those that are getting poorer. These two effects can cancel one another out. That is why current research does not show any link between inequalities and savings rate for developed or developing countries (Schmidt-Hebbel and Serven, 2000). But, at low levels of income the increase in national savings, provided that productivity is constant, is possible only through redistribution from poor to rich, because at low levels of income elasticity of savings on income is very low: a reduction of the income of the poor does not lead to a decline in savings (which are extremely low to begin with), whereas an increase in the income of the rich leads to an increase in savings.

At $500 per capita income (in 1990 dollars) it is easy to understand why inequalities cannot be high. Assuming that the subsistence minimum was equal to half of the average (i.e. about $250), the maximum level of inequality possible without putting people below the subsistence minimum—the *inequality possibility frontier* (Milanovic, Lindert, and Williamson, 2007)—is one where the Gini coefficient is below 50%. In a Malthusian growth regime the wealth and might of the country equals the number of its citizens (determining the number of soldiers that could be mobilized for the war), so high inequality undermines the army size, increasing the chances of defeat in a future war. In the Malthusian world, success meant the faster growth of population, as happened under the emperor Qianlong in China in the eighteenth century, whose rule (1735–96) was marked by a dramatic increase in the share of China in the world population—from 23% in 1700 to 37% in 1820 (Maddison, 2008; see next chapter for details).

There is a clear negative relationship between the growth of a population and the growth of per capita GDP (Fig. 2.1); in fact, this is one of the most robust relationships revealed by empirical studies of economic growth. It is explained by the need to devote more savings/investment to creating jobs for new entrants into the labour force, which leaves less investment for an

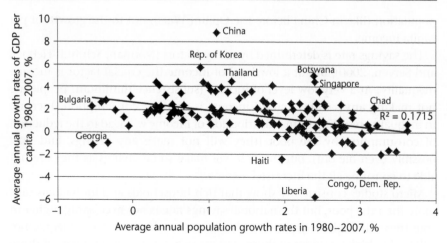

Figure 2.1. Annual average growth rates of population and GDP per capita in 1980–2007, percent
Source: WDI.

increase in *K/L* and hence suppresses productivity growth. It is precisely the reason for the 'one child policy' in China, which is widely considered to have been successful in promoting growth, even by its opponents.

There was also an inverse relationship—per capita GDP dynamics influencing population growth rates—in the Malthusian growth regime, before the demographic transition that occurred with the Industrial Revolution. In the first edition of his book, Malthus suggested that lower income leads to increased mortality, but in subsequent editions he stressed the link between income and birth rate. Recent advances in the reconstruction of population dynamics in the pre-statistical period, particularly in Britain in the sixteenth to nineteenth centuries from parish registers, shed some new light on this relationship (see Saito, 1996, for a survey).[2]

Attempts to break the Malthusian vicious circle were probably made more than once (Greece, Rome, and Byzantium), but all ended up in losing wars with foreign invaders. Countries that tried to eliminate collectivist

---

[2] The decrease in population growth in economically difficult times is due not to increased mortality (a so-called positive check), but to lower fertility (a preventive check). It has been demonstrated that there is no link between mortality and the dynamics of real wages, but that there is a correlation between real wages and birth rate, and this correlation is due to variations in the marriage age (Saito, 1996, referring to Wrigley and Schofield, 1981): when times are bad economically, celibacy and marriage age increase leading to fewer births. It has also been shown that fertility decreases during famines due to a variety of mechanisms. 'It is not so much that famines, both historic and contemporary, killed a vast number of people, but chiefly that the immediate effect of a famine was to reduce the number of conceptions, regardless of how deadly it was' (Saito 2006). Even rich families seem to have less children during bad economic times (Cinnirella, Klemp, and Weisdorf, 2012).

institutions and to put the interests of the individual ahead of the interests of the community experienced growth in income and wealth inequality, which allowed an increase in savings and investment, but only at the cost of polarizing the society and undermining population growth, which was essential for maintaining the military might of the empires. When income levels were about $500–600 per capita (in 1990 dollars), the increase in income inequality put too many people below the subsistence minimum and led to increased mortality. Such an experiment at low income levels could have been largely successful by chance—two to three centuries of dramatic social restructuring (growing income inequality) without backlash revolts of disadvantaged classes and foreign conquests. This chance was realized only in Northwestern Europe in the sixteenth to nineteenth centuries.

The West was the first to exit the Malthusian trap without being conquered by neighbouring countries with collectivist institutions. Making individual rights and freedoms sacred resulted in growing income inequality and an increase in mortality, but allowed an increase in savings and investment and the *K/L* ratio, overcoming the limits of the two-dimensional Malthusian world (greater population => higher GDP).[3] The statistics available on Britain tell the story of the huge costs of transition to modern economic growth between the sixteenth and nineteenth centuries. The enclosure policy and the Industrial Revolution resulted in a dramatic increase in income inequality, a rise in mortality, and weakening of institutions.

Despite the acceleration of productivity growth in 1500–1800 in the UK (to about 0.2% a year, so that GDP per capita in the UK more than doubled over three centuries),[4] the living standards of workers did not improve. 'The single most important fact is that there is no evidence of any significant rise in material living standards for average workers in any societies before 1830' (Goldstone, 2007). Real wages actually fell between 1500 and 1800 (Saito,

---

[3] The Solow model is a model with exogenous technical progress (*A* is not explained, but just assumed). In endogenous growth models, *A* depends on the rate of capital accumulation (investment in R&D and innovations spur technical progress), so a higher investment rate leads to faster growth not only because capital/labour ratio, *K/L*, rises, but also because of the increase in the technical level, *A*. So the acceleration of technical progress due to higher investment becomes another reason for faster growth.

As Charles Feinstein noted, it is essential that a society 'should be able both to organize the process of production so as to incorporate the new techniques in appropriate assets, and to save a sufficient sum to provide the finance for those acquiring capital goods. Without this it would be not possible to benefit from technical progress however readily the knowledge might be available. In this sense at least the process of capital accumulation must still occupy a central role in any explanation of growth of output and productivity' (Feinstein, 1981).

[4] GDP per capita in the UK increased in constant 1990 international Geary–Khamis dollars from $714 in 1500 to $974 in 1600, to $1250 in 1700, and to $1706 in 1820 (Maddison, 2008).

2009). This is consistent with the story of rising income inequality, accumulation of wealth in the hands of a few, and increasing savings and investment rates (the latter increased during the Industrial Revolution from a mere 6% in 1760 to 12% in 1831—Galor, 1998).[5] This is also consistent with the fact that Chinese standards of living in the eighteenth century were comparable or even superior to those found in Europe: in public health and sanitation, medicine, caloric intake, life expectancy, and domestic consumption, China was at about the same level as Europe (Pomeranz, 2000).

The divergent paths of Europe and China in 1500–1800 were not so much seen in the dynamics of consumption, but in the dynamics of income inequality, savings, and accumulation (investment). In England, by 1800, two thirds of the workforce was proletarian, in China 10% (Pomeranz, 2008). According to Brenner and Isett (2002: 614), in England,

> economic agents of the sort found in the Yangtze delta—both possessing peasants and lordly takers of rent by extra-economic means—though dominant during the medieval period, had largely been eliminated...The main economic agents throughout the economy—especially tenant farmers—although in possession of their means of production (tools, animals, and so on) were separated from their full means of economic reproduction, specifically the land.

Dramatic redistribution of property (land) is documented by the changing average size of farms: in Britain, it increased from 14 acres in the thirteenth century to around 75 acres in 1600–1700 and to 151 acres in 1800, whereas in China, it decreased from 4 acres in 1400 to 3.4 acres in 1650 and to 2.5 in 1800 (in the big Yangtze delta—from 4 in 1400, to 2 in 1600–1700, and to 1 in 1800). In China, growing populations in the countryside were given land at the expense of existing owners; in England, farmers were deprived of land and turned proletariat (Brenner and Isett, 2002: Table 1). The share of urban population in England increased from 6% in 1600, to 13% in 1700, and to 24% in 1800, whereas in China it fell from over 20% in the thirteenth century to as low as 5% in the early 1800s (Fig. 1.3; Brenner and Isett, 2002: Table 4).

To put it differently, the escape from the Malthusian trap and the transition to the modern growth regime in Britain, and later in other Western countries, became possible not so much because of inventions that led to the acceleration of technological progress. A necessary component of the transition was the elimination of collectivist institutions and the resulting increase in inequality that allowed increased savings and investment to the point that accumulation of physical capital started to exceed the growth of population,

---

[5] According to C. Feinstein, the savings rate as a percent of GDP was below 8% in the first half of the eighteenth century. It started to rise in the 1740s or 1750s and reached 13–14% in 1810–60 (Feinstein, 1981).

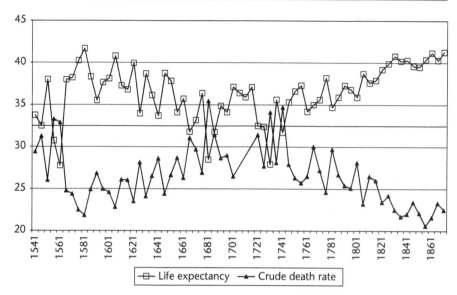

Figure 2.2. Mortality rates and life expectancy (at birth) in the course of early urbanization: England 1540–1870

Source: Wrigley and Schofield, 1981, p. 231.

so that the capital/labour ratio started to rise. The costs of this transition were extremely high—rising income inequality and weakening of institutional capacity (high murder rate) leading, among other factors, to a decline in life expectancy from about 35 to 40 years to about 30 to 35 years in 1560–1730 (Fig. 2.2). Annual average population growth rates in Britain fell from 0.7% in 1000–1500, to 0.4% in the sixteenth century, and to 0.3% in the seventeenth, before increasing to 0.9 and 0.8% in the eighteenth and nineteenth centuries. The respective figures for 29 West European countries were: 0.8, 0.3, 0.1, 0.5, and 0.7% (Maddison, 2008).

To summarize the difference from the traditional explanation, my scheme assumes that the demise of traditional institutions increased income inequalities, which led to higher savings and investment rates, which in turn contributed to both sources of growth—increase in the capital/labour ratio, K/L, and technical progress, A. My scheme does not deny the acceleration of technical progress, but presupposes that this acceleration was the result of higher investment into R&D, innovations, and capital rather than the result of unleashing entrepreneurial talents and creative forces of the human mind.

The traditional explanation could be described as a shift to intensive growth from an extensive growth regime (in this latter regime the country was doomed to remain in the vicious circle of the Malthusian trap). My

29

explanation assumes an increase in extensive efforts (capital accumulation) that only later speeded up technical progress.

It is a fact that most of the discoveries in fundamental science were not made in pursuit of profit. Natural human curiosity was to a greater extent the mother of discoveries, and even inventions, than necessity. The pace of the progress in fundamental research was and is determined not so much by profit motive and existing economic stimuli, but by the amount of R&D financing. The USA, Japan, South Korea, and large European countries spend today about 2–3% of their GDP on R&D (as much as the USSR before collapse), but even if a country spends less than 1% of GDP the pace of advancement in fundamental research can be quite high. In many ancient societies the level of knowledge and fundamental research was much higher than the level of the technologies that predominated in production. Silk and the compass, powder and paper, porcelain and the printing press—all these inventions were made in China in Middle Ages or earlier, but by no means became widespread because the proliferation of inventions depends first and foremost on the savings (invest-ment) rate, which determines how quickly ideas and engineering designs are transformed into fixed capital stock. Many important inventions in human history were not transformed into innovations or had only very limited applications for dozens or hundreds of years. The first steam engines were, for nearly 100 years—up to the end of the eighteenth century—used for nothing more than pumping water out of the mines.

If inventions and discoveries could determine the speed of technical pro-gress, developing countries would have caught up with the Western levels of productivity a long time ago. Or would have nearly caught up—there are generally no patents for inventions made 25 years ago. In African villages land is cultivated with hoes not because nobody knows about tractors, but because there is no money to buy these tractors.

For speedy proliferation of new technologies, the savings/investment rate in developing countries should be not only higher than 5% (which is approxi-mately the level needed to replace retiring elements of fixed capital stock and to create jobs for the new entrants into the labour force), but most probably higher than 20%. If not, the rate of renovation of fixed capital stock will not keep up with the speed of materialization of inventions in developed coun-tries, so developing countries will fall behind or will at least will not catch up.

Borrowing an expression from Paul Krugman that was used on a different occasion,[6] one can say that the West got rich due to 'perspiration', not

---

[6] Krugman referred to the Asian economic miracle—the acceleration of growth rates in East Asian countries, Japan, Korea, Taiwan, Singapore, and Hong Kong, that, he believed, was due to high growth rates of physical capital resulting from high investment ('perspiration'), not to high growth rates of total factor productivity ('inspiration').

'inspiration'. Or, to be more precise, due to a merciless 'big push': an increase in capital accumulation that was only made possible by the increase in income inequalities, which—at this low stage of per capita income—involved a lot of pain and sacrifice by putting a substantial portion of the population below the subsistence level. And, as was argued earlier, in the endogenous growth model 'inspiration' also depends on 'perspiration. 'Inspiration' coming from individual freedom, entrepreneurship, free flow of ideas, and so on does not get you too far if it is not supported by 'perspiration'—increased investment in R&D and innovations that become possible due to the increased savings rate caused by growing inequalities. It is a more prosaic explanation of the speed of the technical progress, but it is supported by the evidence.

The hard fact is that savings and investment rates until 500 years ago were very low, less than 5% of GDP only, so that investment was barely enough to replace the retiring elements of fixed capital stock and create jobs for new entrants into the labour force. There wasn't much left to increase the capital/labour ratio—the key determinant of the productivity—so per capita GDP virtually did not grow over time.

Could it be that the Egyptian pyramids, the Great Chinese Wall, and other impressive structures created by ancient societies were built with a savings rate of just 5%? It is very likely that the answer is actually yes. Today's estimates of the costs of the Great Pyramid of Cheops range, according to different sources, from $250 million to $5 billion[7] (the amount of concrete for such a construction would be similar to the Hoover Dam in Nevada, which was evaluated at $729 million in 2012 prices). The GDP of Egypt in the first millennium was about 2.5–2.7 billion in prices of 1990 (Maddison, 2008—no earlier estimates), so about $5 billion in prices of 2012. Even assuming that the price of the pyramid was indeed as high as $5 billion and that construction really was completed in just 20 years, as historical records suggest (every 5 minutes, day and night, a new 2.5-ton block was installed), this operation would require an investment equivalent to 5% of GDP over the course of 20 years. With a national savings rate of 5% this basically means that all national savings went into the construction of the pyramid for a good 20 years, with nothing left for the repair of irrigation systems and other elements of productive fixed capital stock. This is exactly one of the theories for the fall of the 4th Dynasty, which ended with the death of Cheops. And there is also a more general theory of the life cycle of the Asiatic mode of production (Nureyev, 1993)—all savings are used by the despot for cult structures or for war => degradation

---

[7] What if we built the Great Pyramid today? Howstuffworksexpress. 2003–2012 (<http://express. howstuffworks.com/mb-pyramid.htm>); Natalie Wolchover. How Much Would It Cost to Build the Great Pyramid Today?, Date: 22 February 2012 (<http://www.livescience.com/18589-cost-build-great-pyramid-today.html>).

of irrigation system and decline in living standards => uprising or foreign conquest, leading to the emergence of new rulers that divert investment to fixed capital stock in production, but later start to invest in pyramids and war activities.

There were about 1 million people working on the construction of Great Chinese Wall during the reign of Qin Shi Huang (221–210 BCE), the first Chinese emperor who united the country and started the construction of the Great Wall,[8] whereas the population of China at that time has been estimated at 20 million people.[9] This means that roughly 10% of the labour force was taking part in the construction project, which roughly corresponds to an investment rate of 10%. This could have been possible probably only for a few years, during which time the production fixed capital stock of the country was totally run down. Estimates of the number of workers that were working on the construction of the Wall in the sixth–seventh century AD (1–1.8 million),[10] when the population of China was 50–60 million, correspond to 3–7% of the workforce.

Even in the second half of the nineteenth century, national savings amounted to just 10–15% of GDP in major European countries and in Japan; only in the United States did savings and investment rates steadily exceed 20% in 1874–1899 (Taylor, 1996). In 1890–1913, gross savings rates in Australia, Canada, France, Japan, and the UK were estimated in the range of 9 to 15% (Table 2.1) only.

Today, many developing countries, especially the least developed ones, have very low domestic savings and investment rates (Fig. 2.3, 2.4). Normally, growth rates of such countries are low or even negative—the relationship between savings rate, investment rate, and growth rates of GDP is one of the most robust in empirical research of economic growth (Fig. 2.5). For such countries, mobilization of domestic savings or savings from abroad—from either traditional or innovative sources—is a pre-condition for successful development and catching up with rich countries.

Developing countries entered the period of modern economic growth (Kuznets, 1966) with high savings and investment rates one or two hundred years later than the developed ones. Even Argentina, that was considered to belong to the rich country club between the two world wars, never had a 10 year savings rate of over 10% before the 1930s (Fig. 2.3) In India before independence

---

[8] <Http://www.ccnt.com.cn/culture/greatwall/lishi/huati/huati03.htm>; <http://www.thechinaexpat.com/how-many-people-worked-on-the-great-wall-of-china/>.

[9] Duan Chang-Qun, Gan Xue-Chun, Jeanny Wang, and Paul K. Chien. Relocation of civilization centers in Ancient China: environmental factors—*Ambio*, Vol. 27, No. 7 (November, 1998), pp. 572–75.

[10] <Http://www.ccnt.com.cn/culture/greatwall/lishi/huati/huati03.htm>.

Table 2.1. Total gross savings as a ratio of GDP at current market prices, percent

Period/Countries	1870–89	1890–1913	1914–38	1939–49	1950–73	1974–88
Australia	11.2a	12.5a	12.2	24.3	22.0	13.8
Canada	9.1b	12.2b	14.4b	22.5	21.4	19.3
France	12.8	14.7	n.a.	n.a.	23.4	22.1
Germany	n.a.	n.a.	l2.8c	n.a.	26.7	22.4
India	n.a.	5.8d	7.4	6.7	12.8	20.3
Japan	12.4e	12.4e	16.7e	24.8e	32.8	32.8
Korea	n.a.	n.a	4.3f	n.a.	8.1g	27.9
Netherlands	n.a.	n.a.	15.2i	n.a	26.6	22.1
Taiwan	n.a.	9.6j	25.5k	n.a.	19.9	33.2
UK	13.9	13.6	8.8	2.5	18.4	18.5
USA	n.a.	18.0	17.0	15.2	19.6	17.9

a) excludes inventories; b) 1870–1926 excludes inventories; c) 1925–38; d) 1900–13; e) 1885–1940 excludes inventories and first entry is for 1885–89; f) excludes part of inventories; g) 1953–73; h) 1953–9; i) 1921–38; j) 1903–13 and excludes part of inventories; k) excludes part of inventories.

Source: Maddison, 1992.

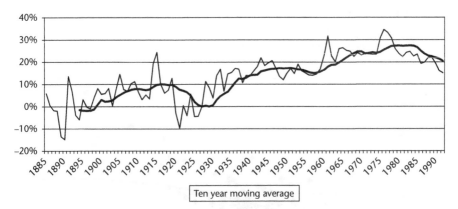

Figure 2.3. Total savings in Argentina, percentage of GDP
Source: Taylor (1996).

(1900–49) the savings rate stayed at a level of 6–7% only; in Korea in 1914–38 it was only 4% of GDP (Table 2.1).

It is the Lewis model of economic growth that assumes unlimited supplies of labour in agriculture that keep wages low despite rapid accumulation of capital in industry. In the words of Arthur Lewis:

> the central problem in the theory of economic development is to understand the process by which a community which was previously saving and investing 4 or 5% of its national income or less, converts itself into the economy where voluntary saving is running at about 12 to 15 percent of national income or more. This is the central problem because the central fact of economic development is capital accumulation (Lewis, 1954).

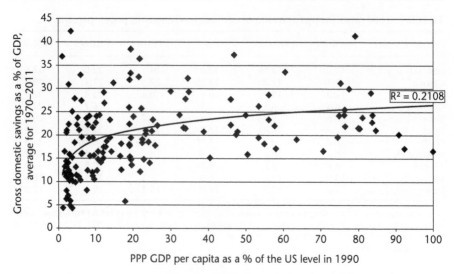

Figure 2.4. Domestic savings as a percentage of GDP in 1970–2011 and PPP GDP per capita as a percentage of the US level in 1990
Source: World Development Indicators database.

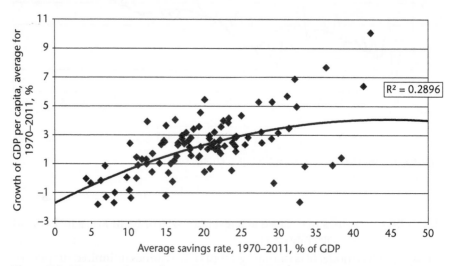

Figure 2.5. The ratio of gross domestic savings to GDP and average annual growth rates of GDP per capita in 1970–2011, percent
Source: World Development Indicators database.

How countries of the South exited the Malthusian trap

After the West began growing rich, non-Western regions of the world, including the most advanced regions like China, stayed on a different trajectory of development—preservation of 'Asian values' and slow, hand-in-hand growth of GDP and population. We can only speculate now what the outcome of this other trajectory, where the population size was the major determinant of competitiveness, could have been. The colonial expansion of the West interrupted logical development along the second trajectory.

Colonization of Sub-Saharan Africa, South America, and, to a lesser extent, South Asia led to complete or near complete destruction of traditional (community) structures that were only partially replaced by new Western-style institutions. Colonialism held back the development of the South not only through the direct extraction of resources from colonized countries (slave trade, unequal exchange, etc.), but also because, in most instances, it ruined collective institutions and increased inequality, which turned out to be extremely detrimental at the low level of development.

Among large geographical regions, only East Asia, MENA, and, to an extent, South Asia managed to retain traditional community institutions despite colonialism. It could be hypothesized that those countries and regions that preserved traditional institutions in the difficult times of colonialism and imposition of Western values retained a better chance of catch-up development in the future than the less fortunate regions of the world periphery, where continuity of traditional structures was interrupted (Scheme 2.3). Transplantation of institutions is a tricky business that works well only when tailored to local traditions, so that it does not interrupt institutional continuity (Polterovich,

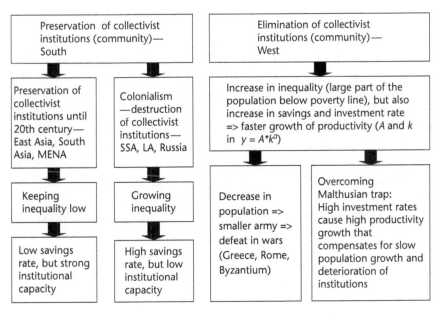

Scheme 2.3. Three ways out of Malthusian regime

2001). Otherwise, it leads either to complete elimination of local structures (the USA, Canada, and Australia) or to a non-viable mixture of old and new institutions that is not very conducive to growth (SSA and LA).

The westernization of the Americas, the Russian Empire, and South Africa led to the transfer of knowledge and human capital, and increased inequality and savings rates, but ruined traditional institutions that were instrumental in maintaining law and order, a stable business climate, and social peace. In SSA the results were the worst: it was poorer than other regions of the global South at the time of colonization and received very little technology and human capital afterwards, so was not able to increase the savings rate, but had to experience all the negative consequences in the form of rising inequalities, institutional degradation, and a rise in social tensions.

The institutional capacity of the state, according to a narrow definition, is the ability of the government to enforce laws and regulations. While there are a lot of subjective indices (corruption, rule of law, government effectiveness, etc.) that are supposed to measure the state institutional capacity, many researchers do not think they help to explain economic performance and consider them biased (Khan, 2007). The natural objective measures of state institutional capacity are the murder rate—non-compliance with the state's monopoly on violence[11]—and the shadow economy—non-compliance with the economic regulations. China is rather unique on both measures—one of the lowest indicators in the developing world comparable to developed countries (see Fig. 2.6).

With less than 3 murders in 2002 per 100,000 inhabitants and less than 1.5 in 2008 (against 1–2 in Europe and Japan and over 5 in the USA) China looks more like a developed country. Only a few developing countries, mostly in the MENA region, have such low murder rates, normally they are higher by an order of magnitude, like in LA, SSA, and many FSU states. By way of comparison, it took Western countries 500 years to bring the murder rate down from about a hundred to just a few (1 to 3) per 100,000 inhabitants (Fig. 2.7). Even in the seventeenth century, the murder rates in Western Europe generally exceeded 10 per 100,000 inhabitants— more than in many developing countries with a similar level of GDP per capita today. In fact, among developing countries today, we find two major patterns—a low murder rate (1–3 per 100,000 inhabitants) in Eastern Europe, China, and MENA countries (Fig. 2.6), and a high murder rate

---

[11] Crimes are registered differently in different countries—higher crime rates in developed countries seem to be the result of better registration of crimes. But serious crimes, like murders, appear to be registered quite accurately even in developing countries, so an international comparison of murder rates is well warranted. See Popov, 2011b.

(10–60 murders per 100,000 inhabitants) in FSU, Latin America, and Sub-Saharan Africa (Fig. 2.6). India (3.5 murders) and some Southeast Asian countries (about 5–10) murders fall between the two groups.

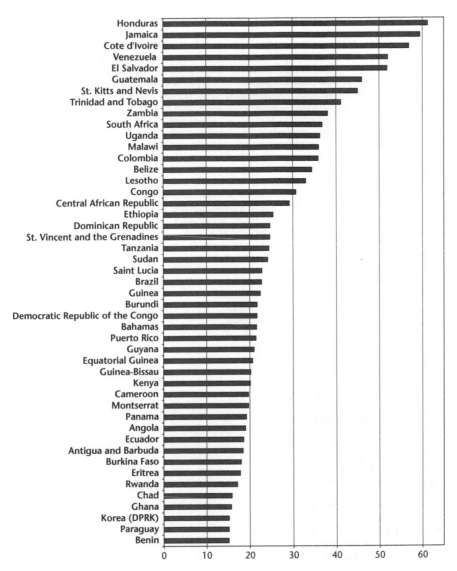

Figure 2.6. Murder rate per 100,000 inhabitants in 2008. Countries with over 10 murders per 100,000 inhabitants.
Source: WHO.

The argument is that countries that preserved collectivist institutions (East Asia, MENA countries, and India) were able to retain institutional capacity of the state, whereas countries that eliminated these institutions while only partly replacing them with individual responsibility systems (FSU, Latin America, and Sub-Saharan Africa) paid a high price in terms of diminished

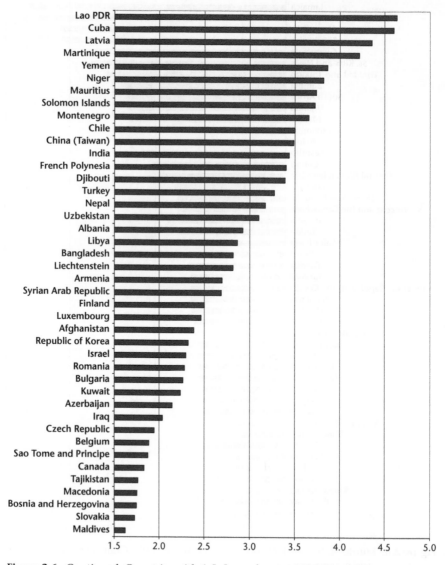

Figure 2.6. Continued. Countries with 1.5–5 murders per 100,000 inhabitants.

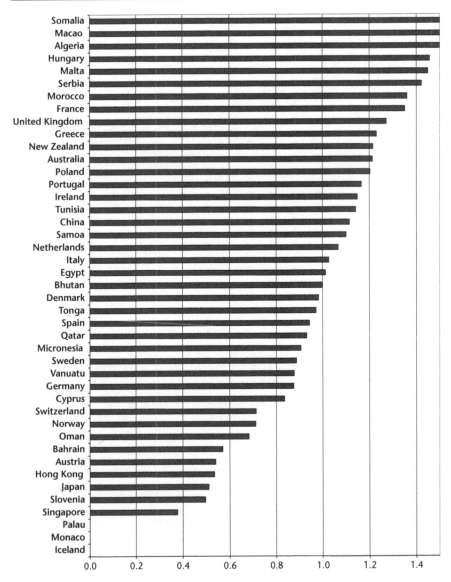

Figure 2.6. Continued. Countries with fewer than 1.5 murders per 100,000 inhabitants.

institutional capacity. Eastern Europe (but not the FSU states) could be the exception that proves the rule: it went through a period of low institutional capacity—high murder rates in the fifteenth to seventeenth centuries, like Western Europe (although direct evidence here is lacking—all observations for Fig. 2.7 are from Western Europe—England, Belgium, Netherlands,

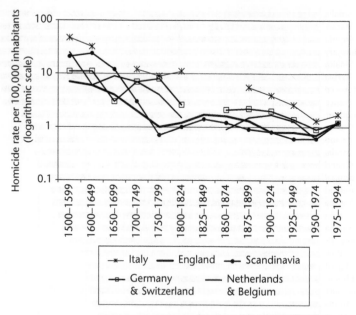

Figure 2.7. Long-term homicide rates in Europe per 100,000 inhabitants
Source: Eisner, 2003.[12]

Scandinavia, and Italy).[13] The same is true of the shadow economy: it is less than 17% of the Chinese GDP, lower than in Belgium, Portugal, Spain; whereas in developing countries it is typically around 40%, sometimes even over 60% (Fig. 2.8). Only a few developing countries have such a low share of shadow economy, in particular, Vietnam and some MENA countries (Iran, Jordan, Saudi Arabia, Syria).

Not surprisingly, these two objective measures of the strength of the state institutional capacity—the murder rate and the share of shadow economy— are strongly correlated (Fig. 2.9).

Another piece of evidence on the cost of breakdown in institutional continuity comes from data on income and wealth inequalities in pre-modern societies.

---

[12] All 398 local estimates are from the History of Homicide Database; national series for Sweden, England and Wales, Switzerland, and Italy.
[13] Another piece of evidence of the strength of the collective institutions in East Asia, South Asia, and MENA countries is the virtual absence of urban slums (Pomeranz, 2008) and homeless children, which are found in abundance in LA, SSA, and FSU. In 2010, there were more 'official' orphans in Russia than during the Second World War, 697,000 against 678,000 in the 1940s. Two thirds of orphans are in fact 'social orphans', children taken from their birth family because of alcoholism, domestic violence, or rejection by the parents (<http://www.asianews.it/news-en/Russia-facing-an-orphanage-and-adoption-crisis-18587.html>). The number of orphans in Russia is probably higher than in China, although the Chinese population is nearly 10 times larger. There are no definitive estimates on the number of orphans in China, though Children's Hope International believes there are around 600,000, with 70,000 of them in state-run programmes (<http://www.thedailybeast.com/newsweek/2007/12/12/faces-of-the-abandoned.html>).

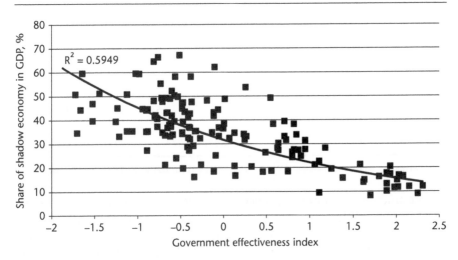

Figure 2.8. Share of the shadow economy in GDP in 2005, percent, and government effectiveness index in 2002

Source: World Bank. Data on shadow economy are from: Friedrich Schneider. Shadow economies and corruption all over the world: new estimates for 145 countries. *Economics*. Open Access, Open Assessment E-Journal, No. 2007–9 July 24, 2007 (measures of the shadow economy are derived from divergence between output dynamics and electricity consumption, demand for real cash balances, etc.).

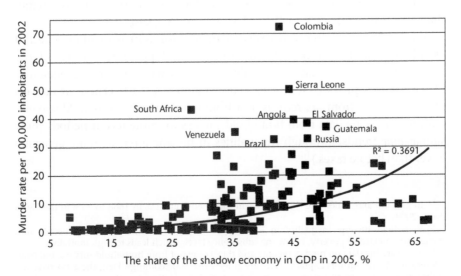

Figure 2.9. The share of the shadow economy in GDP in 2005, percent, and the murder rate per 100,000 inhabitants in 2002

Source: WHO; Schneider, 2007.

Table 2.2. Gini coefficients around particular years in Western countries, percent

Years	14	1000	1290	1550	1700	1750	1800	2000
Rome	39							
Byzantine		41						
Holland				56		63	57	30.9
England			36.7		55.6	52.2	59.3	37.4
Old Castille/Spain						52.5		34.7
Kingdom of Naples/Italy							28.1	35.9
France							55	33

Source: Milanovic, Lindert, and Williamson, 2007; Modalsli, 2013; data for 2000 are sometimes from the WDI.

The destruction of communal, collectivist institutions that was first carried out in Western countries in the sixteenth to nineteenth centuries was accompanied by an increase in income inequality. The available data (Milanovic, Lindert, and Williamson, 2007) suggest that in England, Holland, and Spain in the eighteenth century, the Gini coefficient of income distribution was at a level of 50 and even 60% (Fig. 2.10)[14]—an extremely high level according to today's standards and, most probably, according to the standards of the distant past (about 40% in Rome in the first century and in Byzantium in the eleventh century— Table 2.2).[15] In Denmark—a country with very good statistical records—the share of top 10% in total income in 1870–1920 was always over 40% (reaching 54% in 1917), whereas the Gini coefficient for this period was always higher than 40%, exceeding 70% in 1917 (Atkinson and Søgaard, 2013).

Only in the twentieth century was the trend towards increase in income and wealth inequalities temporarily interrupted, most probably because of the checks and balances that the socialist countries with very low inequalities (25–30% Ginis) provided for the capitalist system (Fig. 2.10). (These are data on pre-tax incomes from tax returns, not from representative household surveys, but more accurate data from household surveys for more recent periods show similar *time* trends, although inequalities in income after taxes are generally lower than before taxes.)[16]

---

[14] In England and Wales, the Gini coefficient increased from 46% in 1688 to 53% in the 1860s (Saito, 2009).

[15] Very high income inequality in low-income countries means that many people find themselves in extreme poverty, below the subsistence level, which leads to high mortality.

[16] These are the data on pre-tax income and they come not from household surveys, but from tax returns. As the authors explain, there are at least two shortcomings. First, these tax data 'are collected as part of an administrative process, which is not tailored to the scientists' needs, so that the definition of income, income unit, etc., are not necessarily those that we would have chosen. This causes particular difficulties for comparisons across countries, but also for time-series analysis where there have been substantial changes in the tax system, such as the moves to and from the joint taxation of couples. Secondly, it is obvious that those paying tax have a financial incentive to present their affairs in a way that reduces tax liabilities. There is tax avoidance and tax evasion. The rich, in particular, have a strong incentive to understate their taxable incomes. Those with wealth take steps to ensure that the return comes in the form of

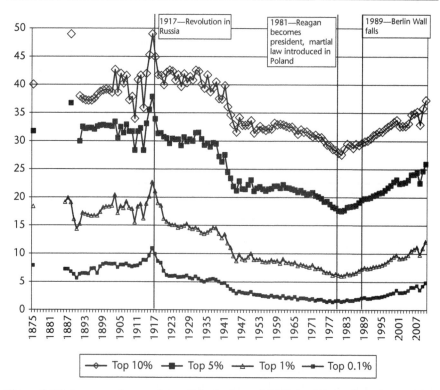

Figure 2.10. Income shares of top 0.1, 1, 5, and 10% in 17 developed countries, unweighted average

Source: Alvaredo, Facundo, Anthony B. Atkinson, Thomas Piketty and Emmanuel Saez, The World Top Incomes Database, <http://g-mond.parisschoolofeconomics.eu/topincomes>, 25 April 2012.

asset appreciation, typically taxed at lower rates or not at all. Those with high salaries seek to ensure that part of their remuneration comes in forms, such as fringe benefits or stock-options which receive favorable tax treatment. Both groups may make use of tax havens that allow income to be moved beyond the reach of the national tax net. These shortcomings limit what can be said from tax data, but this does not mean that the data are worthless. Like all economic data, they measure with error the "true" variable in which we are interested'.

They also point out that the data are 'fairly homogenous across countries, annual, long-run, and broken down by income source for several cases. Users should be aware also about their limitations. Firstly, the series measure only top income shares and hence are silent on how inequality evolves elsewhere in the distribution. Secondly, the series are largely concerned with gross incomes before tax. Thirdly, the definition of income and the unit of observation (the individual vs. the family) vary across countries making comparability of levels across countries more difficult. Even within a country, there are breaks in comparability that arise because of changes in tax legislation affecting the definition of income, although most studies try to correct for such changes to create homogenous series. Finally and perhaps most important, the series might be biased because of tax avoidance and tax evasion. For the details, we refer users to the original papers' (Alvaredo, Facundo, Anthony B. Atkinson, Thomas Piketty, and Emmanuel Saez, The World Top Incomes Database, <http://g-mond.parisschoolofeconomics.eu/topincomes>, 25 April 2012. See also Atkinson, Piketty, and Saez, 2011).

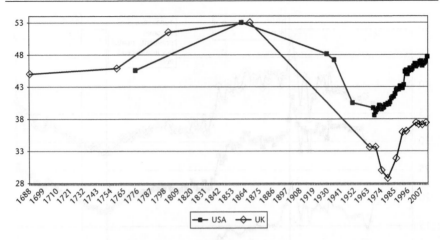

Figure 2.11. Inequality in the USA and UK over the long term, Gini coefficient, percent

Source: Ginis are computed by B. Milanovic from social tables before the twentieth century and from household survey and tax returns afterwards (Milanovic, 2013; Milanovic, Lindert, and Williamson, 2007; and personal correspondence with B. Milanovic).

Data for Britain and the the USA, based on the reconstruction of the social tables for the pre-modern period, provide a similar picture—an increase in inequalities before the 1860s and a decline in the 1930s–1980s (comparable data on the 1867–1929 period are missing)—Fig. 2.11.

In the United States, income and wealth inequalities were initially, in the late eighteenth century, most probably lower than in Europe due to the absence of large accumulated fortunes in the New World and the abundance of free land. In the late eighteenth century, the top 10% of wealth holders accounted for only 45% of total wealth in the USA as compared to 64% in Scotland and 46–80% in Finland, Norway, Sweden, and Denmark (Soltow, 1989: 238). But it appears that inequalities increased greatly in the nineteenth century, reaching a peak in between the two world wars. Soltow (1989: 251) finds some decrease in income inequality in 1798–1850/60 in the USA, and slight or no increase in the wealth inequality in the same period, but the ratio of the largest fortunes to the median wealth of households (Phillips, 2002) tells a different story (Fig. 2.12). This ratio increased from 1000 in 1790 (Elias Derby's wealth was estimated at $1 million) to 1,250,000 in 1912 (John D. Rockefellers's fortune of $1 billion), fell to 60,000 in 1982 ('only' $2 billion fortune of Daniel Ludwig), and increased again to 1,416,000 in 1999 ($85 billion fortune of Bill Gates). Turchin (2013) regards this dynamics as 'repeated back-and-forth swings', but recognizes that the decline in inequality after 1917 was associated with the rise of the workers movement in the USA and 'the lure of Bolshevism'.

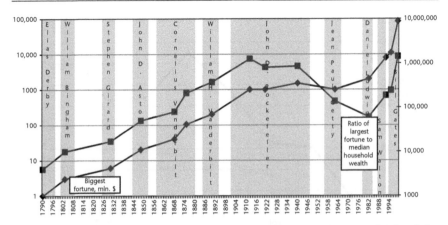

Figure 2.12. Largest fortunes in the USA in million dollars and as a multiple of the median wealth of households, log scale

Source: Phillips, 2002, p. 38.

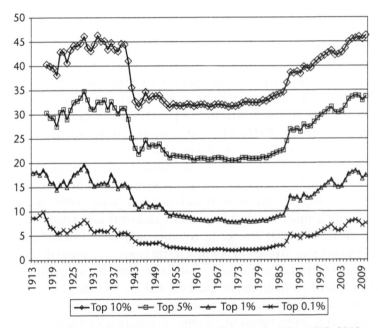

Figure 2.13. Long-term trends in income inequalities in the USA, 1913–2010

Source: Alvaredo et al. (2012).

Besides, data on pre-tax income from income tax returns show very high income inequalities in the USA before the Second World War, in 1913–1940 (Fig. 2.11, 2.13).

The income inequality story for developing countries is quite consistent with the dynamics of institutional capacity: in SSA, LA, and FSU, where

Figure 2.14 Predicted inequality in Latin America 1491–1929[17]
Source: Williamson, 2009.

institutional continuity was interrupted and institutional capacity weakened, inequality increased and remains high today. Extrapolation from regressions, linking Gini coefficients of income distribution to per capita GDP, population density, urbanization, and colonial status (plus some variables to control for different quality of data) suggest that colonialism increased inequality greatly: colonies had Gini coefficients nearly 13 percentage points higher than non-colonies (Williamson, 2009). In LA as a whole, inequality increased from 22.5% in 1491 to over 60% in 1929 (Fig. 2.14).

In the Dutch Cape colony in South Africa, income inequality reached probably the highest level in the world ever—the Gini coefficient was 70–80% in the eighteenth century (Fourie and von Fintel, 2009). And, according to the Engerman–Sokoloff hypothesis (Sokoloff and Engerman 2000), income inequalities that emerge in colonies may be self-sustaining. Initial high inequality may give rise to political institutions that favour the economic elite. Because of the balance of power associated with high inequality, the elite would be able to maintain the institutions that favour them.

On the other hand, India, China, and Japan in the eighteenth–nineteenth centuries had a more balanced income distribution (Table 2.3; Pomeranz, 2000; Saito, 2009).[18] In MENA, India, and East Asia (especially until the 1990s), inequality was noticeably lower (Table 2.3).

---

[17] These are not the actual Ginis, but predicted Ginis reconstructed using the regression equation mentioned in the text.

[18] In Japan, the Gini coefficient allegedly increased from 34% in 1860 to 56% in 1940, but then fell to 30–40% in the 1960s–1990s (Saito, 2009).

Table 2.3. Gini coefficients around particular years in developing countries, percent

Years	1550	1750	1800	1850	1900	1950	2000
Serbia	20.9						32.2
Maghreb					57		40
Bihar/India		48.9	33.5			49.7	32.5
China					24.5		41.6
Indonesia					39.7	32.1	34.4
Japan					39.5		26
Siam/Thailand						48.5	50.9
Kenya					33.2	46.2	44.4
Nueva Espana/Mexico			63.5				50
Brazil				43.3			58.8
Chile				63.7			54.6
Peru (1876)					41		51

Source: Milanovic, Lindert, and Williamson, 2007; Modalsli, 2013; data for 2000 are sometimes from the WDI.

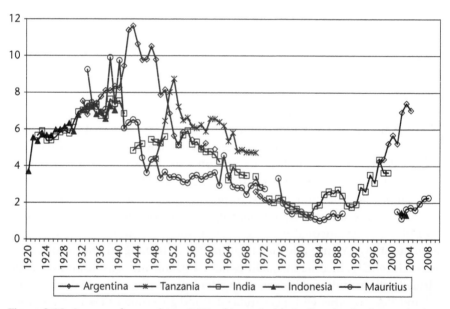

Figure 2.15. Income shares of top 0.1% of households in five developing countries, percent

Source: Alvaredo et al. (2012).

Unlike in developed countries, where income inequalities started to decline or stopped growing after 1917, in developing countries (many of which remained colonies) the turning point was the Second World War (Fig. 2.15). And the share of the rich in total income most of the time was higher in LA and SSA (Argentina, Tanzania) than in Asia (India, Indonesia)—Fig. 2.15. Mauritius, located closer to Africa than to Asia and gaining independence in

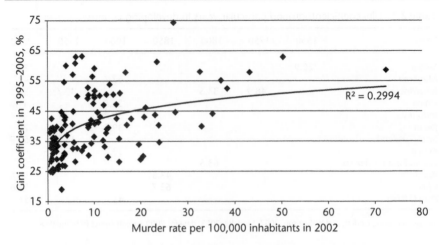

Figure 2.16. Murder rate in 2002 and income inequalities in 1990–2005
Source: WHO, WDI.

1968, may be the exception that proves the rule—low income inequalities and a low murder rate, one of the highest growth rates in the world in the last 40 years, one of the few working democracies in developing world.

Income inequality, of course, goes together with weak institutional capacity, as measured by the murder rate (Fig. 2.16). Subjective measures of the institutional capacity—various indices, such as ICRG (international country risk guide), government effectiveness, rule of law, corruption perception index, doing business index, and so on—are negatively correlated with income inequalities. Islam and Montenegro (2002) claimed that income inequalities do not influence institutional capacity, but they were able to arrive at this result only by introducing dummy variables for LA and SSA—two of the most unequal regions of the world. In a more recent and more accurate study (Alonso and Garcimatrin, 2013), making all efforts to control for endogeneity, income inequalities have a strong and significant impact on virtually all institutional indices even after introducing regional dummies for LA and SSA. Together with per capita GDP and government tax revenues they explain 60 to 80% of variations in the quality of institutions as measured by four out of six indices of the World Bank (government effectiveness, control over corruption, rule of law, regulatory quality, but not political stability and transparency and accountability), the Transparency International Corruption Perception Index, Global Competitiveness Index (Institutions component) of the World Economic Forum, Objective Governance Indicators, and Doing Business Indicators (Alonso and Garcimatrin, 2013).

Wealth inequalities are strongly correlated with income inequalities, although there are some important exceptions (Fig. 2.17). Virtually all countries with income distribution Ginis higher than 50% and wealth distribution

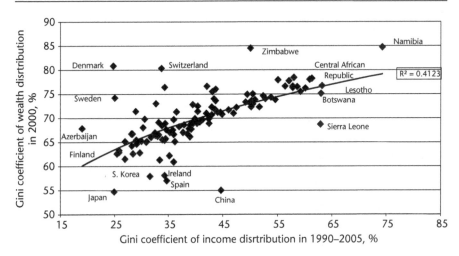

Figure 2.17. Inequalities in income and wealth distribution, Gini coefficients in 1990–2005, percent

Source: WDI database; Davies et al. (2007).

Ginis higher than 70% are in SSA (Botswana, the Central African Republic, Lesotho, Malawi, Mali, Namibia, Niger, South Africa, Swaziland) and LA (Bolivia, Brazil, Chile, the Dominican Republic, Ecuador, Guatemala, Haiti, Paraguay, El Salvador); the only country in the group that does not belong to SSA and LA is Papua New Guinea.

Countries with the lowest wealth inequalities are in Western Europe (Austria, Finland, Italy, Ireland, Norway), Eastern Europe (Albania, Belarus, the Czech Republic, Slovakia, Slovenia), East Asia (China, Japan, Korea), Middle East (Yemen), and Australia, whereas countries with the highest income inequalities are mostly in SSA (Botswana, CAR, South Africa, Swaziland, Mali, Namibia, Zambia, Zimbabwe), LA (Bolivia, Brazil, Chile, Colombia, Ecuador, Guatemala, Nicaragua, Panama, El Salvador, St. Vincent and the Grenadines, St. Kitts and Nevis); the important exceptions in terms of wealth inequalities are Denmark and Switzerland.

There are also statistics on the number of billionaires, published by Forbes annually, that allegedly characterize income distribution at the very top of the wealth pyramid (Table 2.4). The number of billionaires depends mostly on the total size of the country's GDP (per capita GDP is also important, but much less so).[19] The deviations from the predicted values that are shown at Table 2.4

---

[19] The relationship is nonlinear:

Number of billionaires in 2007 = $-0.9 + 0.367y - 0.0049y^2 + 2.6Y^2$, where

y – PPP GDP per capita in thousand \$ in 2005,
Y – PPP GDP in 2005 in trillions.

N= 181, R^2 = 0.95, all coefficients significant at 1% level.

Table 2.4. Number of billionaires in various countries—actual and predicted by regression (see footnote 19)

COUNTRY	Number of billionaires in 2007	Predicted number of billionaires	'Excess' number of billionaires
	(1)	(2)	(3) = (1) – (2)
United States	415	407	8
Canada	23	9	14
Australia	12	7	5
New Zealand	3	5	−2
Japan	24	45	−21
Korea, Rep.	10	7	3
Israel	9	5	4
Western Europe	174	144	29
Austria	3	6	−3
Belgium	2	6	−4
Cyprus	2	5	−3
Denmark	2	6	−4
France	15	15	0
Germany	55	22	33
Greece	1	6	−5
Iceland	2	6	−4
Ireland	4	6	−2
Italy	13	12	1
Monaco	1		
Netherlands	4	7	−3
Norway	4	6	−2
Portugal	1	5	−4
Spain	20	9	11
Sweden	8	6	2
Switzerland	8	6	2
United Kingdom	29	15	14
SA	36	15	21
India	36	15	21
SSA	3	2	1
South Africa	3	2	1
MENA	56	27	29
Turkey	25	2	23
Saudi Arabia	13	5	8
UAE	5	6	−1
Kuwait	4	6	−2
Lebanon	4	2	2
Egypt, Arab Rep.	4	1	3
Oman	1	5	−4
EA	70	93	−31
China	20	75	−55
Hong Kong, China	21	6	15
Malaysia	9	3	6
Taiwan	8		
Singapore	4	6	−2
Thailand	3	2	1
Philippines	3	0	3
Indonesia	2	2	0
LA	38	24	14
Brazil	20	8	12

COUNTRY	Number of billionaires (1)	Predicted number of billionaires (2)	'Excess' number of billionaires (3) = (1) − (2)
Mexico	10	6	4
Chile	3	3	0
Colombia	2	1	1
Venezuela, RB	2	2	0
Argentina	1	3	−2
FSU	65	13	52
Russian Federation	53	10	43
Ukraine	7	1	6
Kazakhstan	5	2	3
EE	8	13	−5
Poland	5	4	1
Romania	1	2	−1
Yugoslavia, FR (Serbia/ Montenegro)	1	2	−1
Czech Republic	1	5	−4
ALL	946	817	120

Source: Forbes billionaires website (<http://www.forbes.com/billionaires/>).

are quite telling. Countries that exceed the predicted number of billionaires considerably (2 times and more) are some developed countries (Canada, Israel, Germany, Spain, the UK), India, Turkey, Saudi Arabia, Egypt, Hong Kong, Malaysia, Philippines, Brazil, Russia, Ukraine, and Kazakhstan. Conversely, countries where the number of billionaires is considerably lower than predicted are Japan, China, most countries of Western Europe, Oman, Argentina, Romania, and the Czech Republic.

This picture is not completely consistent with the previously described pattern of income and wealth distribution—the major difference is the 'excess' number of billionaires in MENA countries that are characterized by a relatively even distribution of income and wealth.[20] It looks like East Asia and MENA countries have different models of wealth distribution: in the former income inequalities are relatively low overall and at the very top, whereas in the latter they are low overall, but not at the very top. To be sure, these differences should matter for social tension and the quality of institutions. But the result that matters most for our current purposes is that East Asia in general, and China in particular, have more even income and wealth distribution on all counts and at all levels—throughout the whole income–wealth pyramid—and at the very top of the pyramid as well.

To summarize, there are two ways to escape the Malthusian trap: (1) eliminating collectivist institutions and allowing for the costly increase in income inequality and savings/investment rate at the very early stages of development

[20] After controlling for total GDP and GDP per capita, such variables as resource abundance and the share of export of fuel in total export, Islam dummy, democracy level in 1972–2002 and 2002–2003 are not significant in explaining the number of billionaires.

at the expense of the consumption of the masses; and (2) maintaining collect-ivist institutions and keeping income inequality relatively low until slow techno-logical progress and a rise in productivity allow capital to be accumulated at a pace surpassing population growth rates. The first route was taken by countries that are now called Western, and was associated with dramatic social costs in the sixteenth to eighteenth centuries. Moreover, it was imposed on part of the developing world in the nineteenth to twentieth centuries during the era of colonialism. In the developing world, this Westernization attempt created an institutional vacuum—traditional, collectivist structures were destroyed, whereas the new modern institutions did not take root, which led to even greater costs than those of the West several centuries before. Other countries that destroyed their egalitarian institutions prematurely (replicating the Western path), experi-enced tremendous declines in institutional capacity and rises in inequality.[21]

In the Russian Empire in the nineteenth century and LA countries in the nineteenth and twentieth centuries, the growth rates were not enough to narrow the gap with the West (Argentina, a developed country in between the two world wars, even fell out of the club after the Second World War). SSA was falling behind the West at least until 2000 (Fig. 1.1. in the previous chapter).

On the other hand, those developing countries that managed to resist Westernization of their institutions and preserved institutional continuity as well as relatively low inequality (East Asia, MENA countries, and India) did not gain much in terms of economic growth before the mid 1900s, but were better positioned to take advantage of growth opportunities as soon as creeping increases in productivity allowed them to escape the Malthusian trap. But even in India and China, this path was associated with periodic mass famines, which did not happen before colonialism due to even distribution of limited food resources by the community institutions.[22]

---

[21] Colonialism, of course, affected the growth of developing world through various other channels, especially via promoting 'Great Specialization' (resources in developing countries were exchanged for Western manufacturing goods). Findlay (2009) calls the Industrial Revolution a 'Faustian bargain with the devil'. He regards slavery and resource specialization, 'Great Divergence' of the nineteenth century, as well as depletion of resources and resulting pollution of the twentieth century as natural, if not inevitable, consequences of the type of industrialization model embarked upon by Western countries. My argument here is more modest: colonialism undermined traditional institutions in developing countries at a time when income levels were low and thus increases in inequality led to mass poverty and famines. Besides, colonialism interrupted the trajectory of institutional development in many Southern countries; this resulted in a weakening of their institutional capacity with predictable negative impact on growth.

[22] 'Even before the onset of the Victorian famines, warning signals were in place: C. Walford showed in 1878 that the number of famines in the first century of British rule had already exceeded the total recorded cases in the previous two thousand years. But the grim reality behind claims to "good governance" truly came to light in the very decades that Ferguson trumpets. According to the most reliable estimates, the deaths from the 1876–1878 famine were in the range of six to eight million, and in the double-barrelled famine of 1896–1897 and 1899–1900, they probably totalled somewhere in the range of 17 to 20 million. So in the quarter century that marks the pinnacle

By the mid twentieth century, there were three groups of countries in the South: (1) relatively rich (LA, the Russian Empire, South Africa) that had relatively high investment rates (higher than other Southern countries, but lower than Western countries). They had high income inequalities and poor institutions, so their growth, even though higher than in the rest of the South, was not enough to catch up with the West; (2) poor SSA (with the exception of South Africa) that in addition to all disadvantages of LA and Russia (high inequalities and poor institutions) had also a low savings–investment rate and were not growing at all; (3) poor East and South Asia and MENA countries that did not have a high savings–investment rate, but mostly preserved collectivist institutions that maintained low inequality and reasonable enforcement capacity. Once these countries of the third group were able to increase their savings rate (either through forced savings, like communist China, or due to a slow increase in income caused by creeping technical progress) they found themselves in a better starting position for fast economic growth. Some of them became economic miracles (many countries in East Asia) and experienced rapid growth (South Asia), others probably possess necessary preconditions to become miracles in the future (MENA countries).

In short, premature dismantling of collectivist institutions, even when allowing overcoming of the Malthusian trap, did not allow for healthy growth. Past and recent research shows that inequalities are associated with an array of negative social consequences—from increase in crime and mortality, to the decline in educational attainments, and proliferation of psychological disorders and obesity (Wilkinson and Pickett, 2010). Besides, inequalities undermine social mobility and lead to the conservation of social stratification: the higher the inequalities, the higher the probability that one's income will closely resemble that of your parents (the Great Gatsby curve). Hence the social, and very often the political, structure of the society becomes less flexible as well.

> The frequent claim that inequality promotes accumulation and growth does not get much support from history. On the contrary, great economic inequality has always been correlated with extreme concentration of political power, and that power has always been used to widen the income gaps through rent-seeking and rent-keeping, forces that demonstrably retard economic growth (Milanovic, Lindert, and Williamson, 2007).

of colonial good governance, famine deaths average at least a million per year' (Chibber, 2005). In China, famines claimed 8,000 lives a year in 1644–1795, 57,000 in 1796–1871, 325,000 in 1871–1911, and 583,000 in 1911–47 during the Republic. The 1876–79 famine alone took at least 10 million lives, twice as many as all famines since 1644 (Xia Mingfang calculations cited in Pomeranz, 2008).

As Joseph Stiglitz explains:

> widely unequal societies do not function efficiently, and their economies are neither stable, nor sustainable in the long run ... When the wealthiest use their political power to benefit excessively the corporations they control, much needed revenues are diverted into the pockets of a few instead of benefiting society at large ... That higher inequality is associated with lower growth—controlling for all other relevant factors—has been verified by looking at the range of countries and looking over longer periods of time (Stiglitz, 2012: 83, 117).

Latin American countries, writes Stiglitz, may show the future to other states that are just stepping on the road leading to growing inequalities. 'The experience of Latin American countries, the region of the world with the highest level of inequality, foreshadows what lies ahead. Many of the countries were mired in civil conflict for decades, suffered high levels of criminality and social instability. Social cohesion simply did not exist' (Stiglitz, 2012: 84).

Developing countries with high income inequalities are more likely than others to end up in a vicious circle—bad equilibrium with poor quality of institutions, low growth, low social mobility, and high social tensions. It may take a revolution to break this vicious circle and to exit the bad equilibrium.

3

Chinese and Russian Economies Under Central Planning: Why the Difference in Outcomes?

The CPE that emerged after the victory of communists in Russia and later in China was a reaction to the rise of income inequalities under wild, unconstrained capitalism. The strongest feature of the CPE is its ability to mobilize domestic savings for growth and to transform them into investment without allowing high inequalities. It is exactly due to the mobilization of these savings and their transformation into investment that China and Russia—who were falling behind the West under capitalism—started to catch up. Lack of savings is the major hurdle for speeding up growth in developing countries—very often it leads to a development trap. Centrally planned economies can force the mobilization of domestic savings via taxes without allowing the increase in income inequality (property income goes to the state as the owner of the means of production).

Long-term perspective on the rise and fall of CPE in Russia and China

The socialist experiment in the two countries in the twentieth century was a continuation of their previous history. In China, Westernization started very late, only after Opium Wars of the mid nineteenth century, and immediately caused widespread resistance—the Taiping Rebellion (1850–64) and Boxer Rebellion (1898–1901), both of which were crushed with the help of the Western armies, de facto disintegration of the country in 1915–27, and civil war between Kuomintang and Communist Party of China (CPC) (1927–50) with the simultaneous Anti-Japanese war of 1937–45. After the start of Westernization in the mid nineteenth century, and before the creation of PRC in 1949, there were barely three decades of peaceful development in China.

Conversely, in Russia, creeping dismantling of community institutions had been going on since at least the seventeenth century, with the critical junction being probably Peter the Great's Westernization reforms (early eighteenth century). The land reform of 1861 (Emancipation Act) freed the serfs without land—small land plots given to peasants were supposed to be purchased from the state and the redemption payments continued until the First Russian Revolution of 1905–07. Large estates—latifundia-type land ownership of aristocracy—continued well into the twentieth century and were not eliminated even by Stolypin's 1906 reforms that were aimed at destroying the agricultural community and facilitating the redistribution of the land from the aristocracy to wealthy peasants.

If in Russia, this gradual Westernization was bound 'to succeed', it would 'succeed' as in Latin America, where income inequalities persisted and did not decrease until the twenty-first century, despite numerous uprisings and revolutions. But it did not succeed, it failed—probably to a large extent by a mere coincidence of events and due to the exceptional stubbornness of the Russian ruling class that was adamant in resisting the radical land reform. It failed because even the democratic February 1917 Revolution that led to the abdication of the Czar and to the establishment of the Provisionary Government did not result in radical land reform. It took the October 1917 Socialist Revolution to initiate radical redistribution of land. But the Bolshevik Government confiscated not only all the land of the large landowners, but also all large and medium size enterprises in various industries.

The Emancipation Act of 1861 had led to a dramatic rise in income and wealth inequalities and had sped up the differentiation of peasantry. As Table 3.1 shows, the share of 'middle class' peasants remained stable at a 50% level in 1600–1860, but fell to 23% by the end of the 1800s at the expense of the increase in the share of wealthy peasants on the one side, and poor peasants on the other. As a result, the number of peasant disturbances increased from 10–30 a year in the early 1800s, to 300 before the Emancipation Act of 1861, to 3000 during the First Russian Revolution (Fig. 3.1), whereas the crime rate increased more than threefold in 1850–1910—from 500 to over 1500 per 100,000 inhabitants (Fig. 3.2).

Table 3.1. Increase in inequalities in Russia in 1600–1900. Social structure of Russian peasantry, percentage of total

Years	Wealthy	Middle	Poor
1600–1750	15	53	32
1751–1800	10	48	42
1801–1860	16	56	30
1896–1900	18	23 ⇓	59

Source: Mironov (1985) cited in Turchin and Nefedov, 2009, p. 277.

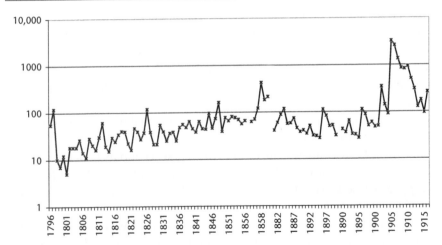

Figure 3.1. The number of peasant disturbances per year in 1800–1920
Source: Dubrovsky (1956), Litvak (1967), Zayonchkovsky (1968) cited in Turchin and Nefedov (2009: 286).

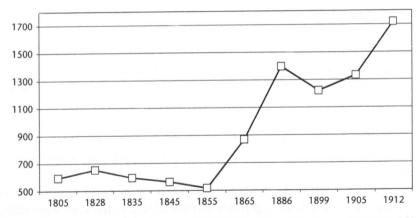

Figure 3.2. Number of total crimes per 100,000 inhabitants in Russia in 1800–1920
Source: Mironov (2000) cited in Turchin and Nefedov (2009: 285).

In the words of Georgi Derluguian,

it is not so wondrous that in the sixteenth century Russia became an empire along the many gunpowder empires of its generation; it is much more wondrous that in 1900 Russia was still a great power. After all, neither China nor India and Iran, not even Turkey or Spain by 1900 could boast the prestige and positions which they had claimed at the start of modern age. The reason for this massive decline of the rest is certainly related to what had come out in the intervening centuries from the far West...Nobody at the time would consider the revolution in Russia unexpected. If anything, such cataclysm had been long and widely anticipated... The revolution struck in Russia whole decades after originally anticipated. (Derluguian, 2013)

The 1905 and 1917 revolutions were a natural reaction to the unfortunate post-1861 reform developments. The great socialist experiment in Russia (1917–91)—the courageous attempt to restore social justice and the institutional capacity of the state—resulted in a decrease in wealth and income inequalities, the crime rate, and the shadow economy. However, once the transition to a market economy occurred in the 1990s, the hidden and suppressed sins of the previous history (income inequalities and poor institutions) came to the surface.

In contrast, the Chinese transition to the market economy benefited from at least two factors that were absent in the Soviet case. First, CPE in China was scrapped after less than 30 years of existence, before it reached its natural limit of efficiency, so China avoided the slowdown of growth that was observed in the Soviet CPE in the 1960s–1980s. And second, the 'Asian values' tradition was too strong to allow the dismantling of the community and the state. The continuity of the collectivist community tradition based on low inequality and the strong state trajectory of Chinese development (up to the mid nineteenth century and from the mid twentieth century) ensured that the transition to the market in China did not produce as much inequality, crime, and shadow economy as it did in the USSR.

Overall, the Soviet economic and social model was quite competitive before the mid 1960s. Despite popular belief that Soviet economic development was a failure, the USSR in 1928–70 was the second fastest growing country in world after Japan (Allen, 2003: 7, Fig. 1.1). Many developing countries all over the world were trying to copy the Soviet model in the 1950s–1960s, even though Soviet assistance at that time was minimal and in any case way below Western assistance. It was probably no less attractive for the developing world than the Chinese economic model today.

Red Plenty, a novel by Francis Spufford, nicely captures the atmosphere of that time—the belief that the gap between the USSR and the West was closing and would disappear soon because socialism was not only a more advanced social system, but also a more competitive economy. During the famous 'kitchen debate' of 1959, Soviet leader Nikita Khruschev famously refused to admit that capitalism could have better innovations at least in some areas. Richard Nixon, the US vice president, opening an American exhibition in Moscow, offered a diplomatic formula—you are ahead in space, we are ahead in coloured TV, let us compete for the benefit of the consumers in both countries. Khruschev, as soon as Nixon's words were translated to him, raised his hand up in objection: we surpassed you in rockets, we'll surpass you in TV, he said (Khruschev and Nixon, 1959). Not only in the Soviet Union, but throughout the world, many people at that time sincerely believed that this was exactly what was going to happen. That was the spirit of the time, when the Soviet system retained its dynamism.

Where has all the Soviet competitiveness gone and why has the Chinese model managed to retain its dynamism? It is important to separate the inherent deficiencies of CPE from the numerous problems resulting from 'bad implementation' and caused by specific historical circumstances.

Theoretically at least, the CPE by keeping inequalities low could have avoided such costs as increase in mortality and deterioration of institutional quality. In practice, of course, in the USSR and in China there were famines due to economic reasons and there was some weakening of institutions in the USSR during the 1970s–1980s, but these features do not look imminent and unavoidable.

Theoretically, the CPE probably could have avoided the huge decline in capital productivity during the emergence of the command economy—in the USSR the growth rates in industry fell from 20% in the 1920s to 10% in the 1930s even though the investment ratio (the share of investment in GDP) increased from 13 to 26% (Shmelev and Popov, 1989). In China, for instance, the emergence of CPE was not associated with such a waste in resources leading to a decline of capital productivity as in the USSR in the 1930s. Besides, the argument about inefficient use of savings makes sense only if these savings are available, whereas many developing countries were unable to mobilize savings in the first place.

Theoretically, industrial policy in the USSR could have been better than the actual import substitution type that was never replaced by export orientation. It is inevitable that a country in need of industrialization starts with import substitution policies (because when newly created industries emerge that were absent before they start by crowding out foreign goods from the domestic market), but there is a need to switch to export orientation at an appropriate point. If enterprises eventually do not become competitive in the international market, they evolve into grandiose, but useless, industrial 'Egyptian pyramids' that can exist only behind a protectionist wall and that go bankrupt as soon as they are exposed to the winds of international competition. But there are examples of export orientation within the framework of the CPE: China started to increase its exports at double digit rates from the early 1970s, well before the market-type reforms.

The inherent deficiency of the CPE is the lack of a mechanism to replace managers and bureaucrats under an authoritarian regime. Neither the Soviet experiments with the *sovnarkhozy* (territorial management bodies created in 1957–65, intended to replace industry branch ministries and to undermine the positions of the ministerial bureaucracy), nor Chinese experiments of replacing the cadres during the Cultural Revolution can be considered successful. However, from a purely economic point of view, this could have become the growth constraint in the future, but it did not really constrain growth in the 1970s–1980s. The quality of state institutions and bureaucracy, despite all problems, at the end of the planning period in China and in the USSR was quite high, higher than in democratic countries at the same level of development. The shadow economy that reached 10–15% of GDP under Brezhnev by most generous estimates, increased to 50% in the 1990s. In the 1980s the corruption perception index (CPI) in the USSR and China was about 5—both countries were in the middle of the list of 54 countries—cleaner than all developing countries and close to countries like Greece, Italy, Portugal, and South Korea. In 1996, after the transition to a market economy and democracy, in the same list of 54 countries Russia moved to the 48th place—between India and Venezuela. In 2011 Russia had a CPI of 2.4, China 3.6, whereas Cuba had 4.2.

What really became the insurmountable and binding growth constraint in the 1970s–1980s in the Soviet Union (but not in China) was the 'ageing' of the CPE resulting from the ageing of the fixed capital stock and the inability of the centrally planned economy to replace the retiring machinery and equipment, buildings and structures. As argued later in this chapter, the CPEs under-invested in replacement of the retiring elements of the fixed capital stock and over-invested in the expansion of production capacities. The task of renovating physical capital contradicted the short-term goal of fulfilling planned targets and, therefore, Soviet planners preferred to invest in new capacities instead of upgrading the old ones. Hence, after the massive invest-ment of the 1930s in the USSR (the 'big push'), the highest productivity was achieved after the period equal to the service life of capital stock (about 20–30 years)—before the need for massive investment into replacing retiring capital stock emerged. Afterwards, the capital stock started to age rapidly, reducing sharply capital productivity, and lowering labour productivity and TFP growth rates.

Among the many reasons for the decline of growth rates in the USSR in the 1960s–1980s, the discussed inability of the centrally planned economy to ensure adequate flow of investment into the replacement of retirement of fixed capital stock appears to be most crucial. What is more important, even if these retirement constraints were not the only reason for the decline in growth rates, they are sufficient to explain the inevitable gradual decline after 30 years of relatively successful development.

If this explanation is correct, a centrally planned economy is doomed to experience a growth slowdown after three decades of high growth following a 'big push'. In this respect, the relatively short Chinese experience with the CPE (1949/59–79) looks superior to the East European experience (1950–91) and excessively long Soviet experience (1929–91). It was only the USSR that fully experienced all the negative consequences of ageing of the CPE. This is one reason to believe that the transition to the market economy in the Soviet Union would have been more successful if it had started in the 1960s.

Was this possible—the transition to a market economy in the USSR in the 1960s? Most probably, yes. It was a junction that happens in development processes from time to time, when the outcome—the route to be taken for the next several decades, if not centuries—is determined not so much by historical necessity but by the confluence of circumstances, by the interplay of minor events that could produce different outcomes. If this transition to the market had been carefully managed, the outcome may have resembled more the Chinese pattern of market-type reforms of 1979 and beyond—without major transformational recession, without dramatic weakening of state institutions and virtual privatization of the state, without the growth of the shadow economy, crime, suicides, and mortality.

But, first, this is only a hypothesis, of course; and it is difficult to test it today, *post factum*. And, second, even if the transition to the market had happened in the USSR in the 1960s, it would not have been as successful as the Chinese transition. Russia would have returned to the pre-1917 trajectory of adopting Western institutions with high income inequalities and polarization of the society (pretty much like it did in the 1990s). Transformational recessions may have been shorter and not so deep, but the weakening of the institutions—increase in crime and shadow economy—would be pretty much inevitable.

What could have been repaired in China in 30 years of socialism, could not have been fixed in Russia even after under 70 years of socialism and 60 years of central planning. Socialism contributed to the restoration of the collectivist institutions in both countries, Russia and in China: income inequalities decreased and the institutional capacity of the state improved. But the legacy of 300 years of Westernization in Russia kicked back once market reforms were carried out in the 1990s after 70 years of socialism: inequalities increased greatly, as did corruption, crime, and the shadow economy. In a sense, it is clear, if only *post factum*, that there were two options in the early 1960s and both of them were bad: (1) to carry out market reforms and see the collapse of the institutional capacity of the state (probably an even greater collapse than occurred in the 1990s), (2) to delay the transition to the market and to preserve socialism, but at a price of a loss of economic and social dynamism.

In reality the second option was chosen: there was no transition to the market in the 1960s, so in the absence of rotation and control from below over managerial cadres, the inability of the CPE to renovate efficiently capital stock, bureaucratization of apparatus and ageing of equipment and structures led to the growth slowdown. The *Sovnarkhozy* reforms (1957–65), designed to renovate cadres and officials, and *khozraschet* reforms (1965), designed to stimulate innovations and growth, basically failed. From the mid 1960s there was a decline of the centrally planned economy in the USSR. Growth of GDP per capita in the USSR continued in the 1970s and 1980s, but the rates of growth were slowing down, so the income gap with the West stopped closing and then started to widen. Life expectancy, after reaching 70 years in 1965, stopped growing, while crimes, murders, suicides began to increase.

It is important to keep in mind the historical perspective, though: as compared to the period of transformational recession of the 1990s, the stagnation of the CPE in the 1970s–1980s looks like a moderate slowdown as opposed to a falling off the cliff. In 1989–98, GDP fell by 45%, from 1987 to 1994 life expectancy fell by 6 years (from 70 to 64), income inequalities, as measured by the Gini coefficient nearly doubled, and the decile ratio more than doubled.

Economic policies of the Soviet period were often bad, but of course not as bad as in the 1990s. The quality of macroeconomic policy deteriorated greatly. In Soviet times, after the new currency, *chervonets*, was introduced in 1922, inflation never reached hundreds or thousands of percent a year like it did in the 1990s—neither during the accelerated industrialization of the 1930s, nor even during the Second World War. And after the 1947 confiscatory monetary reform, and before 1987 when Gorbachev started to pump money into circulation, open and hidden[1] inflation never exceeded 3–5% a year—one of the best records in the world.

Strictly speaking, the late USSR leaders (Brezhnev, Andropov, Chernenko) left the CPE in a good shape for Gorbachev reforms: this CPE was obviously not efficient, but was in a perfect macroeconomic order—low inflation, low government budget deficit, high domestic savings and investment, low domestic and external debt (just about several percent of GDP). Up to the end of the 1980s the Soviet debt was sold at the secondary market at 100% of its nominal value—nobody could have thought that the USSR could default on its debts (in the 1990s Russian debts were sold at 30% and less of the nominal value, and Russia actually defaulted on its debt in 1998).

In general, the late Soviet economy definitely had an accumulated margin of safety (reserve of strength) that was enough to finance the costs of market-type reforms through external and internal borrowing, so that it was possible to limit the adverse impact of these reforms on the welfare of the population. In this sense, the Soviet centrally planned economy was more easily reformable than the Polish one. It just happened, though, that the entire safety margin was quickly and senselessly squandered in the late 1980s–early 1990s, so that 'anesthetic surgery'–transition to the market without the decline in living standards–became impossible.

---

[1] In the CPE, prices were controlled by the planners and often did not reflect the growing gap between the demand for goods and limited supply of goods at controlled prices (hence rationing and/or queues). Hidden (or suppressed) inflation is the increase in prices that would occur, if they were deregulated. The estimates are based on the increase in the gap between money demand and supply of goods at fixed prices (Shmelev and Popov, 1989).

Conversely, the Chinese experience of CPE was much more fortunate. Despite negative growth rates during some years of the Great Leap Forward (1958–61) and Cultural Revolution (1966–76), Chinese GDP per capita increased over 1950–78 on average by nearly 3% a year—quite an impressive record for a developing country. In the five years preceding economic reform (1973–78) per capita income in China was growing at 5% on average, while export was increasing at double digit rates. Chinese life expectancy grew from 35 years in 1950 to 65 years in 1976, and in the year of Mao's death was 13 years higher than in India.

Right before the reforms of 1979, it looked as though China was growing better than in any other previous period of its communist history. Unlike in the USSR, where the economy growth rates were falling before the reforms and fell even faster after the reforms, in China economic growth rates were high and growing before the reforms and increased even more after the reforms. The Chinese story thus looks very much like a virtuous circle as opposed to the Soviet vicious circle. Chinese market-type reforms resulted in an acceleration of economic growth that was already respectable under CPE and even gained momentum. Soviet market oriented reforms were intended to deal with the progressive stagnation that the CPE experienced in the 1970s–1980s, but instead led to the deepest transformational recession.

Soviet economy: from dynamism to stagnation

Soviet catch-up development looked extremely impressive until the 1970s. In fact, from the 1930s to 1960s, the USSR and Japan were the only two major developing countries that successfully bridged the gap with the West (Fig. 1.1, Chapter 1). Before the Soviet period Russia had been permanently falling behind the West in the sixteenth to nineteenth centuries—neither the reforms of Peter the Great in the early eighteenth century, nor the elimination of serfdom in 1861(Emancipation Act), nor Witte's and Stolypin's reforms in the early twentieth century could have changed the trend (Fig. 3.3). Only in the 1920s–1960s did Russia (USSR), for the first time in its history, start to catch up with the West (Fig. 3.3).

But, in the second half of the twentieth century, the Soviet Union experienced the most dramatic shift in economic growth patterns. The high post-war growth rates of the 1950s gave way to a slowdown in growth in the 1960s–1980s, and later to the unprecedented depression of the 1990s associated with the transition from a centrally planned economy (CPE) to a market one. Productivity growth rates (output per worker, Western data) fell from an exceptionally high 6% a year in the 1950s, to 3% in the 1960s, 2% in the 1970s, and 1% in the 1980s (Fig. 3.4). In 1989 a transformational recession

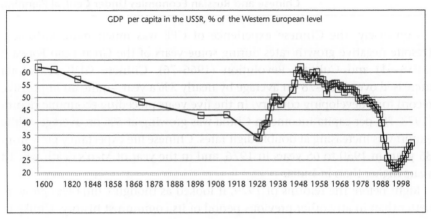

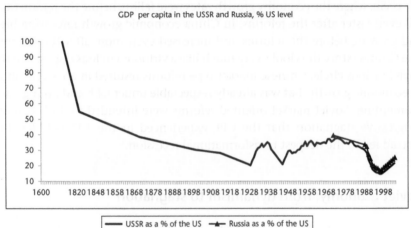

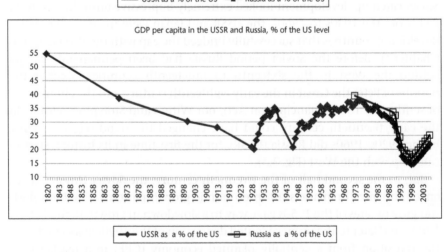

Figure 3.3. PPP GDP per capita in the USSR and Russia, as percentage of Western European and US level

Source: Maddison, 2008.

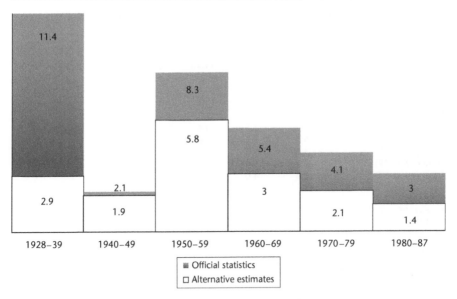

Figure 3.4. Annual average productivity growth rates in Soviet economy, percent
Source: Easterly and Fisher, 1995.

began and continued for almost a decade: output was constantly falling until 1999 with the exception of one single year—1997—when GDP increased by a barely noticeable 0.8%. If viewed as an inevitable and logical result of the Soviet growth model, this transformational recession worsens substantially the general record of Soviet economic growth.

The nature of Soviet economic decline from the 1950s to 1980s does not fit completely into the standard growth theory. If this decline was caused by the over-accumulation of capital (investment share doubled in 1950–85 from 15 to over 30% of GDP), how could it be that Asian countries were able to maintain high growth rates with an even higher share of investment in GDP and higher growth of capital/labour ratios?[2] Why, in the 1980s, as the conventional saying held it, did the Soviet Union maintain the Japanese share of investment in GDP with very 'un-Japanese' results?

If, on the contrary, the Soviet growth decline was caused by the specific inefficiencies of the centrally planned economy, why had CPE been so efficient in the 1950s, ensuring high growth rates of output, labour productivity, and total factor productivity? In the 1950s, Soviet defence spending was already very high and rising (from an estimated 9% of GDP in 1950 to

[2] In China and some Southeast Asian countries, high growth still coexists with high investment/GDP ratios. Chinese growth rates stayed at close to 10% a year for over three decades (1978–2012); the share of investment in GDP during this period increased from 30% in 1970–75 to nearly 50% in 2005 (China Statistical Yearbook).

Table 3.2. Growth in the USSR and Asian economies, Western data, 1928–87 (average annual, percent)

Period/country	Output per worker	Capital per worker	Capital/ output ratio	TPF growth (unit elasticity of substitution)	TPF growth assuming 0.4 elasticity of substitution
USSR (1928–39)	2.9	5.7	2.8	0.6	
USSR (1940–49)	1.9	1.5	−0.4	1.3	
USSR (1950–59)	5.8	7.4	1.6	2.8	1.1
USSR (1960–69)	3.0	5.4	2.4	0.8	1.1
USSR (1970–79)	2.1	5.0	2.9	0.1	1.2
USSR (1980–87)	1.4	4.0	2.6	−0.2	1.1
Japan(1950/57/65/–85/ 88/90)			2.3–3.2	1.7–2.5	
Korea (1950/60/65/–85/ 88/90)			2.8–3.7	1.7–2.8	
Taiwan (1950/53/65–85/ 88/90)			2.6–3.1	1.9–2.4	

Source: Easterly and Fisher, 1995.

10–13% by the end of the decade), whereas Soviet investment spending, although it increased markedly, was still below 25% by 1960. A medium-high share of investment spending and a very high share of defence expenditure is not precisely the kind of combination that could account for high productivity growth rates, even in market economies.

The highest rates of growth of labour productivity in the Soviet Union were observed not in the 1930s (3% annually), but in the 1950s (6%)—Table 3.2. The TFP growth rates by decade increased from 0.6% annually in the 1930s, to 2.8% in the 1950s, and then fell monotonously becoming negative in the 1980s. The decade of 1950s was thus the 'golden period' of Soviet economic growth. The patterns of Soviet growth of the 1950s in terms of growth accounting were very similar to the Japanese growth of the 1950s–1970s and to Korean and Taiwanese growth in the 1960–1980s—fast increases in labour productivity counterweighed the decline in capital productivity, so that the TFP increased markedly (Table 3.2). However, high Soviet economic growth lasted only for a decade, whereas in East Asia it continued for three to four decades, propelling Japan, South Korea, and Taiwan into the ranks of developed countries.

Why did the Soviet economy of the 1950s show better results than today's Russian economy and no worse results than the economies of Asian tigers in the 1950s–1970s? And why did this impressive growth of the 1950s come to an end in the 1970s–1980s? References to oil prices do not help much because these prices fell in 1986 (after Brezhnev's death in 1982 and the Andropov-Chernenko brief interregnum of 1982–85), whereas in 1973–82 world oil prices were exceptionally high, yet this did not result in growth acceleration.

For decades, Soviet experience with economic growth was regarded as a textbook proof of the 'disease of over-investment' resulting in declining factor productivity. It was even referred to as the best application of the Solow model ever seen. The Solow model predicted that growth rates in the long run would not depend on the share of investment in GDP and that the returns on this investment would decline with an increase in investment (growth of capital/labour ratio), making capital more abundant and labour more scarce. Hence, the USSR, as Alice in Wonderland said on a different occasion, had to run two times faster just to remain in the same place. Most estimates of Soviet economic growth found low and even declining TFP (in the 1970s–1980s annual average TFP growth rates were negative) suggesting that growth was due mostly to large capital and labour inputs, and in this sense was extremely costly.

More recently, parallels have been drawn between East Asian and Soviet growth. Krugman (1994), referring to the calculations by Young (1994), has argued that there is no puzzle to Asian growth; that it was due mostly to the accelerated accumulation of factor inputs—capital and labour—whereas TFP growth was quite weak (lower than in Western countries). The logical outcome is the prediction that East Asian growth will end in the same way as the Soviet growth did—over-accumulation of capital resources, if continued, sooner or later will undermine capital productivity. It may have happened in Japan in the 1970s–2000s (where growth rates declined despite the high share of investment in GDP), and may be happening in Korea, Taiwan, and ASEAN countries after the currency crises of 1997. The only other alternative for high growth countries would be to reduce the rates of capital accumulation (growth of investment), which should lead to the same result—slowdown in the growth of output. Radelet and Sachs (1997), however, challenged this view, arguing that East Asian growth would likely resume in two to three years after the 1997 currency crises.

A different approach (based on endogenous growth models and treating investment in human capital as a separate source of growth) would be that, in theory, rapid growth can continue endlessly if investments in physical and human capital are high. According to this approach, all cases of 'high growth failures'—from the USSR to Japan—are explained by special circumstances and do not refute the theoretical possibility of maintaining high growth rates 'forever' with a high investment/GDP ratio.

East Asian growth in Hong Kong, Japan, Singapore, South Korea, and Taiwan slowed down only after they caught up with Western countries in terms of GDP per capita. Even though technical progress was not the major factor of growth, its contribution was no less substantial than in developed countries and much more substantial than in other developing countries (Table 3.3). And these rates of technical progress did not fall even though investment/GDP rates were so high. This means that East Asia basically

Table 3.3. Growth accounting for major regions of the world in 1960–1990, percent

REGIONS	Annual average growth rates, %				
	GDP	Labour (# of workers)	Human capital (labour quality)	Physical capital	TFP (total factor productivity)[*]
East Asia	7.46	2.75	1.33	10.89	0.63–1.00
Latin America	3.27	2.42	0.98	4.51	−0.58–0.46
MENA	5.14	2.43	1.36	6.43	0.22–0.42
South Asia	4.10	2.08	1.51	5.38	−0.96–0.50
Sub-Saharan Africa	3.42	2.61	0.77	3.64	−0.28–0.15
OECD	3.56	1.17	0.63	4.62	0.60–1.27

[*] The lower estimate is obtained after adjustment for labour quality, the highest is obtained without such adjustment.
Source: Hahn and Kim (2000).

manufactured two miracles, not one: it managed to mobilize domestic savings for investment and to keep the share of investment at a very high level (something that other developing countries dream of) and it managed to keep technical progress running at a high speed. The slowdown that happened after they reached the levels of per capita income of rich countries could be logically explained by the approach to the technological frontier (innovations at the cutting edge are more difficult than imitation).

The logical 'special' explanation for the Soviet economic decline would be, of course, the nature of the CPE itself that precluded it from using investment as efficiently as in market economies. But to what extent the Soviet economic slowdown was caused by the specific CPE factors and to what extent it reflected the more general process of TPF decline due to over-accumulation of capital is a controversial issue in the literature. Gomulka (1977), Bergson (1983), Ofer (1987), and others using the Cobb–Douglas production function attributed the slowdown in growth rates to the very nature of the extensive growth model, where the contribution of technical progress to growth was small and falling in line with the accumulation of capital. Weitzman (1970) and Desai (1976), however, pointed out that another explanation is also consistent with the stylized facts, namely constant rates of technical progress, but low capital/labour substitution (CES—constant elasticity substitution—production function) leading to declining marginal product of capital. The debate about the most appropriate form of the production function is summarized in Ofer (1987), Easterly and Fisher (1995), Schroeder (1995), and Guriev and Ickes (2000).

Easterly and Fisher (1995) argue that Soviet 1950–87 growth performance can be accounted for by a declining marginal capital productivity with a *constant* rate of growth of TFP. They show that the increase in capital/output ratio in the USSR was no higher than in fast growing market economies, such as Japan, Taiwan, and Korea (Table 3.2). The reason for poorer Soviet performance is seen in the low elasticity of substitution between capital and labour that caused a greater decline in returns to capital than in market economies. In this case, however, the question of interest would be why exactly the elasticity of substitution was low and whether this low level was related to the nature of the planning system. The endogenous growth models suggest that physical, human, and organizational capital can substitute for labour virtually without limits.

Besides, there is still no exhaustive explanation for the 'golden period' of Soviet growth of the 1950s, when output per worker was growing at about 6% a year both—in industry and in the economy overall—while capital per worker was increasing by 3.9 and 7.4% respectively. An explanation of Soviet economic growth based on low elasticity of capital/labour substitution, has to point out the factors that accounted for the dramatic decline in returns to capital from the 1950s to the 1980s.

A plausible explanation for the low capital/labour substitution may be associated with the inability of the centrally planned economy (CPE) to renovate obsolete capital stock as quickly as the market economy does. It is well documented that, in CPEs, actual service life of fixed capital stock was long, retirement of machinery and equipment and buildings and structures was slow, and the average age of equipment was high and growing (Shmelev and Popov, 1989).

Typically, in the USSR, the service lives of machinery and equipment, buildings and structures were very high, and the retirement rate, respectively, very low. In industry in the 1980s it was just 2–3%, as compared to 4–5% in US manufacturing for all capital stock, and 3–4%, as compared to 5–6% in US manufacturing, for machinery and equipment. Consequently, the major part of gross investment was used not to replace the retiring capital stock (since retirement was low), but to expand it. While in US manufacturing 50–60% of all investment was replacing retirement, and only 40–50% contributed to the expansion of capital stock, in Soviet industry the proportion was reversed: replacing the retiring capital stock required about 30% of gross investment, while over 70% contributed to the expansion of capital stock or to unfinished construction (Shmelev and Popov, 1989 based on *Narkhoz* and *Survey of Current Business* statistics of fixed capital stock in the USSR and the USA).

The production capacities were brought into operation mostly through the construction of new, and the expansion of existing, plants, not through reconstruction of old capacities: of the 16 types of capacities on which data are available, in 15 cases the share of those capacities brought into operation through reconstruction of the old ones was lower than 50% over the whole period of 1971–89; the unweighted average indicator of the share of reconstructed capacities was just 23% (*Narkhoz* for various years).

The reason for massive investment in the expansion of capital stock at the expense of investment to replace retiring stock was a permanent concern of Soviet planners in expanding output and meeting production quotas. Replacing worn out aged machinery and equipment usually required technical reconstruction and was associated with temporary work stoppage and reduction in output. Even if the replacement could be carried out instantly, the resulting increase in output (because of greater productivity of new equipment) was smaller than in case of the construction of new capacities or the expansion of existing capacities: in the latter case there was a hope that the new capacities could be added to the existing ones that would somehow manage to operate for several more years.

Aged and worn out equipment and structures were thus normally repaired endlessly, until they were falling apart physically; capital repair expenditure amounted to over a third of annual investment. The capital stock, meanwhile, was getting older and was wearing out, the average age of equipment and structures increased constantly.

The official statistics suggest that the share of investment into the reconstruction of enterprises (as opposed to the expansion of existing and construction of new enterprises) increased from 33% in 1980, to 39% in 1985, to 50% in 1989 (*Narkhoz*, 1989: 280), but this is not very consistent with other official data. For instance, the retirement ratio in Soviet industry was not only very low (below 2% and about 3% respectively for the retirement of physically obsolete stock and retirement of all assets), but mostly falling or stable in 1967–85 (see Fig. 3.5). Only in 1965–67 (right after the economic reform of 1965) and in 1986–87 ('acceleration' and 'restructuring' policy) was there a noticeable increase in the retirement rate.

The share of investment to replace retirement of machinery and equipment, buildings and structures in total gross investment also stayed at an extremely low level of below 20% for the most part of the 1960s–1980s; only in 1965–67 and in 1985–87 were there short-lived increases in this ratio—up to 30% (Fig. 3.6).

Besides, accumulated depreciation as a percentage of gross value of fixed capital stock (gross value minus net value, divided by gross value) grew from 26% in 1970, to 45% in 1989, and in some industries, such as steel, chemicals, and petrochemicals, exceeded 50% by the end of the 1980s. The average age of industrial equipment increased from 8.3 to 10.3 years in the 1970s–1980s, and actual average service life was 24–28 years (as compared to a 13 year period, established by norms for depreciation accounting). The share of equipment over 11 years old increased from 29% in 1970, to 35% in 1980, and to 40% in 1989, while the share of the equipment used for 20 years and over increased from 8 to 14% (Table 3.4).

The planners' reluctance to modernize existing plants and their heavy emphasis on new construction—a policy that was supposed to increase output

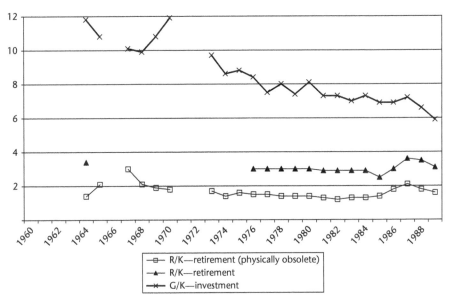

Figure 3.5. Gross investment and retirement in Soviet industry as a percentage of gross fixed capital stock

Source: Narkhoz, various years.

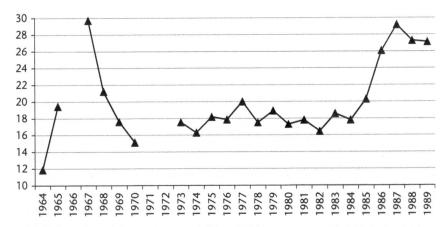

Figure 3.6. Share of investment to replace retirement in total gross investment in Soviet industry, percent

Source: Narkhoz, various years.

as much as possible—in the long run led to declining capital productivity. The capacity utilization rate in Soviet industry was falling rapidly, although official statistics registered only a marginal decrease (Shmelev and Popov, 1989; Faltsman, 1985; Valtukh and Lavrovskyi, 1986). Growing 'shortages' of labour force during the 1970s–1980s may be regarded as a sign of an increasing share

Table 3.4. Age characteristics of equipment in Soviet industry

Years	1970	1980	1985	1989
Share of equipment with an age of:				
- less than 5 years	41.1	36.0	33.7	31.6
- 6–10 years	29.9	28.9	28.5	28.6
- 11–20 years	20.9	24.8	25.5	26.2
- over 20 years	7.8	10.3	12.3	13.7
Average age of equipment, years	8.3	9.31	9.91	10.32
Average service life, years	24.0	26.9	27.9	26.2
Accumulated depreciation as a % of gross (initial) value of capital stock	26	36	41	45

Source: Narkhoz (National Economy of the USSR) for various years.

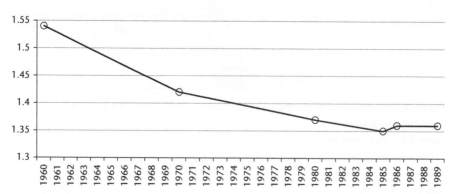

Figure 3.7. Shift coefficient in Soviet industry, 1960–89
Source: Narkhoz (various years).

of unloaded production capacities. On the whole, as was estimated by a *Gosplan* specialist, the excess capacities, not equipped with labour force, constituted in the late 1980s about 1/4 of all capital stock in industry and 1/5 of capital stock in the entire economy. In the mainstream production of all industrial plants, 25% of jobs were vacant, while in the mainstream production of machine-building plants this was up to 45%. In machine-building there were only 63 workers per every 100 machines. The number of these machines exceeded that in the USA by a factor of 2.5, yet each Soviet machine was actually operating half the time in the course of a year of an equivalent American one (Shmelev and Popov, 1989). Meanwhile, the shift coefficient (number of shifts a day) in Soviet industry declined from 1.54 in 1960 to 1.42 in 1970, to 1.37 in 1980, and to 1.35 in 1985 (Fig. 3.7).

It may seem that the whole problem of under-loaded production capacities, or rather 'the shortage of the labour force', as it was usually referred to by Soviet planners, had a simple and feasible solution, especially in a centrally planned economy. To resolve the whole issue of labour shortage, it was necessary to cut the investment in new plants and equipment, increasing the investment in the replacement of obsolete capital stock. Because this type of structural manoeuvre involved a change of macroeconomic (not microeconomic) proportions, it may seem that it could have been carried out quite easily in a directively planned economy.

However, as has already been mentioned, excess investment in new construction resulted not from mismanagement, but from the very idea of directive planning carried out through the setting of production quotas and oriented towards constant increases in output. Shortages were inevitable in such a system and resulted from the disproportions created through central planning almost by definition, while capital investments were regarded as a major means of eliminating the bottlenecks resulting from shortages. So, capital investment was diverted to create new production capacities that would have allowed expanding production of scarce goods. The whole planning procedure looked like an endless chain of urgent decisions forced by emergency shortages of different goods that appeared faster than the planners were able to eliminate them.

This was a sort of a vicious circle, a permanent race against time, in which decisions to make capital investment were predetermined by existing and newly emerging shortages. It turned out, therefore, that any attempt to cut the investment in new plant and equipment led to increased distortions and bottlenecks, resulting, among other things, in a lower capacity utilization rate; while the increased investment in the construction of new production facilities contributed to the widening of the gap between job vacancies and the limited supply of labour force, also causing a decline in the capacity utilization. Under central planning, unfortunately, there was no third option.

As a result, the CPE—with its inherent and unavoidable low capital/labour elasticity trap—was doomed to survive through a life cycle linked to the service life of fixed capital stock. Assuming the service life of capital stock is about 20 years, in the first 20 years of the existence of the CPE the construction of new modern production capacities led to rapid increases of labour productivity, even though the capital/output ratio rose. In the next 10 years, production capacities put into operation 20 years earlier started to retire physically, which contributed to the slowdown of the growth rates, but was compensated for by the continuing expansion of fixed capital stock. After 30 years of the CPE, it entered the stage of decline: over half the capital stock was worn out and falling apart (but not completely replaced), while the newly created production capacities were just barely enough to compensate for the decline in output resulting from ageing of the capital stock.

To summarize, low elasticity of capital/labour substitution is an intrinsic feature of the CPE because it is oriented towards the expansion of the capital stock at the expense of the replacement of the retiring stock. Such an investment strategy will produce its best results in the first 30 years (a period equivalent to 1.5 times service life of capital stock), but later inevitably leads to a rapid decline in capital productivity. Viewed in such a way, CPEs, despite all their inefficiencies and high costs of growth, can support reasonable growth rates, but only in the first several decades of their existence—for the Soviet Union, where the CPE emerged in the early 1930s after the rollback of the New Economic Policy, this was probably the period until the 1960s. Later, the CPE is doomed to witness a severe decline in capital productivity associated with the ageing of fixed capital stock.

There are papers that consider the low ability of the CPE to replace retirement stock as the most important stylized fact; it is used in theoretical models of the CPEs to explain particular features of their performance. Ickes and Ryterman (1997) demonstrate that in the absence of the mechanism of exits of firms inefficient enterprises will tend to be allocated less resources than efficient ones and that this will generate an industrial structure that is bi-modal in nature, one in which inefficient enterprises agglomerate at one end of the size spectrum and efficient enterprises agglomerate at the other end. Iacopetta (2004) explains the gap between the high level of research and invention in the CPEs and poor innovation activity and performance by the perverse Soviet managerial compensation system, which generated incentives for the managers to perform only a modest retooling activity out of fear of breaking the production norm that the planner imposed upon the firm.

The results of the simulation demonstrate more rigorously the intuitively clear effect of the impact of the constraints on investment into the replacement of the retiring elements of the capital stock (Popov, 2007c): in the presence of such constraints, a 'big push' can lead to a temporary increase in the growth rates, but later, after a period equal to the service life of the fixed capital stock, they fall and converge to a low positive level or even to zero (if the investment into the replacement of retirement stock is low enough). The simulation exercise allows us to demonstrate clearly that under very reasonable assumptions (that the productivity of new investment is proportional to the share of investment into the reconstruction of existing production capacities in total investment, and that investment into the reconstruction of these capacities is lower than the actual retirement due to physical wear and tear) growth rates first increase and then fall to a very low level or even zero after a 'big push'—the initial increase in the share of investment in GDP—Fig. 3.8.

The trajectory of the declining rates of growth could also be obtained by assuming that all investments are channelled into the construction of new production capacities (no investment into replacement of retirement of capital stock at all) and that retirement of fixed capital is accelerating with age (i.e. not only physical, but also moral depreciation)—Kosterina (2007).

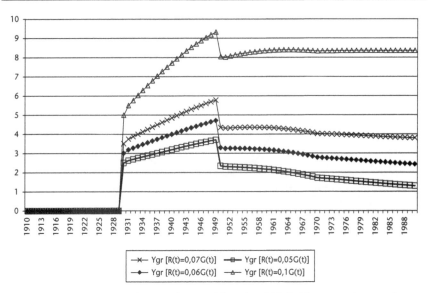

Figure 3.8. Growth rates after the 'big push' in the CPE (with constraints on investment to replace retirement of fixed capital stock), percent
Source: Popov, 2007c.

The fact that growth rates in the USSR started to fall in the 1960s, 30 years after the 'big push', and not 20 years after as the simulation exercise suggests, should probably be explained by the impact of the Second World War that resulted in the destruction of a large portion of fixed capital stock. For 10 years (1940–50) capital stock, in fact, did not increase (first it was destroyed during the war, then increased to the pre-war level during reconstruction), so 10 years should be added to the life cycle of 20 years. Besides, the average service life of capital stock is a very statistically uncertain indicator. In the 1970s–1980s, the service life of machinery and equipment was about 25 years (implying a retirement ratio of 4%)—see Table 3.4, but for the earlier period the statistics are absent. If the service life in the 1930s–1950s was about 30 years, the peak of the growth rates in the 1950s could be explained even without the impact of the war.

When, in the late 1960s, the Soviet catch-up economic development started to experience problems, this immediately affected the area of social development. Life expectancy stopped growing: after reaching 70 years in 1965 (only 2 years less than in the USA), it hovered between 68 and 70 until 1991. The contrast with the previous 50 years (1913–65), when it increased from 35 to 70 years, is striking (Fig. 3.9).

Studies of the stagnation of life expectancy in the USSR in 1965–91, very much like studies of the subsequent mortality crisis (1991–2003), do not provide a uniform answer to the question of why mortality stopped falling

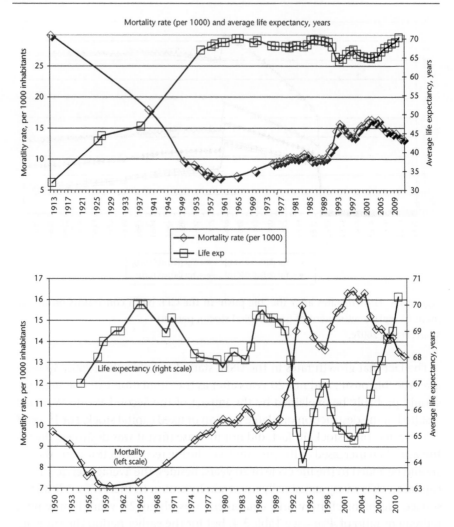

Figure 3.9. Mortality rate and life expectancy in Russia and the USSR
Source: Goskomstat.

and started to grow. Some authors focus on non-material factors (loss of social dynamism in the late Soviet era and the stress of the transition to capitalism and democracy in the 1990s); others regard the increase in the consumption of alcohol as the major cause of the mortality rise (for discussion of the literature see: Popov, 2010–2011; King, Stuckler, and McKee, 2009 and subsequent debate with J. Sachs in the *Economist*).

The dynamics of the mortality rate is readily correlated with the consumption of alcohol, but there are some obvious discrepancies as well (Fig. 3.10). For instance, alcohol consumption in the 1990s was no higher than in the early

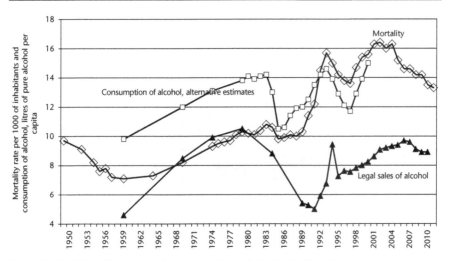

Figure 3.10. Mortality rate and consumption of alcohol in Russia
Source: Goskomstat; *Demoscope*, No. 263–264, October 30–November 12, 2006.

1980s, whereas the mortality rate was 50% higher and more. Besides, alcohol consumption itself is strongly correlated with stress factors (unemployment, job turnover, migration, divorces, income inequalities), so increases in alcohol consumption and mortality can go hand in hand, being driven by stress and loss of social dynamism (Popov, 2007c).

The same reasoning applies to the crime, murder, and suicide rates (Fig. 3.11). There was a creeping increase of these indicators in the 1970s–1980s, only briefly interrupted by the Gorbachev anti-alcohol campaign of 1985–87, and an explosive increase in the 1990s during the transition to capitalism. Correlations with the consumption of alcohol, especially during the anti-alcohol campaign, are apparent (Fig. 3.12), but discrepancies are also visible—in the 2000s, for instance, murders, suicides, and deaths from alcoholic poisoning were falling, while consumption of alcohol increased.

How does the Soviet record in social indicators compare to that of pre-revolutionary Russia and to other countries? The scarce data available suggest that the comparison is not bad. At the beginning of the twentieth century, by European standards of the time, Russia had a very high murder rate—up to 10 and over per 100,000 inhabitants—before the first (1905–07) and second (1917) Russian revolutions. By the 1960s, it was down to 4–6 murders per 100,000 inhabitants (the same as in the USA at that time), even though mortality from other external causes increased markedly. Since the mid 1960s, however, it has been on the rise, approaching early twentieth century levels by the mid 1980s at about 10 murders per 100,000 inhabitants (Bogoyavlensky, 2001) (Demoscope, № 31–32. 27 August–9 September 2001 <http://demoscope.ru/weekly/2013/0567/index.php>).

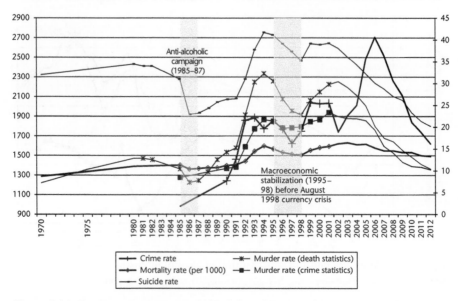

Figure 3.11. Russian crime rate per 1000 (left scale), mortality rate per 1000, murder rate and suicide rate per 100,000 inhabitants (right scale)

Source: Goskomstat.

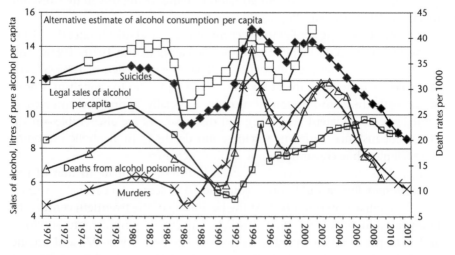

Figure 3.12. Consumption of alcohol and crime, murder, and suicide rates in Russia since 1970

Source: Goskomstat; *Demoscope*, No. 263–264, October 30–November 12, 2006.

The increase in the suicide rate and the rate of deaths from accidents in the 1920s–1960s in the USSR, in the period of successful economic catch-up development, is not an uncommon phenomenon. An increase in accidents and suicides occurred in many countries (including the UK in 1860–1910 and the USA in 1900–30) making the transition from a traditional society to modern society and undergoing industrialization and urbanization. The suicide rate of less than 10 per 100,000 inhabitants in the 1920s and a bit more than 10 in the 1950s–1960s was below the levels that existed at this time in many developed countries. And total mortality from external causes (accidents, suicides, murders) among women (40 per 100, 000 inhabitants) was at the same level as in France, Sweden, the UK, and the USA, whereas the same indicator for men was not much higher (150–170 against 70–130)—(Demoscope, № 29–30, 13–26 August 2001).

To conclude, overall, the record of the Soviet regime in maintaining economic growth and high levels of welfare indicators is quite spectacular, especially until the late 1960s. Since the mid 1960s, however, growth started to slow down, whereas social evils—mortality, crime, murders, suicides, and alcohol consumption—started to increase. In political and social life, the Khrushchev thaw came to an end by the mid 1960s (Khrushchev was removed from power in 1964), and the hopes of transforming the Soviet regime into 'socialism with human face' were buried in 1968, when Soviet troops were moved into Czechoslovakia. The primary reason for the slowdown of growth was the inability of the CPE to replace the retiring fixed capital stock. When in the 1960s, 30 years after the 'big push', time came to make such investment, the economy started to slow down.

The Chinese socialist way

Not only is recent (during and after the Global Recession of 2008–09) Chinese performance robust and respectable, but so is Chinese growth since 1979, when Deng Xiaoping started market-type reforms, and—what is less known—since 1949, when the Communist Party of China (CPC) took power and the People's Republic of China (PRC) was established.

The catch-up development of China since 1949 looks extremely impressive: not only were the growth rates in China higher than elsewhere after the reforms (1979 onward), but even before the reforms (1949–79), despite temporary declines during the Great Leap Forward and the Cultural Revolution, Chinese development was quite successful. According to Maddison (2008), Chinese per capita GDP was about 70% of India's in 1950, rose to about 100% by 1958–59, fell during the Great Leap Forward, rose again to 100% of the Indian level by 1966, fell during the first years of the Cultural Revolution, and

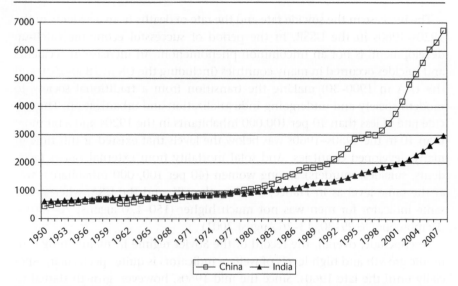

Figure 3.13. PPP GDP per capita in China and India in 1950–2008, 1990 Geary–Khamis international dollars (Maddison, 2010)

Source: Maddison, 2010.

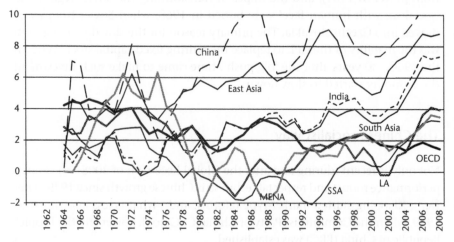

Figure 3.14. GDP growth rates of major countries and regions in 1960–2008, percent

Source: WDI.

rose again to 100% by 1978. By 2008, it was more than two times higher than the Indian per capita GDP (Fig. 3.13).

World Bank estimates (WDI, 2005), however, suggest that, since 1960, Chinese growth rates (five-year moving averages) have always been higher than Indian growth rates (Fig. 3.14) and that in the late 1970s, right before the

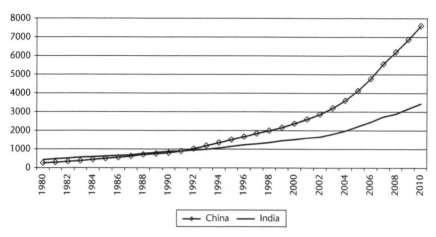

Figure 3.15. PPP GDP per capita in current international dollars, China and India, 1980–2010, World Bank data
Source: WDI.

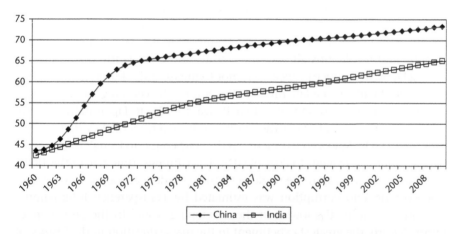

Figure 3.16. Life expectancy at birth, years, China and India, 1960–2010
Source: WDI.

reforms, Chinese per capita GDP was only half of India's, whereas today it is more than two times higher (Fig. 3.15). Life expectancy in China in 1950 was only 35 years, but by the end of the 1970s rose to 65 years—13 years higher than in India (Fig. 3.16), so it is pretty difficult to believe that Chinese per capita GDP was only half of the Indian level; today, it is 73 years—4 years higher than in Russia and 7 years higher than in India.

Thus, by all counts, Chinese development was extremely successful not only during the reform period (1979 onwards), but also since Liberation

(1949 onwards), despite the drawbacks of the Great Leap Forward and the Cultural Revolution.

It is important to realize that the rapid catch-up development of the post-reform period is due not only to, and even not so much to, economic liberalization and market-oriented reforms. The pre-conditions for the Chinese success of the last 30 years were created mostly in the preceding period of 1949–76. In fact, it would be no exaggeration at all to claim that without the achievements of Mao's regime, the market-type reforms of 1979 and beyond would never have produced the impressive results that they actually did. In this sense, the economic liberalization in 1979 and beyond was only the last straw that broke the camel's back. The other ingredients, most importantly strong institutions and human capital, had already been provided by the previous regime. Without these other ingredients, liberalization alone in different periods and different countries has never been successful and has sometimes been counterproductive, like in Sub-Saharan Africa in the 1980s.

As Aiguo Lu (1999) points out, market-type reforms in China in 1979 and beyond brought about the acceleration of economic growth because China already had one of the necessary pre-conditions for growth—an efficient government that was created by the CPC after the Liberation[3]. Through the party cells in every village, the communist government in Beijing was able to enforce its rules and regulations all over the country more efficiently than Qing Shi Huang Di or any emperor since then, not to mention the Kuomintang regime (1912–49). While in the late nineteenth century, the central government had revenues equivalent to only 3% of GDP (against 12% in Japan right after the Meiji Restoration), and under the Kuomintang government they increased to only 5% of GDP, Mao's government left the state coffers to Deng's reform team with revenues equivalent to 20% of GDP. The Chinese crime rate in the 1970s was among the lowest in the world, a Chinese shadow economy was virtually non-existent, and corruption was estimated by Transparency International even in 1985 to be the lowest in the developing world. In the same period, during 'clearly the greatest experiment in the mass education in the history of the world' (UNESCO-sponsored 1984 report), literacy rates in China increased from 28% in 1949 to 65% by the end of the 1970s (41% in India).

The Great Leap Forward (1958–62) and the Cultural Revolution (1966–76) are said to be the major failures of Chinese development. True, output in China declined three times in the whole post-Liberation period: in 1960–62 by over 30%, in 1967–68 by 10%, and in 1976 by 2% (WDI). The Great Leap Forward produced a famine and a reduction in the population. But if these

---

[3] To a lesser extent, this is true for India: market-type reforms in the 1990s produced good results because they were based on previous achievements of the import substitution period (Nayyar, 2006).

major setbacks could have been avoided, Chinese development over 1949–79 would look even more impressive. Most researchers would probably agree that the Great Leap Forward, which inflicted the most significant damage, could have been avoided in the sense that it did not follow logically from the intrinsic features of the Chinese socialist model. There is less certainty about whether the Cultural Revolution could be excluded from the 'package' of subsequent policies—this mass movement was very much in line with socialist developmental goals and most probably prevented the inevitable bureaucratization of the government apparatus that occurred in other communist countries.[4] But the point to make here is that, even without excluding these periods, Chinese development in 1949–79 was much better than that of most countries in the world and that this development laid the foundations of the truly exceptional success of the post-reform period.

From this perspective, growing inequality in income distribution (Fig. 3.17) constitutes a major threat to China's seemingly flawless development path. Unlike in the initial years of economic reforms (1979–85), inequality has been growing since the mid 1980s, exceeding the level of Japan and South Korea and even the level of Russia, and approaching Latin American and African levels.

Recent data from a representative nationwide household survey[5] suggest that the Gini index in China may be even higher (47–49% in 2003–12), but has not really grown in the last decade (Fig. 3.17). It is important, though, to take into account the size of the country—in terms of both territory and population. Three Chinese provinces (Guangdong, Shandong, Henan) have populations over 95 million, another seven have over 50 million, that is bigger than most states, so China should be compared with multistate regions, like the European Union or ASEAN, rather than with particular states. In the EU 27, for instance, the coefficient of income inequality around 2005 was about

---

[4] On 15 June 1976, when Mao's illness became more severe, he called Hua Guofeng and some others in and said to them: 'I am over eighty now, and when people get old, they like to think about post-mortal things…In my whole life, I have accomplished two things. One is the fight against Jiang Jieshi [Chiang Kai-shek] for several decades and kicking him out onto a few islands and fighting an eight-year resistance war against the Japanese invasion that forced the Japanese to return to their home. There has been less disagreement on this matter…The other thing is what you all know, that is, launching the "Cultural Revolution." Not very many people support it, and quite a number of people are against it. These two things are not finished, and the legacy will be passed onto the next generation. How to pass it on? If not peacefully, then in turbulence, and, if not managed well, there will be foul wind and rain of blood. What are you going to do? Only heaven knows' (People's Web, 2003).

[5] Previously, Chinese National Bureau of Statistics (NBS) had separate household surveys for rural and urban areas, so Ginis for the whole country were computed by researchers based on certain assumptions on rural–urban income disparities. By December 2012, the NBS had collected samples of 140,000 urban and rural households from 31 provinces, autonomous regions, and municipalities. The NBS set up a new sample system and began to collect samples from 400,000 households starting from 1 December 2012. (Zhao Qian. NBS reveals Gini coefficient methods.— *Global Times*, 4 February 2013).

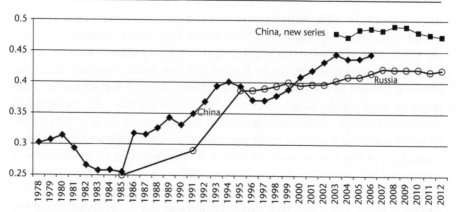

Figure 3.17. Gini coefficient of income distribution in China and Russia, 1978–2012
Source: Chen, Hou, and Jin, 2008; Goskomstat; *China Daily*, January 19, 2013.

40% with 23 percentage points (p.p.) coming from between-country inequalities. In China (29 provinces) it was over 40% with 24 p.p. coming from between-province disparities. In the USA, the inequality coefficient was similar (over 40%), but only 6 p.p. came from disparities in income between the states (Milanovic, 2012). If China manages to reduce the income gap between its provinces (and the EU-between member countries) to a level close to the disparities between US states, the general inequality between citizens will fall to quite a low level.

The number of billionaires in China has also grown fast: before the 2008–09 recession, in April 2007, according to Forbes' list, China had 20 billionaires (Fig. 3.18); in 2011, after the recovery from 2008–09 recession, China had 116 billionaires (plus 36 in Hong Kong and 25 in Taiwan), whereas Russia had 'only' 101.

However, as was argued in Chapter 2 (Table 2.4), in 2007 China still had fewer billionaires than predicted by the regression, whereas Russia had more. So the Gini coefficient should not be taken as the ultimate measure of income inequality. The share of 10% richest taxpayers in total income in China was only 30% in 2003 versus 40% in Japan (Alvaredo et al., 2012), even though the Japanese Gini at that time was way below Chinese—about 30 and 40% respectively.

And if the murder rate is an indicator of the institutional capacity, it seems as though in recent years it has actually improved, not deteriorated. From the mid 1990s the murder rate has declined despite growing/high inequalities (Fig. 3.19).

* * *

To summarize, by the end of the 1970s, China had virtually everything that was needed for growth except some liberalization of markets—a much easier

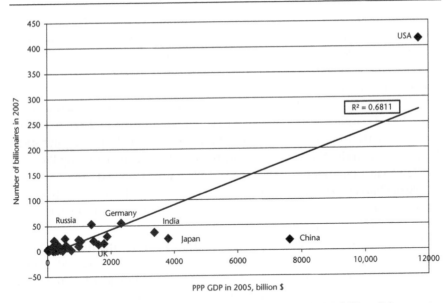

Figure 3.18. Number of billionaires in 2007 and PPP GDP in 2005 (billion $) by country
Source: WDI; Forbes billionaires website (<http://www.forbes.com/billionaires/>).

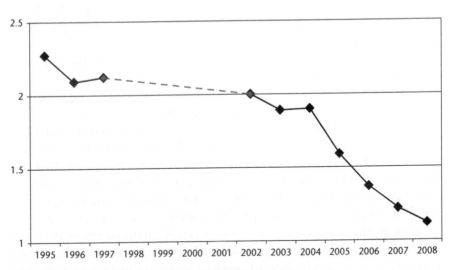

Figure 3.19. Murder rate in China per 100,000 inhabitants
Source: UNODC (2012).

ingredient to introduce than human capital or institutional capacity. But even this seemingly simple task of economic liberalization required careful management. The USSR was in a similar position in the late 1980s. True, the Soviet system lost its economic and social dynamism, growth rates in the 1960s–80s were falling, life expectancy was not rising, and crime rates were slowly growing,

85

but institutions were generally strong and human capital was large, which provided good starting conditions for reform. Nevertheless, economic liberalization in China (since 1979) and in the USSR, and later Russia (since 1989), produced markedly different outcomes (Popov, 2000, 2007a, 2009).

Unlike Russia after 1991, it so far seems as if China in 1979–2013 managed to better preserve its strong state institutions—the murder rate in China was below 3 per 100,000 inhabitants, compared to about 30 in Russia in 2002 and about 1–2 against 10–15 in Russia in 2010–12 (WHO; UNODC Homicide Statistics). In the 1970s, under the Maoist regime, the murder rate in Shandong Province was less than 1 (Shandong, 2005), and in 1987 it was estimated to be 1.5 for the whole of China (WHO, 1994). The threefold increase in the murder rate during the market reforms is comparable with the Russian increase, although Chinese levels are nowhere near the Russian levels.

Why did China manage to preserve relatively strong institutions during economic liberalization, while in Russia state institutions collapsed? Part of the answer, as argued in the following chapter, is the impact of democratization on the quality of institutions: democratization carried out in a poor rule of law environment (weak state institutions) is associated with further weakening of institutions and worsening of macroeconomic policy, which has a negative impact on growth and does not allow the creation of a stable democratic regime, especially in resource-rich countries (Polterovich, Popov, 2007; Polterovich, Popov, and Tonis, 2007).

Another, and the most important, explanation is probably the long-term development trajectory of institutions in China and Russia. The Chinese 1949 Liberation was similar to the Russian 1917 Revolution not only because communists came to power in both countries, but also because traditional collectivist institutions, ruined by the preceding Westernization, were re-established and strengthened. However, in Russia, the 1917–91 communist regime only interrupted the process of transplantation of Western institutions that had been going on since at least the seventeenth century, whereas in China, the Liberation of 1949 returned the country to the long-term institutional trajectory that was briefly (and only partly) interrupted after the Opium Wars.

To put it differently, Russia had already been Westernized before 1917, and collectivist institutions that were introduced in Russia by the 1917 Revolution had already been largely alien to previous long-term institutional development. On the other hand, China aborted the unsuccessful Westernization attempt (1840s–1949) and returned to collectivist (Asian values) institutions.[6] What was a passing episode and a deviation from the trend in Russia was a

---

[6] The continuity and restoration of 'Asian values' could also be seen in the 'revolution's promise that every man, no matter how poor, could become a household head and carry on his family line' (Pomeranz, 2008).

return to mainstream development and the restoration of a long-term trend in China. Hence, economic liberalization from 1979 onwards in China, even though accompanied by growing income inequality and crime and murder rates, did not result, at least until today, in institutional collapse.

The uniqueness of China is that it looks very much like a developed country today in terms of the institutional capacity of the state, even though it is a developing country according to GDP per capita. Indeed, China should be compared with developing countries today or developed countries 100 years ago, when their GDP was at the current Chinese level, and this comparison is very much in favour of China.

As argued earlier, institutional capacity of the state in a narrow definition is the ability of the government to enforce laws and regulations, and the natural objective measures of the state institutional capacity are the murder rate—non-compliance with the state's monopoly on violence—and the shadow economy—non-compliance with economic regulations. China is rather unique on both measures—one of the lowest indicators in the developing world comparable to developed countries (see Figs 2.6, 2.8, 2.9 in the previous chapter).

The roots of the exceptional strength of Chinese institutions lie in the historical trajectory of its institutional development—like many MENA, South Asian, and East Asian countries China was less affected by Western colonialism and had better chances to preserve collectivist institutions and institutional continuity than most of the countries of LA, SSA, and FSU.

Formally, China was not a colony, although after losing the Opium Wars in the middle of the nineteenth century it became a semi-colony of the West for nearly a century. The fact is, however, that at the beginning of the nineteenth century, China was definitely the most successful country in the framework of the Malthusian growth regime—when increases in productivity due to technological advances were all 'eaten up' by the increased growth of the population, so that technical progress did not lead to higher GDP per capita but to a larger population. The share of China in the total population of the world increased in the eighteenth century from a long-term average of 22–26% to 37% (Fig. 3.20)—a truly remarkable achievement by the standards of the pre-industrial world.

Actually, before the Opium Wars in the mid nineteenth century, Chinese performance was extremely impressive—not in terms of growth of productivity and per capita GDP, but in terms of the population growth (which, of course, was the top criteria of performance in the Malthusian growth regime) that made China the most populous nation on Earth. It was only in the 100 years following Opium Wars that the Chinese performance was utterly disappointing from all points of view (Lu, 1999).

To put it differently, China was extremely successful within the Malthusian growth regime: its population had previously risen several times to a ceiling of

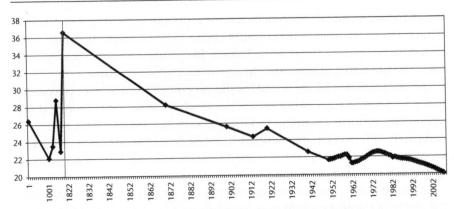

Figure 3.20. Share of China in world population, percentage of total
Source: Maddison, 2010.

100–150 million only to fall back, whereas, by 1800, it rose to nearly 400 million. 'This was clearly a world demographic landmark'—notes Sugihara—'and its impact on world GDP far outweighed that of post-Industrial Revolution Britain, whose share of world GDP in 1820 was less than 6 percent' (cited in Arrighi, 2007). The world was probably heading towards a population balance of one Chinese per one non-Chinese. The comparison with Western Europe is very telling: in 1700 the Chinese population was 1.5 times larger than that of Western Europe and by 1820, it became 2 times larger.

But the rapid growth of population in China—breathtaking success in the Malthusian growth regime—took its toll in the form of decline in the capital/labour ratio and lower government spending per capita. While the Japanese population, after reaching 30 million in the early eighteenth century, stagnated until the Meiji Restoration of the 1860s, the Chinese population grew from 120 million in 1650, to over 200 million in 1750, and to over 400 million in 1850 (Fig. 3.20). Limited savings were barely enough to invest in the creation of jobs for the expanding labour force, and not enough to support the increase in the capital/labour ratio, the expansion of infrastructure, and the improvement of government administration. Per capita revenues and the expenditure of the government (especially non-military spending) in Qing China fell dramatically in the eighteenth–nineteenth century and in real terms (*kokus* of rice) declined to just 15–20% of the Japanese level; the per capita numbers of civil servants was much lower than in Tokugawa shogunate; road construction, provision of urban public goods, and production of coins by the mints were way lower in per capita terms (Sng and Moriguchi, 2012). The result was the weakening of the government administration and the capacity to build up the capital/labour ratio and productivity: by 1900

Japanese per capita income was two times higher than Chinese, whereas in 1850 the difference was barely noticeable.

In the early nineteenth century, even though productivity was already two times lower than in the West, China still accounted for over a third of the population and about a third of the GDP and industrial output. It clearly recognized itself as the self-sufficient centre of the world and was not interested in developing contacts with the 'barbarians' from the outer world. 'Tremblingly obey and show no negligence'—this is how the Chinese emperor Qianlong, ruling for the major part of the eighteenth century (1736–96), ended his famous response to the letter of the British King George III in 1792 with the proposal of trade cooperation.[7]

The problem, however, was that the rules of the game in the world economy had changed: the productivity growth rates in the West increased and the Malthusian growth regime came to an end. Military strength was now more determined by technology than by the size of the population, so that the outcome of military confrontation with the West was pre-determined: China experienced a humiliating defeat in the Opium Wars (1840–42 and 1856–60) and had to accept globalization on Western terms. Chinese GDP per capita fell from about half of the US level in the early nineteenth century to a meager 5% in 1950 (Fig. 1.1); the ratio of Chinese GDP to that of Western Europe fell from 2:1 to 1:5 in the same period.

However, subsequent Chinese development differed from that of other colonies and semi-colonies. Being the largest and most powerful country of the pre-industrial age, China was better able to preserve the continuity of its traditional institutions. In a sense, Britain is called the country of traditions by mistake. It is China that managed to preserve the continuity of traditional values more than any other nation of the world.[8] The Liberation of 1949 thus led to a breakthrough: temporary protection from foreign influence imposed by the CPC (1949–79) allowed traditional institutions to strengthen and development to continue along the lines of the millennium-old trajectory.

This development is not without precedent: earlier, five countries/territories based largely on the Chinese tradition (Japan, Korea, Taiwan, Singapore, and

---

[7] Ch'ien Lung, (Qianlong) Letter to George III (1792). <Http://www.history.ucsb.edu/faculty/marcuse/classes/2c/texts/1792QianlongLetterGeorgeIII.htm>.

[8] China was conquered by outsiders only twice—by Mongols in the twelfth century (who later established the Yuan Dynasty—1279–1368) and by the Manchu (who established the last Qing Dynasty—1644–1911), but in both cases, the conquerors were quickly 'china-ized' ('chinafied') and assimilated by the more powerful Chinese culture. Sinologists agree that the continuity of the Chinese civilization makes it truly unique in at least three respects: many nations started with pictograms (characters), but only the larger Chinese world (Japan and Korea included) preserved characters throughout most of their history; the number of ancient manuscripts and the amount of factual information on its ancient history is at least by an order of magnitude greater than in any other nation of the world; respect to the ancestors and elderly and Confucian values seem to matter more than in other cultures.

Hong Kong) succeeded in catching up with the West without sacrificing their traditional values. But there is no doubt that the Chinese successful catch-up will have a far greater impact on the world. This is firstly because the previous cases of catch-up were generally supported by the West and were sometimes even called 'development by invitation', whereas the rise of China did not happen 'by invitation' by any stretch of the imagination. And it is secondly because the successful catch-up of China cannot be interpreted as extraordinary and exceptional due to the sheer size of the country. If successful, Chinese catch-up will truly be the ultimate and most persuasive evidence of the advantages of institutional continuity.

4

Chinese and Russian Economies Since Reforms: Transformational Recession in Russia and Acceleration of Growth in China

In 1995, in the book *China's Rise, Russia's Fall*, Peter Nolan argued that Russia was wrong in following the 'shock therapy' approach, while China was right in pursuing a policy running counter to the transition 'orthodoxy' shaped by the Bretton-Woods institutions. He claimed that 'the selection of different policies in Russia could have produced rapid growth of output and a large improvement in popular living standards' and that, had China applied the orthodox policies, it 'could have produced a political and economic disaster' (Nolan, 1995: 302).

Most authors, however, tended to explain the impressive Chinese success through initial conditions (large rural population and agricultural sector, advantages of backwardness, etc.), not through gradualist policy, as the shock therapy approach was considered superior and was usually credited for allowing East European countries to do better than former Soviet republics (see references further).

Generally, the debates of the 1990s juxtaposed the shock therapy strategy to gradualism. The question of why Russia had to pay a greater price for economic transition was answered differently by those who advocated shock therapy and those who supported gradual piecemeal reforms. Shock therapists argued that much of the costs of the reforms should be attributed to the inconsistencies of policies followed, namely to slow economic liberalization and to the inability of the governments and central banks to fight inflation in the first half of the 1990s. Conversely, the supporters of gradual transition stated exactly the opposite, blaming the attempt to introduce a conventional shock therapy package for all the disasters and misfortunes.

In Popov (2000, 2007a) various explanations for the transformational recession are discussed and an alternative explanation is suggested: the collapse of output was caused primarily by several groups of factors, all of which were linked to institutional capacity. *First*, by greater distortions in the industrial structure and external trade patterns on the eve of the transition: it was possible to overcome these distortions under the gradual transition strategy, but under shock therapy a deep recession was inevitable. Gradualism, in turn, was possible only with strong institutional capacity. *Second*, by the collapse of state and non-state institutions, which occurred in the late 1980s–early 1990s and which resulted in chaotic transformation through crisis management instead of organized and manageable transition. And *third*, by poor economic policies, which basically consisted of bad macroeconomic policy and import substitution industrial policy. Strong institutional capacity was a necessary, although not a sufficient, condition for carrying out good policies—all countries with poor institutions (plus some countries with strong institutions) had bad policies, but not all countries with strong institutions managed to adopt good macro and industrial policies.

Transformational recession of the 1990s

After the Soviet Union collapsed (December 1991) and market reforms were initiated, the economic performance of the successor states was more than disappointing. By the end of 1998, output (GDP) in Russia had fallen by 45% as compared to the highest pre-recession level of 1989 (Fig. 4.1)–investment had dropped even more; income inequalities had risen greatly so that real incomes declined dramatically for the majority of the population; death rates had increased from 1% in the 1980s to 1.5% in 1994 and had stayed at this high level until 2003 (which was equivalent to over 700,000 additional deaths annually), whereas life expectancy had declined markedly. Over the period of several years such population losses could be likened to the impact of a big war. The crime rate, murder rate, and suicide rate in the 1990s grew several-fold.

By way of comparison, during the Second World War national income in the USSR fell only by 20% in 1940–42, recovered to its 1940 level in 1944, fell again by 20% in 1944–46, during conversion of the defence industry, but had exceeded its 1940 level by nearly 20% already in 1948. In some of the FSU states that were affected by military conflicts (Armenia, Azerbaijan, Georgia, Moldova, Russia, and Tajikistan) GDP in 2000 was only 30–50% of pre-transition levels; in Ukraine, even without the military conflict, GDP fell by nearly two thirds (Fig. 4.1).

By way of another comparison, in East European countries (EE) the reduction of output continued for 2–4 years and totalled 20–30%, whereas in China

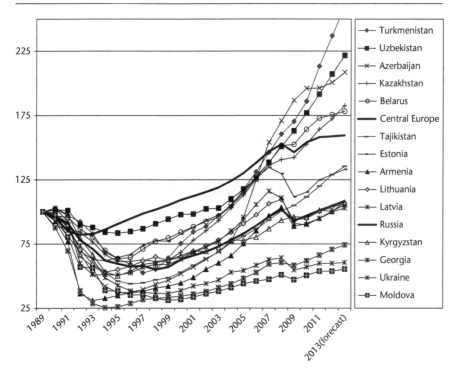

Figure 4.1. GDP change in FSU economies, 1989 = 100%
Source: EBRD Transition Reports for various years.

and Vietnam there was no transformational recession at all—on the contrary, from the very outset of reforms economic growth accelerated.

Post factum, the reduction of output that occurred in the FSU during the 1990s should be considered as an exceptional case in world economic history. Never and nowhere, to the best of my knowledge, has there occurred such a dramatic decline in output, living standards, and life expectancy without extraordinary circumstances, such as wars, epidemics, or natural disasters. Even during the Great Depression (1929–33), GDP in Western countries on average fell by some 30% and by the end of the 1930s had recovered to its pre-recession levels.

Among countries in transition, Russia experienced the greatest increase in the murder rate; it quadrupled during 1987–2002, increasing from 8 to 33 per 100,000 inhabitants (Fig. 4.2). In EE countries and most FSU states, the increases were much less pronounced. In fact, in 2002, Russia became number 1 in the world for suicide, accident, and death rates from external causes, and number 4 in the world for murder rates (Table 4.1).

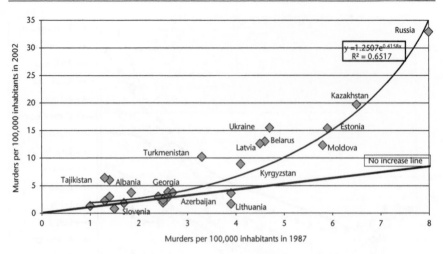

Figure 4.2. Murders per 100,000 of inhabitants in 1987 and in 2002 in post-communist countries (WHO statistics)
Source: WHO.

Table 4.1. Number of deaths from external causes per 100,000 inhabitants in 2002: countries with highest rates in the world

Country	Deaths from external causes, total	Including deaths from			
		Accidents	Suicides	Murders	Other*
Russia	245	158	41	33	11
Sierra-Leone	215	148	10	50	7
Burundi	213	64	7	18	124
Angola	191	131	8	40	13
Belarus	172	120	38	13	0
Estonia	168	124	29	15	0
Kazakhstan	157	100	37	20	0
Ukraine	151	100	36	15	0
Cote D'Ivoire	148	86	11	27	24
Colombia	134	36	6	72	19
Niger	133	113	6	14	0

* Deaths due to unidentified external causes, wars, police operations, executions.
Totals may differ slightly from the sum of components due to rounding.
Source: WHO (<http://www.who.int/entity/healthinfo/statistics/bodgbddeathdalyestimates.xls>)

Since 1979, China has managed to limit the increase in the murder rate, in 2008 it was only 1.1 per 100,000 inhabitants, as compared to about 30 in Russia in 2002 and about 10 in 2012 (Popov, 2007d). National statistics on murders under the Mao regime are not available, but there is data for some provinces. In the 1970s, the murder rate in the Shandong Province was less than 1 (Shandong, 2009), and in 1987 it was estimated at 1.5 for the whole of China (WHO, 2004). The WHO reported ratio for 2004 is 2.1 (WHO website), whereas UNODC reports a murder rate of 1.1 to 2.6 in 2003–08 (UNODC Homicide Statistics Trends, 2003–08). A two-to-threefold increase in the murder rate during the market reforms is comparable with the Russian increase, but the Chinese levels are lower than Russian ones by an order of magnitude.

Why has the reduction of output and incomes in FSU been so deep and so long? To what extent was this collapse caused by the initial conditions and circumstances that were predetermined and barely avoidable, and to what extent was it 'man made', that is the result of poor economic policy choices? If it is the wrong economic policy that is mostly responsible for the collapse, future historians may refer to the FSU transition as the biggest 'man made' economic disaster ever to happen.

The ubiquitous and virtually universal feeling is that 'things went terribly wrong' and that with different policies it would have been possible to avoid most of the misfortunes that struck the former Soviet republics in the 1990s. After all, most other transition economies did better than Russia and other FSU states, and it is difficult to accept the idea that the exceptional length and depth of recession in post-Soviet states was predestined and inevitable.

However, when it comes to the discussion of particular policies, there is much less agreement among scholars. The question why FSU had to pay a greater price for economic transition is answered differently by those who advocate shock therapy and those who support gradual piecemeal reforms. Shock therapists argue that much of the costs of the FSU reforms should be attributed to inconsistencies of the policies followed, namely to the inability of the governments and the central banks to fight inflation in the first half of the 1990s. Conversely, the supporters of gradual transition state exactly the opposite, blaming the attempt to introduce a conventional shock therapy package for all the disasters and misfortunes.

Quite a number of studies were undertaken with the intention of testing whether fast liberalization and macro-stabilization pay off and finally lead to better performance (see: Popov, 2000, 2007b for a summary of the debate). To prove the point, the authors regressed output changes during transition on liberalization indices developed in De Melo et al. (1996) and by EBRD (published in its Transition Reports), inflation, and different measures of initial conditions.

The conventional wisdom was probably summarized in the 1996 World Development Report (WDR) *From Plan to Market*, which basically stated that differences in economic performance were associated mostly with 'good and bad' policies, in particular with the progress in liberalization and macroeconomic stabilization. 'Consistent policies, combining liberalization of markets, trade, and new business entry with reasonable price stability, can achieve a great deal even in countries lacking clear property rights and strong market institutions'—was one of the major conclusions of the WDR 1996 (World Bank, 1996).

The conclusion did not withstand the test of time, since by now most economists would probably agree that because liberalization was carried out without strong market institutions it led to the extraordinary output collapse in CIS states. Liberalization may be important, but the devil is in the details, which often do not fit into the generalizations and make straightforward explanations look trivial.

At first glance, there seems to be a positive relationship between liberalization and performance (Fig. 4.3). However, a more careful consideration reveals that the link is just the result of a sharp difference in the magnitude of the recession in EE countries, as a group, and FSU states, also as a group (Fig. 4.3). Within these groups the correlation, if any, is much weaker, not to speak about China and Vietnam, which are outliers. The Chinese index of economic freedom (measured on a scale from 1 to 5 by the Heritage Foundation) was about the same in the 1990s as the Russian one, but the performance of the two countries has differed markedly (Fig. 4.4).

Take the example of Vietnam and China—two countries that shared many similarities in initial conditions and achieved basically the same results (immediate growth of output without transformational recession) despite different reform strategies. While Chinese reforms are normally treated as a

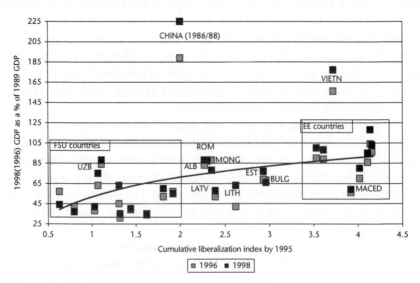

Figure 4.3. Economic liberalization and output change

Source: EBRD Transition Report, various years.

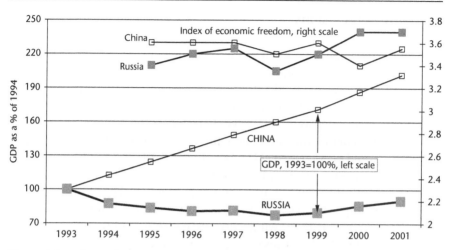

Figure 4.4. Indices of economic freedom and GDP growth in Russia and China
Source: Heritage Foundation; WDI database.

classical example of gradualism, Vietnamese reformers introduced Polish style shock therapy treatment (instant deregulation of most prices and introduction of convertibility of the dong) even before Poland did, in 1989, and still managed to avoid a reduction of output.

Or, take the example of the differing performance of the former Soviet Union (FSU) states. The champions of liberalization and stabilization in the region are definitely the Baltic States (cumulative liberalization index by 1995—2.4–2.9), whereas Uzbekistan (with the same index of 1.1) is commonly perceived to be one of the worst procrastinators. However, in Uzbekistan the reduction of output in 1990–95 totalled only 18% and the economy started to grow again in 1996, while in the Baltics output fell in the early 1990s by 36–60% and, even in 1996, two years after the bottom of the recession was reached, was still 31–58% below the pre-recession maximum.

Overall, attempts to link differences in output changes during transition to the cumulative liberalization index and to macro-stabilization (rates of inflation) have not yielded any impressive results. Studies that have tried to take into account a number of initial conditions (repressed inflation—monetary overhang before deregulation of prices, trade dependence, black market exchange rate premium, number of years under central planning, urbanization, over-industrialization, and per capita income) found that in most cases liberalization becomes insignificant (De Melo et al., 1997; Heybey and Murrell, 1999; Krueger and Ciolko, 1998; Popov, 2000, 2001).

The alternative explanation of the collapse of output in the FSU, accepted in this book, is that the recession was caused primarily by several groups of factors that were all linked to the institutional capacity of the state.

Typology of recessions

Economists distinguish between supply-side and demand-side recessions, the former being caused by supply shocks, the latter by demand shocks. The framework is the AS–AD model, the AS curve characterizes the positive relationship between output and prices (the higher the prices, the larger the supply of goods), whereas the AD curve characterizes the negative relationship between the demand for goods and prices. The demand is the *aggregate* demand; it could be increased (AD moves to the right) by expansionary fiscal and monetary policy. The supply is the aggregate supply; in the long run the AS curve is vertical (given full utilization of production capacities and labour and the level of productivity), but in the short run the AS curve is positively sloped (firms respond to growing prices by expanding output and employment, but eventually this causes wages to increase, so costs catch up with growing prices and output returns to the equilibrium level).

A negative demand shock occurs when there is a decline in the demand for the country's export, or when investors decide to cut spending on new projects, or when consumers decide to save more and buy less—the AD curve moves to the left, as shown on Scheme 4.1 below. Luckily, the government and the central bank can respond to the shock by expansionary fiscal and monetary policy, and can return the AD curve back to its initial position. There is an agreement among economists that the Great Depression of the 1930s was caused by the demand factors (the debate is whether it was poor monetary or fiscal policy that failed to put back the AD curve).

A supply shock occurs when costs increase—either the workers ask for higher wages or fuel producers abroad increase prices for fuel that is imported into the country, or the bridge collapses due to an earthquake. The AS curve then moves to the left (adverse supply shock), and the government does not have the power to affect its position in the short run. The only thing the authorities can do to restore output is to absorb the supply shock by increasing

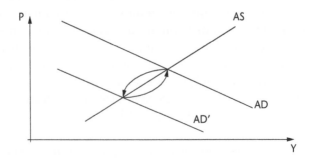

Scheme 4.1. Adverse demand shock and government reaction

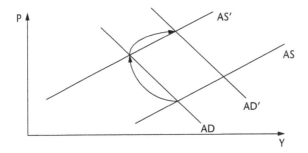

Scheme 4.2. Absorption of the adverse supply shock

aggregate demand (moving the AD curve to the right, restoring output at a cost of higher prices—Scheme 4.2).

Structural recessions—those caused by the decline of one (non-competitive) sector and the rise of another (competitive) sector—would not be recessions at all if the transfer of resources (capital and labour) from the first sector to the second sector could be instant and effortless. But, in reality, such a transfer of resources is associated with higher costs (retraining of employees, replacement of fixed capital stock), so the structural recession (whatever the reasons are— supply side or demand side) becomes a typical general supply-side recession.

This is not to say, however, that all supply-side recessions are structural (i.e. associated with the reallocation of resources from particular industries and regions to the other). Imagine that workers ask for higher wages in all regions and industries, so that profits contract by the same amount in all companies, so employees are fired and output cut. When unemployment grows, real wages fall, profits increase, and output is gradually restored to the previous level. We have a supply-side recession and a recovery without the reallocation of capital and labour from one sector (industry, region) to another.

This is true with respect to demand-side recessions as well. There may be a fall in demand for the products of particular industry, and then there is a need to reallocate resources from this industry to other sectors. But one could imagine a demand-driven recession caused by an absolutely even contraction of demand for all products (say, due to the excess tightening of monetary policy)—in this case we have a temporary decline in output (and prices) that comes to an end as wages fall and the previous profit rate is restored at the new (lower) level of prices and wages.

So, there may be recessions, supply-driven and demand-driven, not associ-ated with the need to reallocate resources between sectors. The important difference between these 'structural' and 'general' recessions is that in the latter case there is no need to reallocate resources, so there is no need for new investment. First, universally across industries, contraction of output occurs, so that there is unemployment and unloaded production capacities;

later, during recovery, employment and capacity utilization rates increase universally across industries.

Recessions in post-communist countries were mostly structural supply side—due to changes in relative prices after deregulation (Popov, 2007b). But appropriate (inappropriate) government policies could have eased (aggravated) these structural recessions. Thus, it has been argued, for instance, that the impact of demand-side factors (excessively tight demand management) on output decline in Poland has been much more pronounced than the impact of supply-side factors (Rosati, 1994).

For non-(former) communist countries, the same question—whether the recession is supply side or demand side—is of course of major importance as well. If the former, an increase in inflation rate may be warranted (to absorb the adverse supply shock); if the latter, good policy would be to stick to the pre-recession inflation rates.

There are objective constraints for the transfer of resources from one sector to the other, in particular the size of savings and investment that could be used to reallocate capital (Popov, 2007b).

Consider a country where deregulation of prices (or elimination of trade tariffs/subsidies) leads to a change in relative price ratios and thus produces an adverse supply shock for at least some industries. Capital should be reallocated from industries facing declining relative prices and profitability to industries with rising relative prices. Assume that 50% of the total output is concentrated in non-competitive industries: this whole sector should disappear either gradually or at once depending on how fast relative prices will change; capital is not homogeneous and cannot be moved to the competitive sector, whereas labour (for the sake of the argument) can be reallocated to the competitive sector without costs.

If prices are liberalized instantly, then the whole non-competitive sector becomes unprofitable overnight and output falls immediately by 50%; later, savings for investment are generated only by the competitive sector, so it takes a number of years to reach the pre-recession level of output. If reforms are carried out slowly (gradual price deregulation or elimination of tariffs/subsidies), so that every year output in the non-competitive sector falls by, say, 10%, this fall could be largely compensated by the increase in output in the competitive sector. *The best trajectory, of course, is the one with such a speed of deregulation of prices that leads to the reduction of output in the non-competitive sector at a natural rate, that is as its fixed capital stock retires in the absence of new investment.*

This example illustrates that there is a limit to the speed of reallocating capital from non-competitive to competitive industries, which is determined basically by the net investment/GDP ratio (gross investment minus retirement of capital stock in the competitive industries, since in non-competitive industries the retiring capital stock should not be replaced anyway). It is not reasonable to wipe away output in non-competitive industries faster than capital is being transferred to more efficient industries.

Market-type reforms in many post-communist economies created exactly this kind of a bottleneck. Countries that followed the shock therapy path found themselves in a supply-side recession that is likely to become a textbook example: an excessive speed of change in relative prices required a magnitude of restructuring that was simply non-achievable with the limited pool of investment. Up to half of their economies were made non-competitive over- night due to the change in relative prices after deregulation. Output in these non-competitive industries fell for several years and fell in some cases to virtually zero, whereas the growth of output in competitive industries was constrained, among other factors, by the limited investment potential, and was not strong enough to compensate for the output loss in the inefficient sectors.

Hence, at least one general conclusion from the study of the experience of transition economies appears to be relevant for the reform process in all countries: *provided that reforms create a need for restructuring (reallocation of resources), the speed of reforms should be such that the magnitude of required restructuring does not exceed the investment potential of the economy.* In short, the speed of adjustment and restructuring in every economy is limited, if only due to the limited investment potential needed to reallocate capital stock. This is the main rationale for gradual, rather than instant, phasing out of tariff and non-tariff barriers, of subsidies, and of other forms of government support of particular sectors (it took nearly 10 years for the European Economic Com- munity and for NAFTA to abolish tariffs).

The problem is that the option of gradual transition may not be available for countries with weak institutions. In particular, keeping relative prices at a level different from the market equilibrium level (or using subsidies or other means to preserve output in inefficient sectors) requires that the state capacity is strong enough to prevent the agents from trading in the shadow economy at market clearing prices. The model developed by Murphy, Shleifer, and Vishny (1992) shows that, if the state is not strong enough to prevent the transfer of critical resources from the state sector to the private sector (even assuming that these resources are used more efficiently in the private sector), the result may be the general reduction of output (reduction in the state sector exceeding increase in the private sector). The authors refer to the example of China (successful gradual transition) and Russia (gradual Gorbachev reforms in 1987–91 that led to a decline in output in 1990–91) concluding that the Chinese government 'has managed to control the diversion problem by strict enforcement of delivery quotas between state enterprises. Such controls require a much stronger government than Russia had in 1991' (p. 906).

In fact, the gradual economic transition in its classical form was carried out only in China. The policy consisted of two components: (1) gradual deregulation of prices (dual track price system); and (2) no privatization of existing enterprises, but allowing the private sector to emerge from scratch (growing out of socialism). Countries like Belarus, Turkmenistan, Uzbekistan, and Vietnam—that are usually regarded as procrastinators—deregulated most prices at once and experienced a transformational recession.[1] They are considered gradualist mostly due to the slow pace of privatization and other structural reforms.

Distortions in industrial structure—the heritage of the CPE

In the first approximation, the economic recession that occurred in FSU states was associated with the need to reallocate resources in order to correct the industrial structure inherited from the centrally planned economy (CPE). These distortions included over-militarization and over-industrialization, perverted trade flows among former Soviet republics and Comecon countries, and the excessively large size and poor specialization of industrial enterprises and agricultural farms. In most cases these distortions were more pronounced than in Eastern Europe, not to speak about China and Vietnam—the larger the distortions, the greater the reduction of output (Fig. 4.5). The transformational recession, to put it in economic terms, was caused by an adverse supply shock similar to the one experienced by Western countries after the oil price hikes in 1973 and 1979, and similar to post-war recessions caused by conversion of the defence industries (Popov, 2000, 2007b). The essence of this adverse supply shock boils down to the fact that the reduction of output in non-competitive industries proceeds faster than the increase in output in competitive industries because the reallocation of capital and labour from the former to the latter is associated with costs (mostly in the form of the investment into restructuring).

Distortions in industrial structure (militarization, over-industrialization, etc.) and distortions at the micro level (the size and specialization of enterprises) are more difficult to overcome if they are embodied in fixed assets, and if these fixed assets are sizeable compared to GDP. It may be argued that in poor agricultural economies distortions were not 'cast in stone', since the relatively primitive fixed capital stock was less susceptible to distortions and, even if distorted, was not so large in comparison to GDP as it was in more

---

[1] While Vietnamese industry, excluding constantly and rapidly growing oil production, experienced some downturn in 1989–90 (-6% in 1989 and 0% in 1990) agricultural growth remained strong, such that GDP growth rates virtually did not fall (5–6% a year)—Montes (1997).

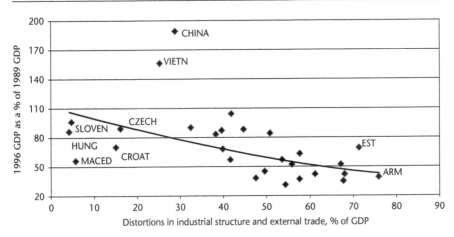

Figure 4.5. Aggregate distortions in industrial structure and external trade before transition and GDP change during transition

Source: Popov, (2000).

advanced industrialized transition economies. Hence, restructuring in more backward countries did not require as much investment (as a percentage of GDP) as in more advanced transition economies.

Distortions are very much linked to the level of development, but not always (for example, Slovenia, a republic of the former Yugoslavia, had the highest income per capita among FSU and EE countries, but very low distortions). However, given the same magnitude of distortions, it is more difficult to overcome these in a more developed country, where these distortions materialize in a more voluminous fixed capital stock.

Ceteris paribus, the low level of economic development (in particular, the lower capital/output ratio) is an asset rather than a liability, that is there are some 'advantages of backwardness'. The conventional understanding of this term introduced by Gerschenkron (1962) implies that countries with lower levels of economic development (lower GDP per capita) can benefit from the technological achievements and the experience of richer countries through international exchanges and hence may enjoy higher rates of growth that allow them to 'catch up' (converge) with the richer countries. With respect to transition economies, this general argument has an additional dimension. Because of distortions in infrastructure and other fixed capital stock, created by decades of central planning, the magnitude of the required restructuring was greater in the socialist economies with higher capital/output ratios, that is a higher level of economic development.

This interpretation suggests, for instance, that Chinese reformers, in most cases, were not overburdened by the legacy of the CPE in the sense that they were not constrained by distorted infrastructure in industry and especially in agriculture. Chinese agricultural communes, with very little fixed capital stock (except land), proved to be much more amenable to reform than were Soviet and East European collective and state farms with a huge super-centralized infrastructure poorly suited to family farming; whereas the township and village enterprises, which became the major growth sector of the Chinese economy, emerged mostly from scratch.

This argument is supported by the example of Vietnam, which followed a different reform path (the overnight deregulation of most prices and the unification of multiple and black-market exchange rates in March 1989), but which also managed to avoid transformational recession. It is also partially supported by the example of the two former Soviet Central Asian republics of Uzbekistan and Turkmenistan, which did not enjoy the advantages of back-wardness and, thus, failed to avoid transformational recession under the more gradual reforms carried out by authoritarian regimes.

In contrast to China and Vietnam (and to Albania and Mongolia to some extent), the East European countries, the Baltic States and, even more so the CIS states—where CPEs existed for a longer time than elsewhere—entered the transition period with huge distortions in fixed capital stock and thus were doomed to experience transformational recession. Even in China, large state enterprises in heavy industry proved to be the bottleneck in the whole reform process. There is a correlation between the share of state enterprises in total output and the rates of economic growth by province: the larger the share of state enterprises in total provincial output, the lower the rates of growth.

Institutional capacity and performance

The additional reason for the extreme depth of the transformational recession, as was argued earlier, was associated with the institutional collapse. After factoring in the impact of distortions in industrial structure and trade patterns inherited from the era of central planning, the institutional weakening measured by the decline of government spending, or as the increase in the share of the shadow economy, explains the bulk of the decline in output. Given the weak institutional capacity of the state, that is its poor ability to enforce its own regulations, economic policies could hardly be 'good'. Weak state institutions usually imply import substitution and populist macroeconomic policies (subsidies to non-competitive industries, budget deficits resulting in high indebtedness and/or inflation, overvalued exchange rates), which have devastating impact on output.[2]

---

[2] Of course, strong institutional capacity does not lead automatically to responsible economic policies. Examples range from the USSR before it collapsed (strong import substitution and periodic

Distortions \ Institutions	Strong	Weak
High	East European countries	FSU
Low	China, Vietnam	Albania, Mongolia

Scheme 4.3. Major factors determining performance during transition

This 2 x 2 matrix (Scheme 4.3) is a simplification, but a useful one. The best performing countries are those with low distortions and strong institutions (China, Vietnam), whereas the worst performance is exhibited by countries with high distortions and weak institutions (former Soviet Union). In between are 'half fortunate' countries with strong institutions, but large distortions (Eastern Europe) and low distortions, but weak institutions (Albania, Mongolia).

This scheme explains what was lacking in FSU and present in EE (strong institutions) that allowed the EE countries to do better than FSU, no matter whether they pursued more or less gradual transition. This scheme also explains why it is wrong to claim that the low level of development per se and the large agrarian sector allowed China and Vietnam to avoid transformational recession. Albania and Mongolia were roughly at the same level of development and their rural population was even larger than in China, but they experienced a reduction of output during transition nevertheless.

The differences between EE countries and FSU in terms of institutional capacity of the state are striking. The adverse supply shock came not only from the change in relative prices but also from inability of the state to perform its traditional functions—to collect taxes and to constrain the shadow economy, to ensure property and contract rights, and law and order in general. Naturally, poor ability to enforce rules and regulations did not create a business climate conducive to growth and resulted in increased costs for companies.

It is precisely this strong institutional framework that should be held responsible for both the success of gradual reforms in China and shock therapy in Vietnam, where strong authoritarian regimes were preserved and centrally planned economy (CPE) institutions were not dismantled before new market institutions were created; and for the relative success of radical reforms in EE countries, especially in Central European countries, where strong democratic regimes and new market institutions emerged quickly. And it is precisely the collapse of the strong state and institutions which began in the USSR in the late

outbursts of open or hidden inflation) to such post-Soviet states as Uzbekistan and Belarus, which seem to have stronger institutional potential than other FSU states, but do not always demonstrate better policies (macroeconomic instability, for instance).

1980s and continued in the successor states in the 1990s that explains the extreme length, if not the extreme depth, of the FSU transformational recession.

In other words Gorbachev's reforms of 1985–91 failed not because they were gradual but because of the weakening of the state institutional capacity leading to the government's inability to control the flow of events. Similarly, Yeltsin's reforms in Russia, as well as economic reforms in most other FSU states, were so costly, not because of the shock therapy, but due to the collapse of the institutions needed to enforce law and order and carry out manageable transition. It turns out that the FSU transition model (with the partial exemption of Uzbekistan, Belarus, and Estonia–see below) is based on a most unfortunate combination of unfavourable initial conditions, institutional degradation, and inefficient economic policies, such as macroeconomic populism and import substitution.

The decline of institutional capabilities contributed a great deal to Russia's and CIS's poor economic performance. If regression equations that account for initial conditions only are used to predict economic performance (GDP change), it turns out that China and Vietnam did much better than expected, the EE and Baltic states on average did not so well—but still a bit better than expected, whereas most CIS states did much worse than expected. Exceptions within CIS prove the rule: Uzbekistan and Belarus, that is exactly those countries that are not only known for proceeding with slow reforms, but are also believed to have the strongest state institutions among all CIS states. The Ukrainian example, on the other hand, proves that it is not the speed of reforms per se that really matters: being a procrastinator, it nevertheless did worse than expected due, arguably, to poor institutional capabilities (trust in political institutions in Ukraine is markedly lower than in Belarus).

In most FSU and Balkan countries the collapse of the institutions is observable in the dramatic increase of the share of the shadow economy; in the decline of government revenues as a proportion of GDP; in the inability of the state to deliver basic public goods and appropriate regulatory framework; in the accumulation of tax, trade, wage, and bank arrears; in the demonetization, 'dollarization' and 'barterization' of the economy, as measured by high and growing money velocity, and in the decline of bank financing as a proportion of GDP; in poor enforcement of property rights, bankruptcies, contracts, and law and order in general; in increased crime rates; and so on. Most of the mentioned phenomena may be defined quantitatively, with the remarkable result that China and Vietnam are closer in this respect to EE countries than to CIS. However, the construction of the aggregate index of the efficiency of institutions is problematic because the rationale for choosing weights is not clear.

One possible general measure is the trust of businesses and individuals in various institutions—here FSU states rank much lower than East European countries in all available surveys. In a global survey of firms in 69 countries on the credibility of the state institutions, CIS had the lowest credibility, below that of Sub-Saharan Africa (World Bank, 1997: 5, 35). Especially striking was the gap between EE and CIS countries: differences in the credibility index between South and Southeast Asia and EE were less pronounced than differences between Sub-Saharan Africa and CIS.

Another good proxy for measuring the institutional capacity of the state is the financial strength of the government—the share of state revenues in GDP. Though much has been said about 'big government' and too high taxes in former socialist countries, by now it is rather obvious that the downsizing of the government that occurred in most CIS states during transition went too far. This argument has nothing to do with the long-term considerations of the optimal size of the government in transition economies. It is true that in most of them government revenues and expenditure as a share of GDP are still higher than in countries with comparable GDP per capita. But whatever the long-term optimal level of government spending should be, the drastic reduction of such spending (by 50% and more in real terms in the course of just a few years) cannot lead to anything else but institutional collapse.

In Kolodko's (2004: 259) words 'there can be no doubt that during the early transition there was a causal relationship between the rapid shrinkage in the size of government and the significant fall in output'. Keeping the government big does not guarantee favourable dynamics of output, since government spending has to be efficient as well. However, the sharp decline in government spending, especially for 'ordinary government', is a sure recipe ensuring the collapse of institutions and a fall in output accompanied by growing social inequalities and populist policies.

When real government expenditure falls by 50% or more—as happened in most CIS and Southeast European states in the short period of time under discussion—there is practically no chance to compensate for the decrease in the volume of financing by increased efficiency of institutions. As a result, the ability of the state to enforce contracts and property rights, to fight criminalization, and to ensure law and order in general, falls dramatically (Popov, 2009). Thus, the story of the successes and failures of transition is not really a story of consistent shock therapy and inconsistent gradualism. The major plot of the post-socialist transformation 'novel' is the preservation of strong institutions in some countries—from Central Europe (CE) and Estonia to China, Uzbekistan, and Belarus[3]—and the collapse of these institutions in

---

[3] Countries like Belarus and Uzbekistan fall into the same group with CE countries and Estonia—with small reduction of state expenditure as a percentage of GDP during transition, good quality of governance, little bribery, a small shadow economy, and low state capture index (Hellman et al.,

others. At least 90% of this story is about government failure (strength of state institutions), not about market failure (liberalization).

Before transition in former socialist states, not only were government regulations pervasive, but also the financial power of the state was roughly the same as in European countries (government revenues and expenditure amounted to about 50% of GDP). This allowed the state to provide the bulk of public goods and extensive social transfers. During transition, tax revenues as a proportion of GDP decreased markedly in most countries. However, Central European countries and Estonia managed to arrest this decline, while Russia (together with Lithuania, Latvia, and several Southeast Europe and Central Asian states) experienced the greatest reduction. In Vietnam, the share of government revenues in GDP grew by 1.5 times in 1989–93. Chinese government revenues as a percentage of GDP fell by more than 2 times since the late 1970s, but this looks more like a conscious policy choice than a spontaneous process (authoritarian regimes always have better powers to collect tax revenues, if they choose to do so, as did all governments in the CPEs before the transition).

In most CIS states the reduction of government expenditure occurred in the worst possible way—it proceeded without any coherent plan and did not involve the reassessment of government commitments. Instead of shutting down completely some government programmes and concentrating limited resources on the others with an aim to raise their efficiency, the government kept all programmes half-alive, half-financed, and barely working. This led to the slow decay of public education, health care, infrastructure, law and order institutions, fundamental R&D, and so on. Virtually all services provided by the government—from collecting custom duties to regulating street traffic— became symbols of a notorious economic inefficiency. There were numerous cases of government failure that further undermined the credibility of the state, since many government activities in providing public goods were slowly dying and were only being partly replaced by private and semi-private businesses.

Three major patterns of change in the share of government expenditure in GDP, which generally coincide with the three major archetypes of institutional developments—and even more broadly with the three most typical distinct 'models' of transition—are shown in Fig. 4.6. Under *strong authoritarian regimes* (China), cuts in government expenditure occurred at the expense of defence, subsidies, and budgetary financed investment, while

2000). In 2005, Belarus and the Slovak Republic were the only two countries out of 25 surveyed in EE and FSU (BEEPS, Business Environment and Economic Performance Survey) where significant improvement was registered in 2002–05 in all seven areas of economic governance (judiciary, fighting crime and corruption, customs, trade, business licensing and permits, labour regulations, tax administration); EBRD (2005).

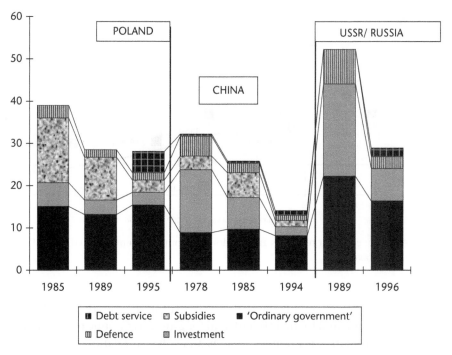

Figure 4.6. Government expenditure during transition, percentage of GDP
Source: Popov (2000).

expenditure for 'ordinary government' as a percentage of GDP remained largely unchanged (Naughton, 1997); under *strong democratic regimes* (Poland), budgetary expenditure, including that for 'ordinary government', declined only in the pre-transition period, but increased during transition itself; finally, under *weak democratic regimes* (Russia), the reduction of the general level of government expenditure led not only to a decline in the financing of defence, investment, and subsidies, but also to the downsizing of 'ordinary government', which undermined, and in many instances even led to the collapse of, the institutional capacities of the state.

While in China total budgetary expenditure and that for 'ordinary government' were much lower than in Russia and Poland, they were sufficient to preserve the functioning institutions since the financing of social security from the government budget was traditionally low. In Russia, however, though expenditure for 'ordinary government' seemed to be not that much lower than in Poland, the pace of its reduction during transition exceeded that of GDP: to put it differently, given the various patterns of GDP dynamics, while in Poland 'ordinary government' financing grew by about one third in real terms in 1989–95/6 (and while in China it nearly doubled), in Russia it fell

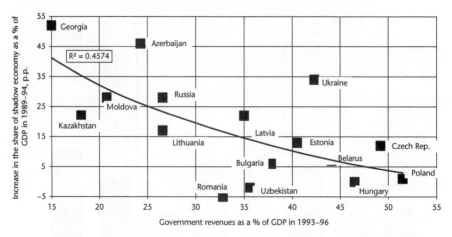

Figure 4.7. Government revenues and shadow economy, percentage of GDP, 1989–96
Source: Popov (2000).

by about two thirds! The Russian pattern of institutional decay proved to be extremely detrimental for investment, and for general economic performance.

Normally in market economies there is a positive correlation between the level of taxation, the share of government revenues in GDP, and the size of the shadow economy: if taxes are excessive, economic agents tend to avoid taxation through underground activity, including non-reported barter operations (Gardner, 1988: 24). In transition economies the opposite is true: the state revenues are lower the larger the shadow economy is (Fig. 4.7). In fact, there was a nearly one-to-one crowding-out effect: for every 1 p.p. of the reduction of the share of state revenues in GDP the share of the shadow economy increased by 1 p.p. Put another way, the dynamics of the share of government revenues in GDP in transition economies is a rather accurate measure of the ability of the state to enforce rules and regulations.

The decline in government revenues was obviously correlated with performance (Fig. 4.8).

There was only one group of transition economies where the share of state revenues in GDP remained relatively stable during transition—Central European countries (Fig. 4.9). Outside Central Europe, there were only four countries where the share of government revenues in GDP did not fall markedly: Belarus, Estonia, Uzbekistan, and Vietnam. In the 1990s the first three were also the top three performers in the FSU region, whereas Vietnam's performance is second only to that of China.

It is noteworthy that Belarus and Uzbekistan, commonly perceived as procrastinators, nevertheless show better results than more advanced reformers. On the other hand, this is an alternative explanation of the Estonian success

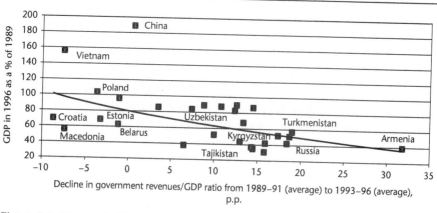

Figure 4.8. Change in GDP and in the share of government revenues in GDP
Source: Popov (2000).

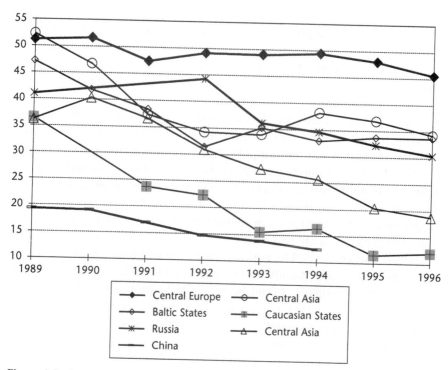

Figure 4.9. Consolidated government revenues as a percentage of GDP
Source: EBRD.

in economic transformation as compared to most CIS states and even to neighbouring Baltic States: the usual interpretation, focusing on the progress in liberalization, may overlook the impact of strong institutions.

The importance of the institutional factor has been pointed out more than once for various countries and regions, including transitional economies (Polterovich, 1999). Rodrik (1996) found that nearly all variations in the rates of growth in labour productivity in Southeast Asian countries in 1960–94 can be explained by per capita income in 1960, average length of education, and the index of the quality of institutions derived from surveys conducted in the 1980s. Similarly, it was found that 70% of the variations in investment in 69 countries can be explained by only two factors: GDP per capita and institutional capacity index (World Bank, 1997). In the late 1990s, Joseph Stiglitz (1997) started to talk about the emerging post-Washington consensus with the greater emphasis on the role of institutions, whereas Holmes (1997) believed that the major lesson to be learned by Western democracies from recent Russian developments was exactly that of the crucial importance of the state institutions: whereas the Soviet Union proved that a non-market economic system with the strongest state cannot be efficient, Russia in the 1990s was proving that a market without a strong state degrades to the exchange of unaccountable power for untaxable wealth, leading to economic decline. Similarly, Campos (1999) found evidence that government expenditures are positively, not negatively, associated with economic growth in transition economies.

A close analogy is that by Wassily Leontief (1974), who noted that an economy using the profit motive, but without planning, is like a ship with a sail but no rudder. It may move rapidly, but cannot be steered and might crash into the next rock. A purely planned economy that has eliminated the profit motive is like a ship with a rudder but no sail. It could be steered exactly where one wanted it to go, if only it moved. To move forward while avoiding dangerous pitfalls, an economy needs both some reliance on the profit motive and some planning: a sail and a rudder.

Reforms that are needed to achieve success are different for countries with different backgrounds. Manufacturing growth is like cooking a good dish—all the necessary ingredients should be in the right proportion; if just one is under- or over-represented, the 'chemistry of growth' will not happen. Fast economic growth can materialize in practice only if several necessary conditions are met at the same time.

Rapid growth is a complicated process that requires a number of crucial inputs—infrastructure, human capital, even land distribution in agrarian countries, strong state institutions, economic stimuli, among other things. Once one of these crucial necessary ingredients is missing, growth just does not take off. Rodrik, Hausmann, and Velasco (2005) talk about 'binding constraints' that hold back economic growth; finding these constraints is the task of 'growth diagnostics'. In some cases, these constraints are associated with a lack of market liberalization, in others, with a lack of state capacity or human capital or infrastructure.

Why did economic liberalization work in Central Europe, but not in SSA and LA? The answer, according to the outlined approach, would be that in Central Europe the missing ingredient was economic liberalization, whereas in SSA and LA there was a lack of state capacity, not a lack of market liberalization. Why did liberalization work in China and Central Europe and not in CIS? Because in the CIS it was carried out in such a way as to undermine the state capacity—the precious heritage of socialist past—whereas in Central Europe, and even more so in China, the state capacity did not decline substantially during transition.

Quality of institutions and democratization

Finally, there is the difficult question of what leads to institutional collapse and whether it can be prevented. Using the terminology of political science, it is appropriate to distinguish between strong authoritarian regimes (China, Vietnam, Uzbekistan), strong democratic regimes (Central European countries), and weak democratic regimes (most FSU and Balkan States—Fig. 4.10). The former two are politically liberal or liberalizing, that is they protect individual rights—including those of property and contracts—and create a framework of law and administration; while the latter regimes, though democratic, are politically not so liberal as they lack strong institutions and the ability to enforce law and order (Zakaria, 1997). This gives rise to the phenomenon of illiberal democracies—countries where competitive elections are introduced before the rule of law is established. While European countries in the nineteenth century and East Asian countries recently moved from first establishing the rule of law to gradually introducing democratic elections (Hong Kong is the most obvious example of the rule of law without democracy), in Latin America, Africa, and now in CIS countries, democratic political systems were introduced in societies without a firm rule of law.

Authoritarian regimes (including communist), while gradually building property rights and institutions, were filling the vacuum in the rule of law via authoritarian means. After democratization occurred and illiberal democracies emerged, they found themselves deprived of the old authoritarian instruments to ensure law and order, but without the newly developed democratic mechanisms needed to guarantee property rights, contracts, and law and order in general (upper left quadrant in Fig. 4.10). Not surprisingly, this had a devastating impact on investment climate and output.

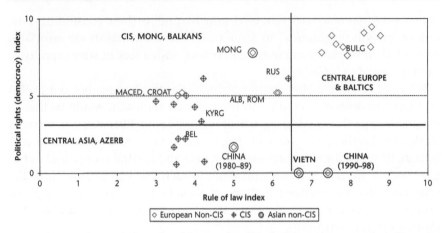

Figure 4.10. Indices of the rule of law and political rights (democracy), 0–10 scale, higher values represent stronger rule of law and democracy
Source: Popov (2000).

In simple words, democratization without strong rule of law, whether one likes it or not, usually leads to the collapse of output. There is a price to pay for early democratization, that is the introduction of competitive elections of government under conditions where major liberal rights (personal freedom and safety, property, contracts, fair trial in court, etc.) are not well established. If the rule of law and democracy indices are included into the basic regression equation, they have predicted signs (positive impact of the rule of law and negative impact of democracy) and are statistically significant (Popov, 2000, 2007b), which is consistent with the results obtained for a larger sample of countries (Polterovich and Popov, 2007). It has been noted that cases of successful simultaneous economic and political reforms are relatively rare (Intriligator, 1998) and that introducing voting in post-communist countries may be detrimental economically (Cheung, 1998). A. Sen (1999) argues that comparative studies that are now available suggest that there is no relation between economic growth and democracy in either direction.

Other studies (Polterovich and Popov, 2007; Polterovich, Popov, and Tonis, 2007, 2008; Zakaria, 1997), show that democratization carried out in a poor rule of law environment (weak state institutions) is associated with further weakening of institutions and with worsening of macroeconomic policy, which has a negative impact on growth and does not allow for the creation of a stable democratic regime, especially in resource rich countries.[4] This is

---

[4] When growth of GDP per capita in 1975–99, *y*, is regressed on the usual control variables (initial income levels, population growth rates, population density, investment/GDP ratios) and various indicators of institutional quality (share of shadow economy, WB indices of rule of law, government effectiveness, etc., corruption perception indices from Transparency International,

only part of the story, however, because there are few examples of fast catch-up development under democratic regimes (Japan after the Second World War, Botswana and Mauritius after gaining independence in the 1960s). Besides, democracy is an institution by itself, and it remains to be explained why some countries adopted it at earlier stages of development while other countries stayed authoritarian, or returned to authoritarianism, after short-lived experiments with democracy. And finally, differences in the institutional capacity of the state in countries with authoritarian regimes (say China, the USSR, Russia) are huge and need to be explained.

A possibly more important part of the story is the long term-trajectory of institutional development, that is the historical path from traditional collectivist institutions to the modern individual responsibility type. Whereas East Europe more or less adopted Western institutions, and China preserved the institutional continuity (traditional 'Asian values' institutions), Russia and some other FSU states found themselves in a 'no man's land'—collectivist institutions were destroyed, but Western law and order institutions did not take root.

investment risk indices) and democratization (increase in democratic ratings from Freedom House), the best result is usually the threshold equation, like the one below:

$$y = \text{CONST.} + \text{CONTR.VAR.} + 0.18\Delta(RL - 0.72),$$

where Δ—democratization (change in index of political rights in 1970–2000), RL—rule of law index (one of the indicators of the institutional capacity).

5

Growth Miracles and Failures: Lessons for Development Economics

As Leo Tolstoy claimed in *Anna Karenina* 'happy families are all alike; every unhappy family is unhappy in its own way'. This wisdom, however, can hardly be applied to the development success of countries: it appears that success stories in the development and transition world are as different as they can be. It is not uncommon to come across contradictory statements about the reasons for economic success. Economic liberalization and free trade are said to be the foundations of rapid growth in some countries, whereas successes of other countries are credited to industrial policy and protectionism. Foreign direct investment, normally considered a factor contributing to growth, did not play any significant role in the developmental success of Japan, South Korea, and pre-1990s China. Privatization of state enterprises, foreign aid, free trade, liberalization of the financial system, democratic political institutions— all these factors, to name just a few, are usually believed to be prerequisites of successful development, but it is easy to point to success stories that are not associated with these factors.

In the 1970s, the breathtaking economic success of Japan, that transformed itself into a developed country in just two post-war decades, was explained by the 'Japan incorporated' structure of the economy—special relations between (1) the government and companies (MITI), (2) between banks and non-financial companies (bank-based financial system), and (3) between companies and workers (life-time employment). After the stagnation of the 1990s, and especially after the 1997 Asian financial crisis that affected Japan as well, these same factors were largely labelled as clear manifestations of 'crony capitalism' that should be held responsible for the stagnation (Popov, 2008).

And during the recent Great Recession of 2008–09 the dominant views changed once again, coming a full circle. The USA resorted to measures that were previously considered inflationary and even socialist—nationalization of the banks, expansion of fiscal deficit and of money supply.

In 1960, Rosenstein-Rodan, widely regarded as the author of the Big Push theory, favoured India, Burma, Argentina, and Hong Kong as nations expected to achieve 3% annual growth per capita for a five-year period. India, Burma, and Argentina all achieved about 1.5% growth, whereas Hong Kong did much better. Chile, Egypt, Ghana, and Jordan were also named for their unusually good growth prospects. But no one seems to have selected South Korea or Taiwan (Toye, 1987).

Ideas matter a great deal. As Karl Marx put it, 'material force can only be overthrown by material force, but theory itself becomes a material force when it has seized the masses' (Marx, 1843: 60). However, the development thinking of the second half of the twentieth century can hardly be credited for 'manufacturing' development success stories. It is difficult, if not impossible, to claim that either the early structuralist models of the Big Push, financing gap and basic needs, or the later neo-liberal ideas of the Washington consensus that have dominated the field since the 1980s, have provided crucial inputs to economic miracles in East Asia, for instance. On the contrary, it appears that development ideas, either misinterpreted or not, contributed to a number of development failures—the USSR and Latin America of the 1960s–1980s demonstrated the inadequacy of the import-substitutions model (the debt crisis of the 1980s in Latin America and the dead end of the Soviet-type economic model in the 1970s–80s), whereas every region of developing world that became the experimental ground for Washington consensus-type theories, from Latin America to Sub-Saharan Africa to the former Soviet Union and Eastern Europe, revealed the flaws in the neo-liberal doctrine by experiencing a slowdown or even a recession in the 1980s–1990s.

To reiterate, neither structuralists, nor neo-classical developmental theoreticians, can claim credit for at least one case of economic miracle. Big Push and import-substitution models, as well as the economic liberalization theories that inspired economic policies in different countries and different periods, never and nowhere led to outcomes that today could be characterized as economic, much less social, success.

In the post-war period one dominant theory replaced another and economic policies in various countries changed accordingly, but neither state-led development doctrines, nor economic liberalization wisdom produced long lasting economic successes in any of the countries that followed these economic theories. In the words of Dani Rodrik:

> Once upon a time, economists believed the developing world was full of market failures, and the only way in which poor countries could escape from their poverty traps was through forceful government interventions. Then there came a time when economists started to believe government failure was by far the bigger evil, and that the best thing that government could do was to give up any pretence of

steering the economy. Reality has not been kind to either set of expectations. Import substitution, planning, and state ownership did produce some successes, but where they became entrenched and ossified over time, they led to colossal failures and crises. Economic liberalization and opening up benefited export activities, financial interests, and skilled workers, but more often than not, they resulted in economy-wide growth rates (in labour and total factor productivity) that fell far short of those experienced under the bad old policies of the past (Rodrik, 2004a).

Meanwhile, economic miracles that surprised the world occurred mostly in East Asia as a result of policies that were not explicitly based on any particular economic doctrine and sometimes seemed even contradictory: relatively low government spending, but high state investment; large foreign direct investment in some countries and territories (China after 1990, Hong Kong, Singapore, Taiwan), but small in the others (China before 1990, Japan, South Korea); rapid increase in exports and foreign trade, but protection of domestic markets. Why did there emerge these gaps between theory and practice?

This chapter examines the impact that development theories have had on development policies, and the inverse impact of actual successes and failures in the global South on development thinking. Low income inequalities and strong institutional capacity are the necessary, but not sufficient, prerequisites for economic miracles. Good policies—macroeconomic and industrial policies (export orientation)—would be other prerequisites and, as was argued earlier, it is up to growth diagnostics to determine what the missing ingredient is of economic growth mechanisms. But, in reality, it usually happens that good policies go hand in hand with good institutions. As a rule of thumb, countries with lower income inequalities and stronger institutions (higher government effectiveness, lower crime and shadow economy) have lower inflation, budget deficits, and government debt, less overvalued exchange rates, and switch to export orientation after a brief period of import substitution. East Asia and MENA countries more often than not have better macroeconomic indicators and export-orientation drive than LA and SSA countries. The crucial question, of course, is why this is the case.

Part of the reason is obviously associated with the political economy of reform. Strong institutional capacity results from consensus in the ruling class; whereas if there are conflicting factions and lobbies, populist macroeconomic policies are likely to be used to temporarily sweep the problems under the carpet. For instance, if there is no consensus among different industrial, regional, or social groups of the ruling class about how to balance the government budget via an increase in taxes or spending cuts, the deficit will very likely persist and will lead to either growing government debt or, if it is financed by money printing, to inflation (Castanheira and Popov, 2001). An overvalued exchange rate is also a variety of macroeconomic populism (and import substitutions orientation as well) because it is, in essence, a policy of stimulating imports at a cost of accumulating external debt or selling tangible assets (land, companies) to foreigners (Dornbush and Edwards, 1989; Sachs, 1989).

But political economy is only part of the explanation, because there are examples of countries with strong institutional capacity pursuing bad policies (for instance the USSR, some South Asian and MENA countries that were pursuing import substitution and sometimes running high budget deficits, debts, and inflation) and countries with weak institutional capacities and reasonable macroeconomic policies (for instance, Colombia, Ecuador, and Paraguay in the last 50 years have never experienced hyperinflation, or even very high inflation, like many other LA countries). This is exactly the area where ideas do matter a great deal—they could help to build coalitions for good economic policies even when the institutional capacity of the state is weak and even where there are powerful lobbies that are not interested in enacting optimal policies.

Finally, at the end of the chapter, I try to formulate a tentative new development paradigm about good policies that may be currently replacing the earlier theories of Big Push and import substitution, on the one hand, and Washington (and post-Washington) consensus on the other.

The 'Big Push': theories and practice

To what extent did development thinking influence actual policies in developing countries? The development efforts of the 1950s and 1960s were dominated by the ideas of 'Big Push', 'Take off', 'Incremental Capital-Output Ratio', 'Two Gaps' (gap between domestic savings and investment and gap between export and imports), and so on, all of which focused on aggregate growth rate to be achieved through large doses of physical capital investment. The logic was seemingly flawless: the savings rate is low in developing countries, so they may stay in a bad equilibrium forever (the development trap—just enough investment to create jobs for the new entrants into the labour force, but not enough to increase capital/labour ratio), unless there is a Big Push—mobilization of domestic savings or import of savings from abroad. The Big Push can ensure a transition to a good equilibrium, where it will be possible to stay on a growth trajectory. The savings gap is another side of the foreign exchange gap: not enough domestic savings to finance investment, not enough foreign exchange earned from export to finance imports of investment goods. What is the answer to lack of savings to create the investment needed to exit the poverty trap? Voluntary or forced mobilization of domestic savings or foreign borrowings to finance import of machinery to carry out industrialization.

The Big Push ideas are usually attributed to Rosenstein-Rodan (1943) and to Murphy, Shleifer, and Vishny (1989), but there were earlier predecessors in the 1920s—'the theory of primitive socialist accumulation' of Preobrazhensky (1926/1965) and the two sector Feldman–Mahalanobis model (Feldman, 1964), which is now acknowledged by researchers[1] and even the omniscient Wikipedia.[2]

The Big Push, in practice, in the 1930s in the USSR, was associated with enormous costs, but is exonerated by many even today as the only possible strategy to create heavy and defence industries in an agrarian country in the short period of time before the start of the Second World War. The share of investment in GDP increased from 13% in the late 1920s to 26% in the 1930s, annual grain procurements by the state doubled from 11 million tons to over 20 million tons over the same period, export of grain—the major source of hard currency needed to pay for the imported machinery—grew from virtually nothing in the 1920s to 5 million tons in 1930–31 (Fig. 5.1). Collective farms created in 1929–30 had to deliver grain to the state at symbolic prices (not even covering 10% of the costs). The result was the reduction of peasants' consumption and the famine of 1932–33 that took 5 million lives. Real consumption, especially that of the peasants, decreased in 1929–32, although total consumption in 1928–37 increased in urban as well as in rural areas by about 30% (Allen, 2003: ch. 7). So, in a sense, the record of the Soviet system in increasing living standards was better than that of British primitive accumulation (no increase in consumption for 300 years, 1500–1800, despite doubling of GDP—see previous chapter). As Robert Allen put it, 'by the late 1930s, urban residents and industrial workers, teachers and bureaucrats had economic reasons for supporting the Soviet state' (Allen, 2003: 152).

Stalin (1976) claimed that this was the only possible strategy of rapid industrialization. 'We are fifty to a hundred years behind the advanced countries. We have to make good this distance in ten years. Either we do this or they crush us . . . '—he said in 1931, exactly 10 years before Nazi Germany invaded the USSR. He even claimed that the elimination of prohibition in

---

[1] Bardhan (1993) writes about the emergence of development economics: 'In the third decade of this century it briefly flourished in the Soviet Union, dwelling on the problems of capital accumulation in a dual economy and of surplus mobilization from agriculture, and on the characteristics of the equilibrium of the family farm: the best products of this period, the dual economy model of Preobrazhensky (1926 [1965]), the two-sector planning model of Feldman (1964) and the peasant economy model of Chayanov (1925 [1966]) came to be regarded as landmarks in the post-World War II literature, after these works were translated into English'.

[2] <Http://www.en.wikipedia.org/wiki/Mahalanobis_model>.

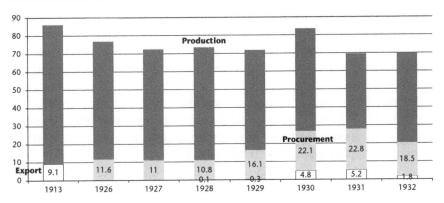

Figure 5.1. Grain production, procurement, and export in the USSR in the 1920s–1930s, million tons

Source: Malafeev, 1964.

1926 (allowing the government to receive excise taxes from sales of alcohol) was the price to pay for the reluctance of Western countries to provide the USSR with credits for industrialization.[3]

There is still a debate going on about whether the USSR would have been able to survive in the Second World War if not for cutting the consumption of the peasants for the sake of increasing the share of investment, industrializing the country, and producing armaments preparing for coming world war (Shmelev and Popov, 1989). Some would say there was no alternative (Klyamkyn, 1987), others claim that had the New Economic Policy (NEP) of the 1920s been continued, the Soviet economy could have reached even higher investment and growth rates with even larger industrial output, including steel, tanks and airplanes, by the beginning of the war (Popov and Shmelev, 1989).

But, in the 1930s, there were no precedents of rapid catch-up development in poor countries. Only after the Second World War did Japan, and later South Korea, Taiwan, Singapore, and Hong Kong, manage to increase their savings and investment rate and to radically raise their growth rates within the market

---

[3] 'When we introduced the vodka monopoly we were confronted with the alternatives: *either* to go into bondage to the capitalists by ceding to them a number of our most important mills and factories and receiving in return the funds necessary to enable us to carry on *or* to introduce the vodka monopoly in order to obtain the necessary working capital for developing our industry with our own resources and thus avoid going into foreign bondage. Members of the Central Committee, including myself, had a talk with Lenin at the time, and he admitted that if we failed to obtain the necessary loans from abroad we should have to agree openly and straightforwardly to adopt the vodka monopoly as an extraordinary temporary measure' (Stalin, 1927).

economy and without forced restraints on rural consumption. In the 1930s it was not clear whether it was possible to do so within the framework of the NEP economy. Not surprisingly, many supported (and even support now) the curtailment of NEP in 1929 and forced industrialization at the expense of the countryside.

One way or another, as was argued previously, the centrally planned economy was able to build new plants and to expand the existing ones, but not to replace retiring equipment. So when the time came to replace the worn out elements of capital stock, growth rates fell. Besides, there was another shortcoming of the Big Push strategy in the USSR—excessive reliance on import substitution. Even in market economies that did not have the problem of replacing capital stock like the centrally planned economies, but that tried to carry out import substitution policies for too long, the results were disappointing. In the 1950s–1970s in Latin America, India, and Africa this strategy more often than not led to the creation of non-viable 'white elephants' and 'industrial dinosaurs' that could operate behind the wall of protection with implicit and explicit subsidies, but that failed to pass the efficiency test once they were exposed to the winds of international competition.

Washington Consensus versus the Big Push

After the debt crisis of the early 1980s, and especially after the Soviet collapse in 1991, Big Push and ISI ideas were totally compromised and the pendulum of development thinking swung to the right—excessive government intervention was proclaimed to be the major reason for development failures. The slogans of the day formulated in the Washington consensus were liberalization, deregulation, macro-stabilization, downsizing of the government, privatization, and opening up of closed economies—elimination of barriers in trade and capital flows (although not in international migration). Even East Asian success was explained mostly by deregulation and the smaller size of the Asian governments.

The Structural Adjustment Programs (SAP) implemented in the 1980s and 1990s focused on reduction of budget deficit, liberalization of prices, privatization of assets, liberalization of trade and investment, and so on. They urged debt-distressed countries to adopt 'sensible economic policies', a term that encompassed not just macroeconomic stabilization on a grand scale but also microeconomic measures of thorough market liberalization. In 1988 this position was formalized; in a concordat aimed at improving policy coherence, the IMF and the World Bank agreed that adjustment lending would be available only to countries undergoing an IMF stabilization programme (Toye, 2009).

The results of the Washington consensus policies were even more frustrating than the results of the Big Push and ISI experiments. Over 1980–2000, the gap between developed and developing countries actually increased for all regions of the South except for East Asia (Ocampo, Jomo, and Vos, 2007). Over the 1980s, the economies of the middle-income developing countries and of Sub-Saharan Africa actually contracted. Transition economies in the 1990s experienced a transformational recession that was either comparable (Eastern Europe) or greater in magnitude (former Soviet Union) than the Great Depression of the 1930s.

Meanwhile, as seen earlier in Fig. 3.14, East Asia was growing several times faster than others. It was growing faster than other regions even in the 1950s–1970s, but this growth accelerated dramatically after Deng's reforms in China in 1979. From the 1980s, India and South Asia became the second fastest growing region—their per capita GDP growth increased to 3% a year in the 1980s, 4% in the 1990s, and 6–7% in 2000–12. Fast Indian growth is sometimes attributed to the deregulation reforms of the 1990s, but it has been shown that it actually started in the early 1980s, well before deregulation reforms were launched (Ghosh, 2007).[4] Like the Chinese, Indian growth was based on the achievements of the 1950s–1970s period of ISI and mobilization of domestic savings: the savings rate (as a percentage of GDP) has doubled over the last 50 years, going up from 12–15% in the 1960s, to 16–20% in the 1970s, 15–23% in the 1980s, 23–25% in the 1990s, and to 24–35% in 2000–08 (WDI database).

With the fast growth of East and South Asia, the understanding that mobilization of domestic savings is crucial may be coming back. Big Push ideas may now be gradually returning, albeit in a renewed form. 'The UN Millennium Project recommended in January 2005 "a big push of basic investments between now and 2015" while its Director suggests that "[A] combination of investments . . . can enable African economies to break out of the poverty trap. These interventions need to be applied . . . jointly since they strongly reinforce one another" (Sachs, 2005: 208). British PM Blair's Commission for Africa launched a report that claims that "Africa requires a comprehensive 'big push' on many fronts at once." In July 2005 the G-8 Summit similarly considered an increase in aid to Africa to finance such a "Big Push"' (Bezemer and Headey, 2006).

In fact, countries that managed to achieve high growth rates were mostly net creditors, not net borrowers; their current accounts were positive, that is they were saving more than they were investing (Fig. 5.2). Even controlling for

---

[4] 'It is now accepted that the shift to a higher economic growth trajectory in India came about not in the 1990s, after neo-liberal economic reforms, but a decade earlier, from the early 1980s' (Ghosh, 2007).

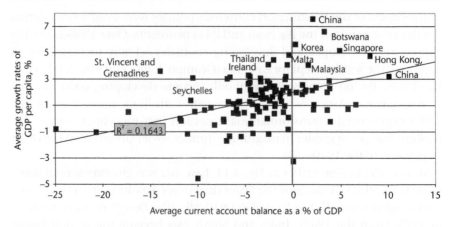

Figure 5.2. Average current account as a percentage of GDP and growth of GDP per capita, percent, in 1970–2007

Source: World Development Indicators.

the level of development, PPP GDP per capita in the middle of the period, 1975, the relationship between the current account surplus and growth rates is still positive and significant.[5] As Prasad, Rajan, and Subramanian (2006) show, foreign financing of developing countries (negative current account) is associated with lower, not higher, growth rates, whereas in developed countries this relationship tends to be positive. They explain the effect by the fact that 'successful developing countries have limited absorptive capacity for foreign resources, whether it be because their financial markets are underdeveloped or because their economies are prone to overvaluation caused by rapid capital inflows'.

This is also known as the Feldstein–Horioka puzzle (Feldstein and Horioka, 1980): high correlation between domestic savings and investment even among countries with relatively open capital accounts, contrary to the prediction of the theory that capital should flow to countries with better investment climate and rates of return on investment. With high domestic savings rates come high investment rates, which usually, although not always, lead to faster growth.

In the words of Paul Krugman (2009), since the early 1980s there have been three big waves of capital flows to developing countries, but none of them resulted in a growth miracle.

---

[5] $GROWTH = 0.68* Ycap + 0.12***CA + 0.05,$
$\quad\quad\quad\quad\quad (1.80) \quad\quad\quad (3.44)$

N=91, R^2 = 0.23, robust standard errors, T-statistics in brackets below, where

$GROWTH$ –annual average growth rates of per capita GDP in 1960–99, %,
$Ycap$—logarithm of per capita PPP GDP in 1975,
CA—average current account to GDP ratio in 1960–99,%.

The first wave was to Latin American countries that liberalized trade and opened their markets in the wake of the 80s debt crisis. This wave ended in grief, with the Mexican crisis of 1995 and the delayed Argentine crisis of 2002.

The second wave was to Southeast Asian economies in the mid 90s, when the Asian economic miracle was all the rage. This wave ended in grief, with the crisis of 1997–8.

The third wave was to eastern European economies in the middle years of this decade. This wave is ending in grief as we speak.

There have been some spectacular development success stories since 1980. But I'm not aware of any that were mainly driven by external finance. The point is not necessarily that international capital movement is a bad thing, which is a hotly debated topic. Instead, the point is that there's no striking evidence that capital flows have been a major source of economic success (Krugman, 2009).

In view of this evidence, the developing country policy choice of a determined attempt to rely on external financing is ironic. It is also ironic that while development economists are preoccupied by 'capital flowing uphill' problem (from developing to developed countries), the best growth record is exhibited exactly by countries with positive current accounts and large reserve accumulation, that is by countries that are generating this uphill movement of capital.

The Marshal plan for Western Europe right after the Second World War may have been the first and the last success story of foreign financing contributing substantially to economic revival. But even in this case it could be argued that without appropriate domestic (European) institutions and mobilization of domestic savings, the (relatively) rapid growth would not have happened.[6] Foreign financing of Japan after the Second World War was insignificant, whereas Japanese post-war growth was more impressive than European.

The same could be said about aid—official development assistance (ODA). Whereas from the point of view of a developing country, it is certainly better to have assistance from abroad than not to have it, aid alone cannot become a crucial factor promoting development. The sheer magnitude of aid (about $100 billion annually) is too small to make a decisive difference (0.3% of GDP of recipient countries, less than total net capital flows by an order of magnitude and several times smaller than just remittances from migrant labour). For most developing countries, ODA is well below private capital

---

[6] The Marshall Plan, designed to support West European countries to help them recover from the devastations of the war, involved assistance of $13 billion in 1948–51. US GDP in 1950 was about $300 billion, so about 1% of annual US GDP was provided to Western Europe in the form of grants and credits during a period of four years. Total American grants and loans to the world in 1945–53 (not only to Western Europe, but also to Japan, Korea, Taiwan, and other countries during occupation of Japan and Korean War), came to $44.3 billion, about 15% of annual GDP, or 2% of GDP a year in the course of 8 years (Marshall Plan. Wikipedia. <Http://www.en.wikipedia.org/wiki/Marshall_Plan>; US Bureau of Economic Analysis NIPA tables).

inflows, such as FDI or portfolio inflows, and below the remittances of migrant workers (Djankov, Montalvo, and Reynal-Querol, 2006). In Latin America, for instance, in 2001–09 only in four countries—Bolivia, Nicaragua, Cuba and Guyana—did ODA constitute over 40% of total inflows of funds consisting of FDI, portfolio inflows, and remittances; for most other countries it amounted only to several percent of total inflows (Gottschalk, 2012).

The irony also is that aid, emergency aid excluded, is usually used efficiently in countries that have relatively good institutional capacity and can mobilize domestic savings themselves, whereas in countries with weak institutions and a lack of domestic savings, where aid is most needed, it is often squandered. In countries that grow fast aid works, in countries that do not grow, aid doesn't help much, except in an emergency.

On top of that, the magnitude of foreign assistance seems to depend mostly not on the needs of the South, but on the attitude of the West towards developing countries and the balance of forces between the West and the South. Plotting the relative size of ODA over the last five decades reveals at least two important trends (Fig. 5.3). First, despite rhetoric and intuition that more aid should be given to poorer countries in difficult times, it appears that aid increased when resource (oil) prices were high, and decreased when they were low. It can be hypothesized that the bargaining positions of the South improved in times of more favourable terms of trade, so the West was trying to ensure that the greater financial independence of developing countries was not translated into more anti-imperialist political orientation. Second, the clear levelling of the volume of aid between 1991 and 2001, after the collapse of the Soviet Union and before the 9/11 terrorist attack, was probably caused by the perception of reduced security threats to the West in the period 'after communism—before terrorism'.

Numerous studies failed to find a correlation between aid and growth and development (Easterly, 2001) or found a significant impact at micro level, but no hard evidence of the impact at the macro level (Channing, Jones, and Tarp, 2010). Arguably, aid is an over-researched issue and is less important than possible gains from any of the following reforms: elimination of Western protectionism and especially agricultural subsidies; more benevolent attitude of the West towards trade and exchange rate protectionism of the South; loosening of the intellectual property rights (IPR) regime for the South; allowing freer international migration of low-skilled labour and efforts to stop brain drain from the South; control over the capital account and over FDI; recognition that the reduction of pollution should be done primarily by the West and that per capita emissions in the South can be as high as in the North; understanding that labour, environmental, and human right standards in the South could differ from that in the North.

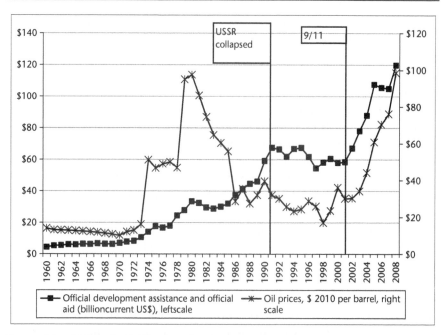

Figure 5.3. ODA and official aid to developing countries in current dollars (left scale) and oil prices per barrel in 2010 dollars (right scale)
Source: WDI database.

Not all countries that pursued the strategy of mobilization of domestic savings achieved a breakthrough, some failed, but without such a mobilization there were no breakthroughs either. The same seems to be true of protectionism and industrial policy: not all the governments that tried to interfere in the allocation of resources by the market managed to succeed, but without such interference there were no economic miracles. To put it differently, mobilization of domestic savings and a government policy of allocating these savings across industries appear to be necessary, although not sufficient, conditions of the development success.

Why doesn't the Big Push work with mostly external savings? One reason may be that domestic savings follow investment opportunities—countries with strong institutions that create a good investment climate raise the national savings rate nearly automatically. The other reason may be the proliferation in the global South of a special type of industrial policy that promotes growth of tradable goods and export sectors—undervaluation of domestic currency via accumulation of foreign exchange reserves. This non-selective industrial policy became very common in Asian countries in the second half of the twentieth century—first in Japan and South Korea in the 1950s–1970s (before the 1985 Plaza Accord), then in China since the 1980s, and later, since the 1997 Asian financial crisis, in virtually all major developing countries. This policy allowed the keeping in check of wages and prices for non-tradables, while giving a huge boost to tradables, exports, profits, savings, and investment (Polterovich and Popov, 2004; Ghosh, 2007; Spiegel, 2007; Rodrik, 2008).

One way or the other, economic miracles happened only in countries that relied on the mobilization of domestic savings, not in countries that were seeking to bridge the financing gap through borrowing abroad. The crucial question then, is how national governments can mobilize domestic savings and alter the allocation of resources in such a way as to achieve rapid, balanced sustainable and equitable growth. This is not only a matter of getting policies right, but also of having the appropriate institutional capacity that allows them to design, adopt, and enforce these right policies.

The Big Push theorists were right in arguing for the mobilization of savings, but their theories had a couple of weaknesses. First, it turned out that foreign savings alone, without mobilization of domestic savings, cannot produce rapid growth. There are no cases of economic miracles based solely on foreign, not domestic, savings. Second, quite a number of national experiments involving mobilization of domestic savings on a massive scale failed. Domestic saving is a necessary, but not a sufficient, condition of fast growth. Mobilization of domestic savings and even successful transformation of these savings into investment, does not guarantee fast growth. Investment should be channelled to projects with the highest externalities and these projects have to finally pass the test of world market competition. The import-substitution strategy can be good at the initial stages of the Big Push, but if it is not later supplemented by export orientation, it leads to a dead end: creation of non-viable industrial complexes that are not able to compete in the world market. Protection is a necessary condition of take-off growth, but should be supplemented with export promotion if growth is to continue.

The Washington consensus was an overreaction to the failure of ISI and the debt crisis of the 1980s—it threw the baby out of the bath together with the bathwater. It denounced not only import substitution (which is a crucial and necessary stage on the road to export promotion), but also all types of industrial policies. And it denounced the need for special efforts to mobilize domestic savings. Meanwhile, the examples of fast growers—Asian tigers, South East Asia, China, and India—all pointed to the need for such mobilization and for industrial strategy.

Undervaluation of domestic currency, accumulation of foreign exchange reserves (FOREX), and export orientation

If both mobilization of domestic savings and export orientation are crucial for growth, there is a policy instrument that allows killing two birds with one stone—undervaluation of domestic currency via accumulation of foreign exchange reserves. It is, in fact, the kind of industrial policy that benefits the producers of tradables and exporters at the expense of the producers of non-tradables and importers. It also leads to an increase in profits, and because wages lag behind, so the share of profits and savings in national income increases. If there are externalities from export and production of tradables (industrialization), undervaluation of the exchange rate resulting from the accumulation of reserves provides a subsidy to these activities and this subsidy is automatic, that is does not require a bureaucrat to select possible beneficiaries. In short, this is a non-selective industrial policy promoting savings and investment, export, and production of tradables that seems to be quite efficient, especially in countries with high corruption and poor quality of institutions (Polterovich and Popov, 2004; Frenkel and Rapetti, 2008; Rodrik, 2008; Bresser-Pereira, 2010; Di Nino, Eichengreen, and Sbracia, 2011; Nouira, Plane, and Sekkat, 2011; Bhalla, 2012).[7]

In Polterovich and Popov (2004) there is a formal model demonstrating how the accumulation of reserves can spur growth, as well as the empirical evidence. It is shown that accumulation of reserves leads to a disequilibrium exchange rate, which in turn causes the increase in export/GDP and trade/GDP ratios, which stimulates growth.[8]

---

[7] In standard macroeconomics, devaluation of the currency is an expansionary policy—it can increase output in the short term, especially if there are unloaded production capacities and unemployment. It is known that countries that stuck to the gold standard during the Great Depression and did not devalue their currencies experienced a greater reduction of output (Eichengreen and Sachs, 1985). A similar pattern was observed during the outflow of capital from developing countries after the Asian Crisis (1997) and during the recent recession (2008–09)—see Popov, 2011c for details. The issue in this chapter is different though—the impact of long-term disequilibrium (undervalued) exchange rate on growth. This impact may be partly associated with the mentioned short-term effect, but mostly is due to the externalities from the development of export sector.

[8] To resolve the chicken and egg problem, we first regress increases in foreign exchange reserves on objective factors that could determine the level of reserves (per capita GDP in the beginning of the period, trade/GDP ratio and the increase in this ratio).

$$delta\ R = 38 - 11.4\log Ycap75us + 0.1(T/Y) + 0.24(delta\ T/Y)$$

(R^2=34%, N=82, all coefficients significant at 0.1% level), where

delta R—increase in the ratio of reserves to GDP in 1975–99 in p.p., *Ycap75us*—PPP GDP per capita in 1975 as a % of the US level, *T/Y*—average ratio of trade to PPP GDP in 1975–99 in %, *delta T/Y*—increase in the ratio of trade to GDP in 1975–99 in p.p.

The residual from this equation is treated as *policy induced accumulation of reserves*, **Rpol**, that is accumulation of reserves above the level required by objective circumstances. Afterwards, we used

And there is strong evidence that accumulation of reserves can spur long-term growth in developing countries, although not in rich countries.[9] The undervaluation of real exchange rate was also found to be good for growth in a panel of 34 countries over 1861–1939 (Di Nino, Eichengreen, and Sbracia, 2011). If all countries use these policies, obviously all will lose in a war of competitive devaluations. On top of that, this policy does not work for developed countries. But for developing countries it works, and there are good reasons why these countries should have sufficient policy space to use this tool to promote catch-up development.

How does the low exchange rate–growth relationship work in practice? There may be several mechanisms at play (Polterovich and Popov, 2004), but the most important one seems to be associated with the externalities from the growth of non-resource and especially high-tech exports, and growth of tradable goods sector, industry, and secondary manufacturing. If there are externalities from these activities (Hausmann, Hwang, and Rodrik, 2006; Rodrik, 2006b), it means that the market alone cannot raise the share of tradables, industry, and secondary manufacturing, as well as the share of non-resource and high-tech export in GDP of developing countries to the optimal level; it takes a special government policy to ensure optimality, and undervaluation of the national exchange rate is one of the best options.

Not surprisingly, empirical research shows that the real exchange rate (RER) is of crucial importance for exports of goods, especially non-resource goods that do not yield resource rent (Polterovich and Popov, 2004). As Rodrik (2008) shows, undervaluation of RER is especially important for boosting the development of the tradable sector, which is smaller than optimal in developing countries but yields greater externalities. And as recent research shows, even for export of services, especially modern services, RER is the decisive factor (Eichengreen and Gupta, 2012). These authors conclude that 'as developing countries shift from exporting primarily commodities and merchandise to

---

the *policy induced change in foreign exchange reserves* as one of the explanatory variables in regular growth regressions with controls for usual variables: initial level of GDP per capita in 1975, indices of institutional capacity, size of the country, population density, and population growth rates.

[9] The resulting equation suggests a threshold relationship:

$$GROWTH = CONST. + CONTR.VAR. + Rpol(0.10 - 0.0015Ycap75us)$$

R^2 = 56%, N=70, all variables are significant at 10% level or less, where

GROWTH—annual average growth rates of GDP per capita, and control variables are population, population density, initial level of GDP per capita in 1975, and population growth rates.

It turns out that there is a threshold level of GDP per capita in 1975—about 67% of the US level: countries below this level could stimulate growth via accumulation of FOREX in excess of objective needs, whereas for richer countries the impact of FOREX accumulation was negative. Di Nino, Eichengreen, and Sbracia (2011) also find a strong positive correlation between undervaluation of the real exchange rate and growth for developing countries and a weak one for developed countries.

exporting traditional and modern services in the course of their development, appropriate policies toward the real exchange rate become even more important' (Eichengreen and Gupta, 2012: abstract).

In macroeconomic textbooks the real exchange rate (RER) is usually considered to be endogenous, that is it is supposed to be determined by objective considerations and cannot be a policy variable. For instance, if the monetary authorities of a particular country try putting downward pressure on the RER by accumulating extra foreign exchange reserves, then either money supply would increase (assuming no sterilization), triggering an increase in domestic prices and an increase in RER, or domestic interest rates would increase (assuming sterilization by the monetary authorities), causing the inflow of foreign capital and appreciation on the nominal and real exchange rates. Hence, there is the belief that there is an automatic mechanism to bring the RER back into equilibrium, if the government or monetary authorities are trying to influence it. Or, to put it differently, there is an 'impossible trinity' (no way to maintain simultaneously the free capital flows, fixed exchange rate, and desired interest rate).

The argument against a policy of low exchange rates is that the accumulation of reserves leads to monetary expansion and hence to inflation. Calvo, Reinhart, and Vegh (1995) argue that undervaluation of the exchange rate is inflationary in theory and was inflationary in practice for Latin American countries in the 1980s. Sterilization is often viewed as a self-defeating policy, since it is achieved only at the cost of higher domestic interest rates, which in turn leads to the greater inflow of capital, the need for the new sterilization, and thus even higher interest rates, and so on. However, in practice sterilization is usually carried out by countries exercising some kind of capital control, either administrative or in the form of the Tobin tax, which makes the sterilization policy efficient. It appears also that countries that accumulated FOREX faster than others usually financed such accumulation with a government budget surplus and thus managed to escape high inflationary pressure. Data for all countries (Polterovich and Popov, 2004) do not show any link between the accumulation of FOREX and inflation.

In the long-term static equilibrium, according to the Balassa–Samuelson effect, because there is a smaller productivity gap between developing and developed countries in the non-tradable goods sector than in tradables, but wages are equal in both sectors, non-tradables will be cheaper in poorer countries than in rich countries. In dynamics, the Balassa–Samuelson effect implies that, if productivity grows faster in sectors producing tradable output (mainly goods) than in sectors producing non-tradable output (mainly services), and if wage rates are equalized across sectors—with the result that economy-wide real wage increases lag behind productivity growth, then the real exchange rate (RER) can appreciate without undermining business profits.

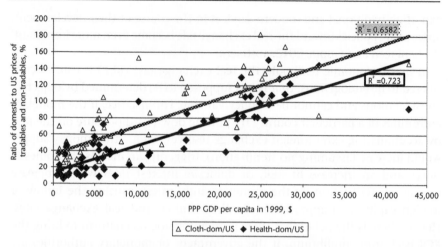

Figure 5.4. PPP GDP per capita in 1999 and the ratio of domestic to US prices of tradables (clothing and footware) and non-tradables (healthcare services) in 1993, percent
Source: WDI.

As Fig. 5.4 suggests, there is an obvious relationship between GDP per capita and the level of national prices to US prices (RER). In fact, this correlation exists not only for non-tradables, but also (although a bit weaker) for tradable goods, which is usually explained by the fact that the price of tradable goods includes a sizeable component of trading costs (that are basically non-tradables).

But it is difficult to detect the effect of RER appreciation for particular countries, even over the period of 25 years—as Fig. 5.5 illustrates, even in fast growing developing countries RER was generally declining, driven more by the deterioration of terms of trade than by the Balassa–Samuelson effect.

Another reason may be that most developing countries, including such important ones as China and India, exercise control over their capital account, so that they can actually pursue successfully the conscious policy of low exchange rates as part of their general export-orientation strategy. Even if formal barriers to the capital movement are absent, capital mobility is never perfect, so the policy of building up reserves can influence the RER. By creating a downward pressure on their currencies through building up foreign exchange reserves, countries are able to limit consumption and imports and to stimulate exports, investment, and growth.

Foreign exchange reserves (FOREX) as a percentage of GDP vary dramatically across different time periods and countries. The share of gold in total reserves of the world has dropped to about 10% today, but in the USA, EU (European Central Bank), and some European countries it exceeds 50%. Net FOREX (excluding gold that is a very volatile component of total reserves

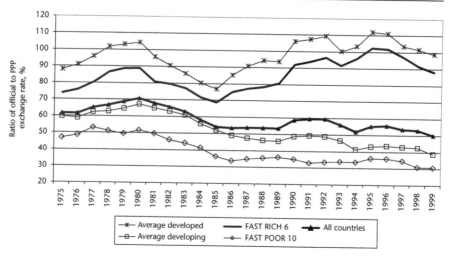

Figure 5.5. Ratio of official to PPP exchange rate in 1975–99 for groups of countries (unweighted average)

Source: WDI.

because its price fluctuates enormously) as a percentage of GDP for the whole world increased from 2% before the collapse of Bretton Woods in 1971 to 4% in the 1970s–1980s, to 6% in the 1990s, and to 12% in 2010 (Fig. 5.6). The increase in the early 1970s is usually linked to the transition from the fixed exchange rates of the Bretton-Woods period to floating rates, even though theoretically floating rates do not require as much reserves as a fixed exchange rate system. The increase in reserves in the 1990s and beyond is usually attributed to increased capital movements due to the liberalization of capital accounts, and to the proliferation of new financial instruments (derivatives) that enhanced the risks of rapid changes in the balance of payments. But the increase in FOREX, as a percentage of GDP, or in months of imports, two to three times in most countries of the world (Fig. 5.6) since 2000 can hardly be explained by just the need to create a cushion against increased volatility.

The variations in relative FOREX across countries are even more impressive. The average ratio of FOREX to GDP for 1960–99 ranged from several percent of GDP for most countries, to several dozen percent for some (Hong Kong—over 40%; Singapore—over 60%; Botswana—69%; by the end of 1999 Botswana had reserves of over 100% of GDP). In East Asia and the Middle East and North Africa countries, the ratio of reserves to GDP on average increased over the course of the most recent four decades, whereas in African and Latin American countries foreign exchange reserves grew roughly in line with GDP. As Fig. 5.6 suggests, Latin America had relatively high reserves in the 1990s, but recently has not accumulated FOREX as fast as EA and MENA countries. Today, LA countries have smaller buffers and hence a weaker ability to manage

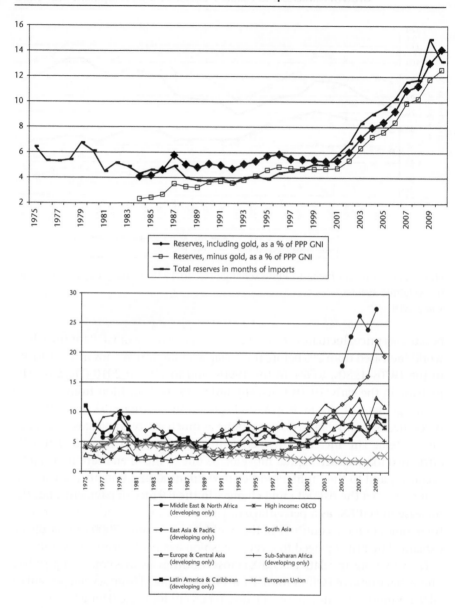

Figure 5.6. Foreign exchange reserves as a percentage of GNI and in months of import in the world as a whole and in major regions
Source: WDI database.

negative trade and financial shocks than East Asia, the Middle East, and North Africa.

The same pattern is observed for Sovereign Wealth Funds (SWF). In 2011, out of $4,814 billion of assets of Sovereign Wealth Funds, nearly 40% were in West Asia oil exporters: Abu Dhabi Investment Authority ($627 billion), SAMA Foreign Holdings of Saudi Arabia ($473 billion), Kuwait Investment Authority ($296 billion), Qatar Investment Authority ($86 billion), UAE, Libya, Algeria, Iran, Bahrain, Azerbaijan, Oman, and Kazakhstan funds ($390 billion); and another 40% in East Asia (China—over 1 trillion; Hong Kong, Singapore—nearly $700 billion; South Korea, Malaysia, Brunei—over $100 billion).

North and South America accounted for just 3% of assets of SWF, and all countries of Latin America for less than 1%: Chile ($22 billion); Brazil ($13 billion); Mexico ($6 billion); Trinidad and Tobago ($3 billion)—Fig. 5.7 and Table 5.1.

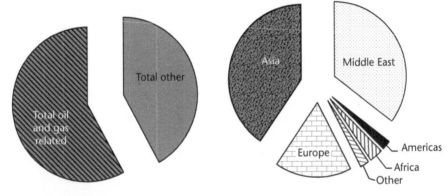

Figure 5.7. Sovereign wealth funds as of November 2011 by funding source and by region, percent of total

Source: Sovereign Wealth Fund Institute (<http://www.swfinstitute.org/fund-rankings/>).

Table 5.1. Largest Sovereign Wealth Funds by assets under management

Country	Fund name	Assets $billion	Inception	Origin
UAE—Abu Dhabi	Abu Dhabi Investment Authority	$627	1976	Oil
China	SAFE Investment Company	$567.9**	1997	Non-Commodity
Norway	Government Pension Fund—Global	$560	1990	Oil
Saudi Arabia	SAMA Foreign Holdings	$472.5	n/a	Oil
China	China Investment Corporation	$409.6	2007	Non-Commodity
Kuwait	Kuwait Investment Authority	$296	1953	Oil

(continued)

Table 5.1. Continued

Country	Fund name	Assets $billion	Inception	Origin
China—Hong Kong	Hong Kong Monetary Authority Investment Portfolio	$293.3	1993	Non-Commodity
Singapore	Government of Singapore Investment Corporation	$247.5	1981	Non-Commodity
Singapore	Temasek Holdings	$157.2	1974	Non-Commodity
Russia	National Welfare Fund	$149.7*	2008	Oil
China	National Social Security Fund	$134.5	2000	Non-Commodity
Qatar	Qatar Investment Authority	$85	2005	Oil
Australia	Australian Future Fund	$73	2004	Non-Commodity
UAE—Dubai	Investment Corporation of Dubai	$70	2006	Oil
Libya	Libyan Investment Authority	$65	2006	Oil
UAE—Abu Dhabi	International Petroleum Investment Company	$58	1984	Oil
Algeria	Revenue Regulation Fund	$56.7	2000	Oil
South Korea	Korea Investment Corporation	$43	2005	Non-Commodity
USA—Alaska	Alaska Permanent Fund	$40.3	1976	Oil
Kazakhstan	Kazakhstan National Fund	$38.6	2000	Oil
Malaysia	Khazanah Nasional	$36.8	1993	Non-Commodity
Azerbaijan	State Oil Fund	$30.2	1999	Oil
Ireland	National Pensions Reserve Fund	$30	2001	Non-Commodity
Brunei	Brunei Investment Agency	$30	1983	Oil
France	Strategic Investment Fund	$28	2008	Non-Commodity
UAE—Abu Dhabi	Mubadala Development Company	$27.1	2002	Oil
USA—Texas	Texas Permanent School Fund	$24.4	1854	Oil & Other
Iran	Oil Stabilization Fund	$23	1999	Oil
Chile	Social and Economic Stabilization Fund	$21.8	1985	Copper
Canada	Alberta's Heritage Fund	$15.1	1976	Oil
USA—New Mexico	New Mexico State Investment Council	$14.3	1958	Non-Commodity
New Zealand	New Zealand Superannuation Fund	$13.5	2003	Non-Commodity
Brazil	Sovereign Fund of Brazil	$11.3	2008	Non-Commodity
Bahrain	Mumtalakat Holding Company	$9.1	2006	Non-Commodity
Oman	State General Reserve Fund	$8.2	1980	Oil & Gas
Botswana	Pula Fund	$6.9	1994	Diamonds & Minerals
East Timor	Timor-Leste Petroleum Fund	$6.3	2005	Oil & Gas
Mexico	Oil Revenues Stabilization Fund of Mexico	$6.0	2000	Oil
Saudi Arabia	Public Investment Fund	$5.3	2008	Oil
China	China–Africa Development Fund	$5.0	2007	Non-Commodity
USA—Wyoming	Permanent Wyoming Mineral Trust Fund	$4.7	1974	Minerals
Trinidad & Tobago	Heritage and Stabilization Fund	$2.9	2000	Oil
USA—Alabama	Alabama Trust Fund	$2.5	1985	Oil & Gas
Italy	Italian Strategic Fund	$1.4	2011	Non-Commodity

UAE—Ras Al Khaimah	RAK Investment Authority	$1.2	2005	Oil
Nigeria	Nigerian Sovereign Investment Authority	$1	2011	Oil
Venezuela	FEM	$0.8	1998	Oil
Vietnam	State Capital Investment Corporation	$0.5	2006	Non-Commodity
Kiribati	Revenue Equalization Reserve Fund	$0.4	1956	Phosphates
Gabon	Gabon Sovereign Wealth Fund	$0.4	1998	Oil
Indonesia	Government Investment Unit	$0.3	2006	Non-Commodity
Mauritania	National Fund for Hydrocarbon Reserves	$0.3	2006	Oil & Gas
USA—North Dakota	North Dakota Legacy Fund	$0.1	2011	Oil & Gas
Equatorial Guinea	Fund for Future Generations	$0.08	2002	Oil
UAE—Federal	Emirates Investment Authority	n/a	2007	Oil
Oman	Oman Investment Fund	n/a	2006	Oil
UAE—Abu Dhabi	Abu Dhabi Investment Council	n/a	2007	Oil
Papua New Guinea	Papua New Guinea Sovereign Wealth Fund	n/a	2011	Gas
Mongolia	Fiscal Stability Fund	n/a	2011	Mining
	Total Oil & Gas Related	$2,703.7		
	Total Other	$2,110.0		
	TOTAL	$4,813.7		

* This includes the oil stabilization fund of Russia.

** This number is a best-guess estimation.

*** All figures quoted are from official sources or, where the institutions concerned do not issue statistics on their assets, from other publicly available sources. Some of these figures are best estimates as market values change day to day.

Source: Sovereign Wealth Fund Institute (<http://www.swfinstitute.org/fund-rankings/>). Updated February 2012.

Global imbalances or capital flowing uphill

Because of this rapid accumulation of foreign exchange reserves by the central banks of developing countries and by the governments in sovereign wealth funds, there emerged a phenomenon known as 'global imbalance'—the inflow of private capital to developing countries became smaller than the export of the 'state capital' in the form of accumulation of foreign currency by the central banks (foreign exchange reserves) and governments (sovereign wealth funds). As a result, the exchange rate of these developing countries fell below equilibrium (the level that balances the balance of payments), the current account of the developing countries as a group turned positive, and the current account of the developed countries as a group became negative (Fig. 5.8).

Basically, the imbalances emerged because East Asian and oil-exporting developing countries (mostly MENA) had a current account surplus of the magnitude of 2% of world gross product to finance the US current account deficit of a similar magnitude. It actually meant that some regions of the global South started to generate more savings than required for their domestic investment, and to provide these savings in the form of credits to countries

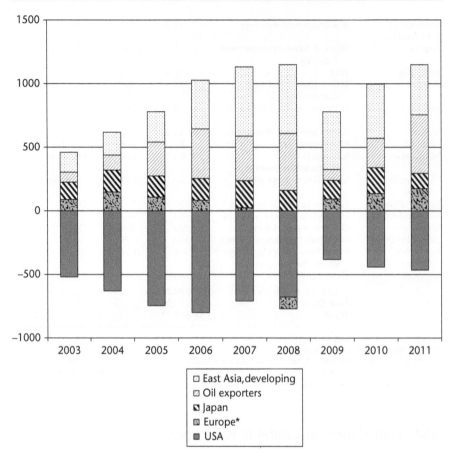

Figure 5.8. Balance of payments on current accounts for some countries and country groups, 2003–2011, billion dollars

* Europe consists of the EU-15, the new EU Member States, and Iceland, Norway, and Switzerland.
Source: World Economic Situation and Prospects. 2013, United Nations, NY, 2013.

(the USA basically) that consumed more than they produced, imported more than they exported, and invested more that they saved. There was a lot of talk of 'capital flowing uphill'—from poor Southern countries to rich Western countries—an obvious paradox because the conventional theory suggested that capital should flow from capital abundant countries to those where capital is scarcer.

In the USA the *conventional view* of global imbalances is that China is a currency manipulator—by accumulating reserves it artificially undervalues its currency, gains unfair trade advantages, and drives the USA into trade deficit and debt accumulation (Goldstein and Lardy, 2009). Even though the US current account as a percentage of GDP decreased somewhat in 2007–09, it

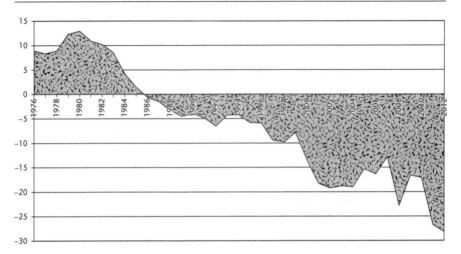

Figure 5.9. Net international investment position of the United States, percentage of GDP

Source: Bureau of Economic Analysis—<http://www.bea.gov/>.

remained large and widened again in 2010–11(Fig. 5.8), and the US net international indebtedness now approaches 30% of GDP (Fig. 5.9).

What are the options for the USA to deal with the problem? It could do nothing and wait until the ratio of external debt to GDP increases to 60% and more, so that foreign creditors will pull their money out of the USA. The US dollar will then depreciate; the adjustment would occur via improvement of the current account. Or, the USA could press China into revaluation of the yuan (the burden of initiating the adjustment would be on China, but the adjustment in the USA would be painful as well). Alternatively, the USA could proceed with unilateral actions, initiating adjustment with domestic policy tools: cut the government budget deficit, impose import duties, promote exports, accumulate foreign exchange reserves in yuans in order to devalue the dollar vs. yuan.

For the USA, the adjustment (less consumption, more savings) is going to be painful in any case, but it is usually assumed that a soft landing is better than a hard landing, and to ensure soft landing it is necessary to start the adjustment sooner rather than later. Also, politically, it seems to be easier to sell the adjustment to the US electorate if it is initiated by the Chinese government, not the US government.

What is the Chinese view of global imbalance? It is interesting that many, if not most, experts in China oppose accumulation of reserves, saying that Chinese money is used for the development of the US economy and that it could be better used at home. Reserves are invested in US treasury bills with very low returns. As Fig. 5.10 suggests, the ratio of foreign exchange reserves to GDP in China has dramatically increased in recent decades, but there are still countries (Botswana,

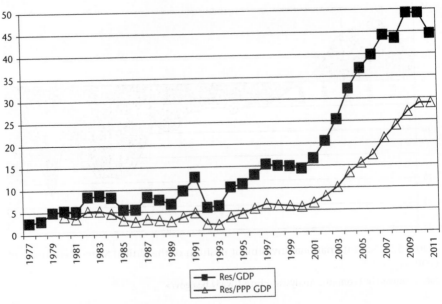

Figure 5.10. Foreign exchange reserves (including gold) as a percentage of GDP and PPP GDP, China
Source: World Development Indicators.

Saudi Arabia, Hong Kong, Singapore), where the ratio of reserves to GDP was higher or about the same on average for the whole period of 1960–2000.

The most vocal opponents of the accumulation of reserves in China are the critics of the government on the Left. A remake of a Russian painting (Popov, 2010b) shows how the Chinese Left view the situation. Mao, with two heroes of Anti-Japanese war (fictional characters from a modern Beijing opera), is coming to get the Chinese gold back from Bush. Gold (actually, foreign exchange reserves are mostly not in gold, but in dollar investment into US treasury bills) was given to Bush by Jiang Zemin, whose portrait is on the wall. At the table are the corrupt former party secretary of Shanghai Chen Liangyu (sentenced to 18 years in prison in 2008) and the liberal economist Zhang Weiying.

Why does the Chinese central bank continue to accumulate reserves despite criticism and US pressure? It appears there is a gut feeling that appreciation of yuan can stop rapid Chinese growth, in the same way as the 1985 Plaza Accord that led to the revaluation of yen allegedly brought to an end rapid Japanese growth. Many believe that among the many reasons for the Japanese stagnation of the 1990s, and the weak growth afterwards, was the appreciation of the national currency (Fig. 5.11).

The non-conventional view of global imbalances that is offered in this chapter is that undervaluation of the exchange rate via accumulation of

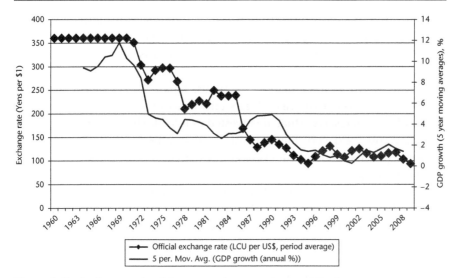

Figure 5.11. Exchange rate of the yen and economic growth in Japan
Source: World Development Indicators.

foreign exchange reserves is in fact an industrial policy to promote export oriented growth. This view is gaining some support in the literature (Dollar, 1992; Easterly, 1999; Polterovich and Popov, 2004; Rodrik, 2008).

This is not a short-term Keynesian effect, but a long-term effect operating through export externality (and strengthened by the subsequent inflow of FDI—Polterovich and Popov, (2004). In developed countries, trade/GDP ratios are already at an optimal level, in developing countries these ratios are below optimal, so a special policy is necessary to reap the benefits of externality from export.

Theoretically, all externalities can be properly managed via taxes and subsidies, but these are selective tools of industrial policy, that is clean bureaucracy is required to use these growth-promoting tools successfully. Undervaluation of the currency is equivalent to import duties for all tradables and to simultaneous subsidies to exporters, but it is a non-selective industrial policy instrument that can be successfully used even in a highly corrupt environment.

Accumulation of reserves means that the country saves more than it invests and produces more than it consumes, providing its savings to finance investment and consumption in other countries. This may sound like a drag on development; it is often argued that capital should flow from rich to poor countries because K/L ratios are lower in developing countries and hence the returns on capital are greater. However, this is only one effect; the other effect is a dynamic one and it works in completely the opposite direction: if a country manages, somehow, to become competitive in the world markets (either via higher productivity or through lower wages or via low exchange rate), it starts to export more than it imports and develops a trade surplus. If this surplus is stored in the form of foreign exchange reserves, the exchange rate becomes undervalued and the trade surplus persists. That is why countries that develop faster than others usually have a trade surplus (the United States in the twentieth century before the 1970s, Japan and Germany after the Second World War, East Asian Tigers and Dragons and China, of course). Accumulation of reserves (that are invested in reliable short-term government securities and yield very low interest rates) implies losses to the national economy (Rodrik, 2006a), but every policy has costs—this is the price to pay for promoting growth.

The argument against the policy of reserve accumulation and undervaluation of the exchange rate for developing countries is the following: if all poor countries pursued this policy, developed countries would finally accumulate unsustainable levels of debt and the inevitable subsequent adjustment would be painful.

But even today the debt of the rich countries is not that high. The USA has net international indebtedness of about 20% of GDP, the Euro area has net international liabilities of just over 10% of GDP (Fig. 5.12), and Japan is a net creditor with net international assets of over 50% of GDP (Fig. 5.13, Table 5.2).

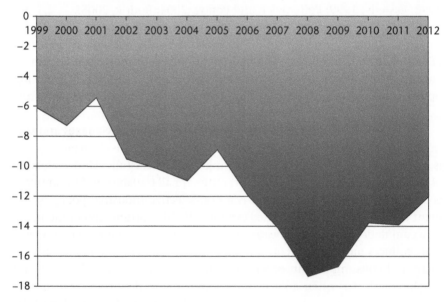

Figure 5.12. Euro area 17 (fixed composition) net international investment position, percentage of GDP

Source: European Central Bank
(<http://sdw.ecb.europa.eu/quickview.do?SERIES_KEY=118.DD.Q.I6.BP_IIP_NT.PGDP.4F_N>).

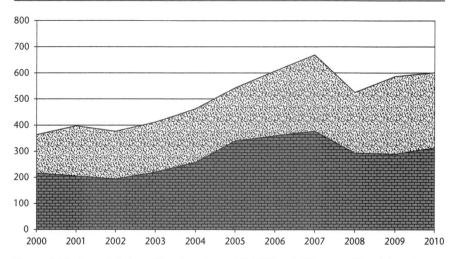

Figure 5.13. Japan's international assets and liabilities, trillion yen (direct investment estimated on a market value basis)

Source: Japan's International Investment Position at Year-End 2010 International Department, Bank of Japan. BOJ Reports and Research papers, August 2011 (<http://www.boj.or.jp/en/research/brp/ron_2011/data/ron110826a.pdf>).

Table 5.2. Net international assets of major countries

Country/year	Net assets as a % of nominal GDP
Hong Kong, 2010	308.6
2007	233.6
Japan, 2010	53.5
2009	56.5
2008	44.4
2007	48.5
Switzerland, 2010	136.1
2008	123.2
China, 2009	36.5
2008	34.5
Germany, 2010	42.1
2008	26.2
Russia, 2009	9.1
2007	−9.4
India, 2007	−6.5%
France, 2010	−11.5
2007	13.4
United Kingdom, 2010	− 13.2
2008	−4.6
Canada, 2010	−16.2
2008	0.8
Italy, 2010	−17.1
2008	−12.9
United States, 2009	−19.4

(continued)

Table 5.2. Continued

Country/year	Net assets as a % of nominal GDP
2007	–17.7
Brazil, 2007	–38.8
Australia, 2010	–58.2
Spain, 2010	–87.1

Note: 'International Investment Position' as released by the central banks of Germany, Switzerland, and Italy, as well as the statistical authorities of China, Canada, and the United Kingdom. Figures for all other countries are from the *International Financial Statistics* of the IMF.

Source: Japan's International Investment Position at Year-End 2008 International Department, Bank of Japan. BOJ Reports and Research papers, August 2009 (<https://www.boj.or.jp/en/research/brp/ron_2009/data/ron0908c.pdf>); Japan's International Investment Position at Year-End 2010. International Department, Bank of Japan. BOJ Reports and Research papers, August 2011. (<http://www.boj.or.jp/en/research/brp/ron_2011/data/ron110826a.pdf>).

As Table 5.2 suggests, it is exactly developing countries that are the major international debtors, whereas developed countries (with some well-known exceptions—like Spain, Greece, and Portugal) are mostly net creditors (Germany, Japan) or modest debtors (the USA and the UK), so there is still room for the West to go into debt.

To conclude, reserve accumulation works as a development tool (theoretically, every externality could be taken care of through taxes, but in practice selective policies rarely work). Because protectionism is currently *de facto* outlawed by the WTO, exchange rate protectionism is the only available tool for promoting catch-up development, in a way the instrument of last resort. Reserve accumulation in poor countries will not continue forever, it will come to an end, once they catch up with the West. Meanwhile, developed countries get a chance to consume more than they produce. Why not go into debt to help the global South catch up with the West sooner?

Maintaining today's global imbalances would help to overcome the major disproportion of our times: the income gap between developed and developing countries. This gap has widened for 500 years and only now, in the last 50 years, are there some signs that it is starting to decrease. The chances of closing this gap sooner rather than later would be better if the West went into debt, allowing developing countries to have trade surpluses that would help them develop faster. Previously, in the sixteenth to twentieth centuries, it was the West that was developing faster, accumulating surpluses in trade with 'the rest' and using these surpluses to buy assets in developing countries, while 'the rest' were going into debt. Perhaps now it is time for 'the rest' to accumulate assets and for the West to go into debt.

Institutional capacity and the new paradigm

Development thinking is at a crossroads. Development theories in the post-war period went through a full circle—from the Big Push and ISI, to the neo-liberal Washington consensus, to the understanding that neither the former, nor the latter, really works in engineering successful catch-up development.

The general principle—that good policies are context dependent and there is no universal set of policy prescriptions for all countries at all stages of development—is definitely shared by most development economists. But when it comes to particular policies, there is no consensus. The future of development economics may be the theory, explaining why at particular stages of development (depending on per capita GDP, institutional capacity, human capital, resource abundance, etc.) one set of policies (tariff protectionism, accumulation of reserves, control over capital flows, nationalization of resource enterprises—to name a few areas) is superior to another.[10] The art of the policymakers, then, is to switch gears at the appropriate time to avoid the development trap. The art of the development theoretician is to fill the cells of the periodic table of economic policies at different stages of development.

The secret of 'good' industrial policy in East Asia, as opposed to 'bad' industrial policy in the former Soviet Union, Latin America, and Africa, may be associated with the ability to reap the benefits of export externality (Khan, 2007; Gibbs, 2007). Exporting to the world markets, especially to developed countries, allows upgrading of quality and technology standards and yields social returns that are greater than returns to particular exporters (Jomo, 1997, 1998). It was shown that the gap between the actual level of development, and the hypothetical level that corresponds to the degree of sophistication of a country's exports, is strongly correlated with productivity growth rates (Hausmann, Hwang, and Rodrik, 2006; Rodrik, 2006b). To put it differently, it pays off to promote exports of sophisticated and high-tech goods. Not all the countries that try to promote such exports succeed, but those that do not try, do not ever engineer growth miracles.

---

[10] Acemoglu, Aghion, and Zilibotti (2002a, b) suggested that appropriate policies depend on the distance to the technological frontier—the larger the productivity gap between the country in question and the most advanced (Western) economies, the more likely that protectionist policy, encouraging investment into 'catch-up' pattern of development, will be beneficial. The authors actually extend these principles to a number of other policy areas (promotion of vertical integration and imitation of technology versus indigenous R&D—the larger the distance to the frontier, the greater the returns from vertically integrated companies and from reliance on imported technology). And there is a whole body of literature that provides evidence that trade liberalization is not always good for growth, especially at the earlier stages of development, whereas protectionism actually can be beneficial (Rodriguez and Rodrik, 1999; O'Rourke and Williamson, 2002; O'Rourke and Sinnoit, 2002; see, for a survey: Williamson, 2002; Polterovich and Popov, 2005; Rodriguez, 2007; Kim and Lin, 2009).

In the words of K.S. Jomo:

EPconEP is our abbreviation for 'effective protection conditional on export promotion'. Basically, it recognizes that for industrial latecomers, import substitution is often necessary for industrial promotion. However, it is very easy for protected industries to become heavily dependent on and protective of trade protection as well as other privileges provided by governments to encourage import substitution in particular sectors or industries. This is the common criticism of rent-seeking, which can easily become entrenched and a long-term burden for the rest of the economy.

Hence, such supported industries must be encouraged, if not forced, to become internationally competitive within a reasonable timeframe. Exports discipline industries, both quantitatively and qualitatively, in that products have to be considered acceptable in terms of quality and have to be price competitive, especially to break into new markets. It is also important to ensure that the ministries or agencies are effectively able to supervise and promote such industries (Jomo, 2013).

Undervaluation of the exchange rate is a universal tool for stimulating the production of tradables at the expense of non-tradables, of industrial goods for exports instead of services for domestic consumption. There is a negative correlation between undervaluation of the currency and the share of services in GDP (Özyurt, 2013); countries with rapid accumulation of FOREX, low exchange rate, and fast growth of export and GDP usually have a small service sector. This is consistent with the stylized fact that economic miracles were based on production and exports of industrial goods, whereas countries with a high share of services, such as trade, finance, real estate, and tourism, did not surprise the world with rapid growth rates.

The emerging theory of stages of development will hopefully put the pieces of our knowledge together and reveal the interaction and subordination of growth ingredients. The New Developmentalism manifesto, that emphasizes the strategic role of the state in providing the institutional framework, mobilization of domestic savings for growth, and prevention of the overvaluation of the exchange rate (New Developmentalism, 2010), makes an important contribution to this approach and may be a sign of an emerging consensus in a new school of development economics (Bresser-Pereira, 2012). The successful export-oriented growth model à la the East Asian tigers seems to include, but is not limited to:

- Building strong state institutions capable of delivering public goods (law and order, education, infrastructure, health care) needed for development.
- Mobilization of domestic savings for increased investment.
- Gradual market-type reforms.

- Export-oriented industrial policy, including such tools as tariff protectionism, subsidies, undervaluation of the exchange rate,

- Appropriate macroeconomic policy—not only in the traditional sense (prudent, but not excessively restrictive fiscal and monetary policy), but also in the exchange rate policy: undervaluation of the exchange rate via rapid accumulation of foreign exchange reserves.

What may be good for developed countries is not necessarily good for countries that are farther away from the technological frontier and are catching up with developed nations. There are quite a number of areas, from trade policy to industrial organization to exchange rate management, where complete deregulation and reliance on market mechanisms is harmful for developing countries even though it pays off for countries operating closer to the technological frontier. Conversely, in other areas, such as the protection of intellectual property rights and migration controls, state intervention that is optimal for Western countries (TRIPS, limits on unskilled labour flows) turns out to be sub-optimal and even ruinous for developing countries. Thus, ideally, reforms in developing countries should not follow Western patterns. But in our interdependent world 'good policies' for developing countries, whether these be trade protectionism or control over short-term capital flows, in most instances cannot be pursued unilaterally without the cooperation of the West or at least without some kind of understanding on the part of the rich countries.

On top of that, the relative importance of different developmental goals in poorer countries is by no means the same as in the rich part of the world. When living standards are low, the marginal returns from improvement of these standards are high: spending an additional $1 a day can take 1 person out of absolute poverty and save them from starving to death. No wonder increases in consumption are often preferred to the clean-up of the environment, to improvement in work conditions, and even to strengthening of human rights and democracy.

The new world economic order, the popular demand of the South in the 1970s–1980s, after the first and the second oil price shocks, may be back on the agenda of North–South negotiations with the rise of China. 'Democratization' of international economic relations—adoption of the rules of the game favourable for the development of the South, together with the proliferation of the new Chinese growth model in the developing world—can finally make globalization 'good for the poor'.

Conclusions

No other economy in the world has developed faster in the last three decades than China—a fact usually attributed to Deng Xiaoping's market-oriented reforms that began in 1979. But economic liberalization reforms alone, of course, cannot explain the breathtaking Chinese performance. Economic liberalization in LA and SSA, let alone post-communist countries of Eastern Europe and former Soviet Union, in the 1980s–1990s never produced such an acceleration of economic growth. Researchers point to other factors: export-oriented industrial policy and prudent macroeconomic policy, foreign direct investment and special economic zones, and so on. The research presented in this book suggests that initial conditions, macroeconomic and industrial policy did indeed matter a great deal, but the most crucial factor was the institutional capacity of the state.

In the recent recession of 2008–09 the Chinese economy also did much better than many other, especially Western, countries. Whereas the latter experienced in most cases a reduction of output, Chinese growth rates decreased only marginally—from 14% in 2007, to 10 and 9% respectively in 2008 and 2009, and increased to 10% in 2010–11. During the recession there was no shortage of articles suggesting that the Chinese model is more viable and that the West should learn from China.

'We in the West have a choice',—wrote Anatole Kaletsky in *The Times*:

> Either we concede the argument that China, in the 5,000 years of recorded human history, has been a much more successful and durable culture than America or Western Europe and is now reclaiming its natural position of global leadership. Or we stop denying the rivalry between the Chinese and Western models and start thinking seriously about how Western capitalism can be reformed to have a better chance of winning.[1]

---

[1] Anatole Kaletsky. 'We need a new capitalism to take on China. If the West isn't to slide into irrelevance, governments must be much more active in taking control of the economy'. *The Times*.

'East is East, and West is West, and never the twain shall meet.' Ever since Rudyard Kipling said it, his words have been extensively cited and debated. A more modest question is this one: does the Chinese economic model today differ radically from the Western one, does it really have magic properties that allow growth amidst a worldwide recession, or did this happen just by a stroke of luck?

To be sure, Chinese economy is no longer either centrally planned or state-owned. On the similarities side we have:

- The dominant role of the private sector: 75% of GDP is produced at non-state enterprises, including joint stock companies and individual private businesses, which are not that different from their Western counterparts.

- A relatively small share of government spending in GDP (about 20%)—lower than in all Western countries and often lower than in developing countries with similar per capita GDP.

- No more free education and health care and relatively high income and wealth inequalities (Gini coefficient of 45% and 122 billionaires only in the mainland, according to the March 2013 'Forbes' count, second place in the world—after the USA with 442, but ahead of Russia with 110).

Differences with the Western economic model seem to be less significant:

- China has a strong export-oriented industrial policy—mostly in the form of undervaluation of yuan through accumulation of foreign exchange reserves. (This is not without precedent, however, since it was used by Hong Kong, Japan, Korea, Taiwan, and Singapore at earlier stages of development).

- Land is still not a private property in China and is not traded, but public ownership of land is not uncommon in other countries, albeit in smaller proportions.

- State property is dominant among the largest enterprises—in 2011, among China's 500 largest companies, state-owned enterprises (SOEs) accounted for more than 90% of the total assets and 85% of revenues (Lu, 2012).[2] It is not uncommon for developing countries to keep the biggest enterprises, especially in resource industries, as state property, but normally the share of state property in these countries is not so high.

---

4 February 2010 (<http://www.timesonline.co.uk/tol/comment/columnists/anatole_kaletsky/article7014090.ece>).

[2] Among China's top 500, 316 are SOEs, accounting for 63.2%. The operating revenue of these SOEs was 30.08 trillion yuan, accounting for 82.84%, while the total asset was 97.74 trillion yuan, accounting for 90.41% (Zhiyong Wang. China unveils new top 500 companies list. China.org.cn, 3 September 2011. <http://www.china.org.cn/business/2011-09/03/content_23344983.htm>).

- China exercises control over the capital account, but it is used by many developing countries now and was used by European countries just half a century ago, after the Second World War.

- China has an authoritarian regime (which, of course, all countries/ territories had before, and some of them, like Spain, Portugal, Taiwan, South Korea, as recently as three to four decades ago).

In the longer-term perspective, the exceptional achievements of China are even more obvious. It was argued that the success of China is not limited to the recent (since 1979 or even since 1949) impressive catch-up in terms of GDP per capita. The other measure of success is its ability to become the most populous nation on the planet and to retain this status even when the country was falling behind the West in terms of GDP per capita (1500–1950). By the integral criteria (total GDP), China today is the most successful developing country and potentially, within a decade or so, the most successful country in the world.

From this longer-term, millennium, perspective, the extraordinary success of China before the Opium Wars (mid nineteenth century) and after the Liberation (of 1949) is due to institutional continuity—the ability to proceed along the evolutionary path without breaking up traditional collectivist structures ('Asian values'). In a sense, Deng's famous 'feeling for the stones while crossing the river' reform strategy is deeply rooted in the millennium-old Chinese tradition and represents this institutional continuity.

China found another, and more painless, exit from the Malthusian trap. Western countries broke traditional collectivist institutions at a low level of development (sixteenth to eighteenth century) and experienced a painful redistribution of income in favour of the rich (rising income and wealth inequality); this allowed the share of savings and investment in income, the K/L ratio, and productivity to rise, but only at the price of high income inequality associated with the deteriorating quality of institutions and increased mortality. China retained traditional institutions and low income inequality for nearly 500 years longer than the West, until technical progress allowed productivity and the share of investment in income to increase without causing mass deprivation of the population.

Why did economic liberalization work in China (1979 onwards) but fail in other countries (Sub-Saharan Africa, Latin America, and the Former Soviet Union)? It was argued that there are several explanations. *First*, Chinese reforms were very different from the Washington consensus package (gradual rather than instant deregulation of prices, no mass privatization, strong industrial policy, and undervaluation of the exchange rate via accumulation of reserves—see Polterovich and Popov, 2004, 2005, 2006). *Second*, the recent Chinese success (1979 onwards) is based on the achievements of the Mao period (1949–76): strong state institutions and efficient government, improved infrastructure, and an increased pool of human capital (Popov, 2007a). *Third*, unlike in the Former Soviet Union, these achievements were not squandered in China due to gradual rather than shock therapy-type economic liberalization and democratization (Popov, 2007b; Polterovich and Popov, 2007). *Fourth* and finally, and probably most importantly, until today, China has never really departed from the collectivist institutions that allowed low income and wealth inequality to be maintained; the short-lived Western-ization attempt (1840s–1949) was aborted. On the other hand, countries that willingly and unwillingly (colonialism) transplanted Western institutions (LA, FSU, and SSA) replicated the Western exit from the Malthusian trap and ended up with high income inequality and an apparent lack of institutional capacity.

It follows that the successful catch-up development of China, if it continues, will become a turning point for the world economy not only due to the size of the country, but also because, for the first time in history, successful economic development on a major scale is based on an indigenous, not a Western-type, economic model.

The litmus test for such an interpretation of economic history is a question on which economists sharply disagree: where will the next economic miracles occur, if at all? If the suggested interpretation is correct, the next large regions of successful catch-up development would be MENA Islamic countries (Turkey, Iran, Egypt, etc.) and South Asia (India), whereas Latin America, Sub-Saharan Africa, and Russia would fall behind.

Today, conventional wisdom seems to point to democratic countries encouraging individual freedoms and entrepreneurship—like Mexico and Brazil, Turkey and India—as future growth miracles, whereas rapidly growing currently authoritarian regimes—like China and Vietnam or Iran—are thought to be doomed to experience a growth slowdown, if not a recession, in the future. The proponents of these views say that without free entrepreneurship and democracy technical progress will always suffer.

According to Jack Goldstone (2009), 'a country encouraging science and entrepreneurship will thrive regardless of inequality: hence India and Brazil, and perhaps Mexico, should become world leaders. But I say countries that retain hierarchical patronage systems and hostility to individualism and science-based entrepreneurship, will fall behind, such as Egypt and Iran.' Many believe that rapid growth can be achieved under an authoritarian regime only at the catch-up stage, not at the innovative stage: once a country approaches the technological frontier and it becomes impossible to grow just by copying the innovations of others, it can continue to advance only with free entrepreneurship, guaranteed individual freedoms, and democratic polit-ical regime (Inglehart and Welzel, 2005).

This may be true or may be not, we still do not have enough evidence for innovation-based growth. For one thing, on all measures of patent activity,

Japan, South Korea, and China are already ahead or rapidly catching up with the USA. The patent office of the United States of America, which has consistently issued the highest number of patents since 1998, was overtaken in 2007 by the patent office of Japan. The patent office of China replaced the European Patent Office as the fourth largest office in terms of issuing grants (the five largest patent offices: the patent offices of Japan, the USA, the Republic of Korea, China, and the EPO accounted for 74.4% of total patent grants). The number of resident patent filings per $1 of GDP and $1 of R&D spending is already higher, sometimes considerably higher, in Japan, Korea, and China than in the USA (WIPO, 2009).

And the evidence for the catch-up growth is controversial to say the least. Successful technical progress and high rates of economic growth (including labour productivity and TFP) in the USSR in the 1950s are not consistent with the view that individual freedom and free entrepreneurship are prerequisites for successful growth. In the 1960s–1980s there was more freedom in the USSR than in the 1950s, but less growth. And in the 1990s individual freedom, entrepreneurship, and flow of ideas really flourished, but it was a period of economic decline, not growth, a period of technical degradation and collapsing R&D. Fundamental research was in disarray, applied research by enterprises virtually stopped, high-tech industries experienced a dramatic decline, the share of machinery and equipment in exports fell. To put it differently, R&D, innovation, and technical progress in the former Soviet Union compares to today's Russia's technological landscape as a mountain peak to a swamp.

And the history of economic forecasting is telling as well. Imagine, for a moment, that the debate about future economic miracles is happening in 1960: some are betting on a more free, democratic, and entrepreneurial India and Latin America, whereas others predict the success of authoritarian (even sometimes communist), centralized, and heavy-handed government interventionist East Asia . . .

What is unknown, however, is whether the gradual weakening in the reform period of the capacity of the Chinese state will continue to weaken further, which will convert China into a 'normal' developing country. In this case, Chinese rapid growth would come to an end and there wouldn't be a question any longer of what was so special about the Chinese economic model.

The continuation of rapid Chinese growth is just one of the possible scenarios, and there are factors that could prevent it from materializing. *First,* there is a controversy among economists about whether 10% annual Chinese growth is sustainable. As was mentioned earlier, parallels have been made between East Asian and Soviet growth by Krugman (1994)—he argued that there is no puzzle to Asian growth; that it was due mostly to the accelerated accumulation of factor inputs—capital and labour, whereas TFP growth was quite weak (lower than in Western countries); and that East Asian growth is going to end in the same way the Soviet growth did—over-accumulation of capital will undermine capital productivity.

Predictions of a coming crash of the Chinese economic model and political system are by no means in short supply. Chang (2001) predicted a collapse within five years back in 2001,[3] whereas Yang (2006), Pei (2006), and Hutton (2007) believed that without democratization Chinese economy is doomed to at least slow down, if not collapse completely.[4] Huang and Khanna (2003) make a different argument: China, they say, as compared to India, lacks home-grown entrepreneurs and is very dependent on FDI, it is behind India in terms of corporate governance, innovations, and access to external financing.[5] Gilboy (2004) shows that China today is still behind Korea and Japan 20 and 30 years ago respectively in terms of the share of high-tech goods produced by domestic, not foreign, firms in total output and export, in R&D spending as a proportion of GDP, and so on. He concludes that China is experiencing growth without development and that technologically it is not able to compete with the USA. Ocampo (2013) believes that technological sophistication is the real measure of development success, and that East Asia is not succeeding in this respect despite rapid catch up in per capita income.

Second, there is a view that China's rise will continue, but it does not really represent the danger to the West because the Chinese model is developing in the direction of the Western liberal democracy and a 'normal' capitalist market economy based on private property (discussions are in: Peerenboom, 2007; Bergsten et al., 2006). Even more so that inside China, very much like in other developed and developing countries, the inequalities in income distribution appear to have been on the rise since the early 1980s.

---

[3] 'Peer beneath the surface, and there is a weak China, one that is in long-term decline and even on the verge of collapse. The symptoms of decay are to be seen everywhere.' Chang believed China had about five years to get its economy in order before it suffered a crippling financial collapse—a timeline he seriously doubted could be met.

[4] 'In the absence of an alternative to the vision of liberal democracy, the authoritarian Chinese ruling elite will find it no easy task to juggle all the competing demands that come its way' (Yang, 2006: 164). 'The lack of democratic reforms in China has led to pervasive corruption and a breakdown in political accountability. What has emerged is a decentralized predatory state in which local party bosses have effectively privatized the state's authority. Collusive corruption is widespread and governance is deteriorating. Instead of evolving toward a full market economy, China is trapped in partial economic and political reforms' (Pei, 2006, cover text).

[5] 'In fact, you would be hard-pressed to find a single homegrown Chinese firm that operates on a global scale and markets its own products abroad' (Huang and Khanna, 2003). This is not factually true—Baosteel, Chery, Cosco, Haier, Konka, Lenovo (Legend)—that recently purchased the PC business of IBM—TCL are just a few examples. Twenty Chinese companies (all under Chinese control and nearly all state controlled) were in Fortune's-500 list of the world's largest companies in 2006, as compared to six Indian companies (USA—170, Japan—70, Britain—38, Germany—35, Russia—5).

The question is whether the Chinese model will evolve gradually into the Western model and, if yes, will it look more like a European state-led model or like an American model with high income inequalities, limited social guarantees, and state involvement in the economy? If the Chinese model evolves in the Western direction, the geopolitical change—China becoming the leader instead of the USA—would look more like a replacement of one state by another within the existing world system (like the USA replacing the UK after the Second World War). But if the Chinese model retains its present characteristics or evolves into something different from the Western model, the consequences for the world economic order would be far reaching. There may be a true democratization of international economic relations and more favourable conditions for the economic development of the global South.

* * * *

By contrast, the Russian economy did not have the advantages of institutional continuity that China had. Even in the Soviet period, the objective indicators of institutional capacity (crime and murder rates) in Russia were never as good as in China. And in the 1990s, during the transition to capitalism, the income inequalities, crime, and shadow economy increased to the levels of Latin America and Sub-Sahara Africa, so differences with China became even more pronounced.

The weakening of state institutions in the 1990s in Russia contributed to the adoption of poor economic policies—macroeconomic populism, lack of industrial policy, sweeping privatization, shock therapy-type deregulation, and opening up of the economy. Even though state capacity is not the sufficient condition for good economic policies, it seems to be a necessary pre-condition, and the weakening of state capacity in the 1990s did not allow the enactment of reasonable economic policies even when there was a political will to do so (preventing the collapse of government revenues, for instance).

The Russian and FSU transition model (with partial exemption of Uzbekistan, Belarus, and Estonia) was based on a most unfortunate combination of unfavourable initial conditions, institutional degradation, and inefficient economic policies, such as macroeconomic populism and import substitution. And the economic performance exhibited by Russia and other former communist states over the last 25 years, since the late 1980s, is about the worst in the world.

In the 1990s, the Russian economy was contracting at an average annual rate that was nearly equal to the average growth rate of the Chinese economy. Only in 2012 did Russian GDP approach its 1989 level, whereas Chinese GDP—with an annual growth of about 10% a year—increased in this period

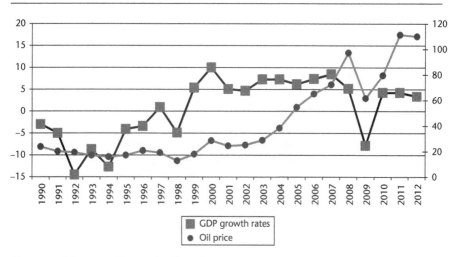

Figure 1. Oil prices (brent, $ a barrel, right scale) and GDP growth rates in Russia (%, left scale), 1990–2012

Source: Goskomstat; BP Statistical Review. (<http://www.bp.com/sectionbodycopy.do?categoryId=7500&contentId=7068481>).

(1989–2012) by more than 8 times. In 2009, during the world economic crisis, Russian GDP fell by 8%—more than in most countries and even more than in most transition economies, even though the crisis originated in Western countries. The reason for the output fall was the decline in world oil prices (terms of trade shock) and the outflow of capital (capital account shock) that was especially pronounced in the case of post-communist countries, the newcomers to the capitalist system. The ability of Russia and other newly emerged market economies to cope with these external shocks left a lot to be desired. Out of 42 countries of the world that experienced a reduction of GDP in 2007–09, 13 were transition economies. Russian growth in recent years has been extremely volatile and very dependent on the level of oil prices (Fig. 1).

In 2004–05, Andrew Schleifer and Daniel Treisman published a short and full version of their article 'A normal country: Russia after communism' (Shleifer and Treisman, 2004). They compared Russia to Brazil, China, India, Turkey, and other developing countries and argued that in terms of crime, income inequalities, corruption, macroeconomic instability, and other typical curses of the third world Russia is far from the worst—somewhere in the middle of the list, better than Nigeria, worse than China. In short—a *normal* developing country. They were right in the sense that Russia degraded to the status of a 'normal developing country' during the 1990s.

The USSR was an *abnormal* developing country. The Soviet Union put the first man into space, and had about 20 Nobel Prize winners in science and literature. Out of about 40 living laureates of the Fields Medal (awarded since

1936 and recognized as the 'Nobel Prize in mathematics') eight came from former Soviet Union (that had only about 5% of world population). The USSR had universal free health care and education (the best among developing countries), low income inequalities, and relatively low crime and corruption. By 1965, Soviet life expectancy increased to 70 years—only 2 years less than in the USA even though per capita income was only 20–25% of the US level (Popov, 2010a).

Market reforms of the early 1990s caused an unprecedented reduction of output and living standards. From 1989 to 1998 Russia experienced a transformational recession—GDP fell to 55% of the pre-recession 1989 level. Over 1999–2008, the Russian economy was recovering at a rate of about 7% a year and nearly reached the pre-recession peak of 1989. But in 2009, due to the collapse of oil prices and the outflow of capital caused by world recession, Russian GDP fell again by 8%. The pre-recession (1989) level of GDP was surpassed only in 2012. For over two decades there has been no improvement in living standards for most Russians.

The transition to the market economy in the 1990s brought about the dismantling of the state—the provision of all public goods, from health care to law and order, fell dramatically. The shadow economy, which the most generous estimates place at 10–15% of the GDP under Brezhnev, grew to 50% of the GDP by the mid 1990s. In 1980–85, the Soviet Union was placed in the middle of a list of 54 countries rated according to their level of corruption, with a bureaucracy cleaner than that of Italy, Greece, Portugal, South Korea and practically all the developing countries. In 1996, after the establishment of a market economy and the victory of democracy, Russia came in 48th in the same 54-country list, between India and Venezuela.

Income inequalities increased greatly—the Gini coefficient increased from 26% in 1986, to 40% in 2000, and 42% in 2007 (42% in 2011). The decile coefficient—the ratio of incomes of the wealthiest 10% of the population to the incomes of the poorest 10%—increased from 8 in 1992, to 14 in 2000, to 17 in 2007 (16 in 2011). But the inequalities at the very top increased much faster: in 1995 there was no person in Russia worth over $1 billion, in 2007, according to Forbes, Russia had 53 billionaires, which propelled the country to the second/third place in the world after the USA (415) and Germany (55)—Russia had 2 billionaires less than Germany, but they were worth $282 billion ($37 billion more than Germany's richest). In 2011, the number of billionaires in Russia increased to 101—more than in Germany, but less than in China, where they increased from 20 in 2007 to 116 in 2011 (plus 36 in Hong Kong and 25 in Taiwan). But Russian billionaires had more wealth than the Chinese—about 500 billion or 1/3 of annual GDP.

Worse of all, the criminalization of the Russian society grew dramatically in the 1990s. Crime had been rising gradually in the Soviet Union since the mid

1960s, but after the collapse of the USSR there was an unprecedented surge—in just a few years in the early 1990s crime and murder rates doubled and reached one of the highest levels in the world. By the mid 1990s, the murder rate stood at over 30 people per 100,000 of inhabitants, against 1–2 persons in Western and Eastern Europe, Canada, China, Japan, Mauritius, and Israel. Only two countries in the world (not counting some war-torn collapsed states in developing countries, where there are no reliable statistics anyway) had higher murder rates—South Africa and Colombia; whereas in countries like Brazil or Mexico this rate was twice as low. Even the US murder rate, the highest in the developed world—6–7 people per 100,000 of inhabitants—paled in comparison with the Russian one.

The Russian rate of deaths from external causes (accidents, murders, and suicides) by the beginning of the twenty-first century had skyrocketed to 245 per 100,000 inhabitants. This was higher than in any of the 187 countries covered by WHO estimates in 2002. To be sure, in the 1980s, murder, suicide, and accidental death rates were quite high in Russia, Ukraine, Belarus, Latvia, Estonia, Moldova, and Kazakhstan—several times higher than in other former Soviet republics and in East European countries. However, they were lower than in many other countries with the same level of development. In the 1990s these rates rapidly increased, far outstripping those in East Asia, South Asia, and MENA, reaching the levels of Latin American and Sub-Sahara Africa.

The mortality rate grew from 10 per thousand in 1990 to 16 in 1994, and stayed at a level of 14 to 16 per thousand until 2011. This was a true mortality crisis, a unique case in history when mortality rates increased by 60% in just five years without wars, epidemics, or eruptions of volcanoes. Never in the post-war period had Russia had such a high mortality rate as in the 1990s (Fig. 4.7). Even in 1950–53, during the last years of Stalin's regime—with a high death rate in the labour camps and the consequences of war-time malnutrition and wounds—the mortality rate was only 9–10 per thousand as compared to 14–16 in 1994–2010.

Russia became a typical 'petrostate'. Few specialists would call the USSR a resource-based economy, but Russian industrial structure changed a lot after the transition to the market. Basically, the 1990s were a period of rapid deindustrialization and 'resourcialization' of the Russian economy, and the growth of world fuel prices since 1999 seems to have reinforced this trend. The share of output of major resource industries (fuel, energy, metals) in total industrial output increased from about 25% to over 50% by the mid 1990s and stayed at this high level thereafter. Partly this was the result of changing price ratios (greater price increases in resource industries), but also the real growth rates of output were lower in the non-resource sector.

The share of mineral products, metals, and diamonds in Russian exports increased from 52% in 1990 (USSR), to 67% in 1995, and to 81% in 2007, whereas the share of machinery and equipment in exports fell from 18% in 1990 (USSR), to 10% in 1995, and to below 6% in 2007. The share of R&D spending in GDP that was 3.5% in the late 1980s in the USSR, fell to about 1% in Russia today (China—1.3%, USA, Korea, Japan—2–3%, Finland—4%, Israel—5%). So, from this angle as well, Russia really looks like a 'normal resource abundant developing country'.

To understand Russia today one has evaluate the record of the last 20 years. In the late 1980s, during Gorbachev's perestroika, the Soviet Union aspired to joining the club of rich democratic nations, but instead degraded in the next decade to the position of *a normal* developing country, considered neither democratic nor capable of engineering a growth miracle. For some outsiders a 'normal developing country' may look better than an ominous superpower posing a threat to Western values.

Insiders, however, feel differently. Most Russians want to find a way to modernize the country so as to make it prosperous and democratic. But they also feel that something went very wrong during the transition; the policies and political leaders of the 1990s are totally discredited. And that is why Putin–Medvedev's policy was getting a 50% plus approval rate even in the midst of economic recession.

The reconstruction of the state capacity in the 2000s can give some grounds for optimism, however. By 2012 the economy finally surpassed the pre-recession level of 1989. Government consumption of goods and services has reached the late 1980s level, and even though investment was only 50% of the level of the late 1980s, personal consumption on average was nearly 50% higher than in the late 1980s. Unemployment dropped from 13% in 1999 to 6% in 2007 and, after an increase during 2008–09 recession (to 8.4%), dropped again to 6% in 2012. Inflation declined from over 2500% in 1992 and 84% in 1998 to single digits in 2009–12.

The budget deficit turned into a surplus in 2000–08, and government revenues and expenditures as a percentage of the GDP began, ever so slowly, to rise; foreign debt as a percentage of the GDP decreased, capital flight decelerated, and currency reserves expanded. During and after the recession of 2008–09, the consolidated government budget, as could have been anticipated, went into the red, but it returned to balance in 2011; foreign exchange reserves fell from nearly $600 billion in 2008 to $380 billion in mid 2009, but later recovered to about $500 billion and stayed at this level until late 2012, even though the capital flight continued.

The most important result of the last 12 years is probably this: the growth of the economy and the stability of leadership have finally led to increased order and an improvement in the social climate. The number of murders, having hit a sky-high peak in 2002, has dropped back down by over 50% since then; the number of suicides has also been on the decline (Fig. 2); the birth rate, which

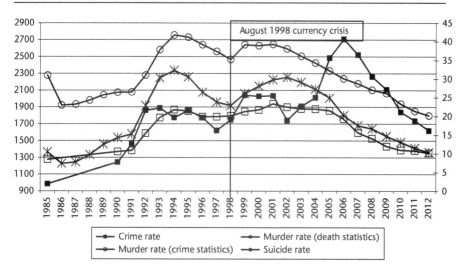

Figure 2. Crime rate (left scale), murder rates and suicide rate (right scale) per 100,000 inhabitants
Source: Goskomstat.

hit a 50-year low in 1999, has begun to rise, as has the number of registered marriages (although this is partly a result of the demographic wave of the 1970s); the divorce rate, having reached a maximum after many years, is now on a downward slope. The Russian population, that fell from 148.5 million in 1993 to 141.9 million in 2009, started to grow from 2010 for the first time in nearly 20 years. In effect, this means that Russia is gradually backing away from the edge of the abyss of anarchy and chaos into which it systematically descended in the 1990s. Income inequalities, at least Gini and decile coefficients of income distribution, have not grown since 2007.

It is these very improvements in the social sector in the past few years that are most encouraging. Economic growth and low inflation alone cannot prevent the disintegration of the country if social inequality and crime increase. Building the verticality of power and intensifying centralization may not be able to stop the collapse of the state, if they don't bring about stronger law and order and limit the shadow economy. In fact, Putin has been criticized precisely for taking all the power into his own hands without greater order resulting. Well, now, it seems that the first signs have appeared of a real, rather than an ephemeral, stabilization: crime and suicide rates are falling, the mortality rate has levelled out, the number of marriages and the birth rate are rising, and the divorce rate is down.

The future, of course, harbours many dangers. The current real exchange rate of the rouble (the ratio of domestic to world prices) is too high. Therefore, a drop in world energy prices could easily provoke a new currency crisis and interrupt economic recovery, despite what would seem to be the major contribution to stability provided by the large currency reserves. Domestic fuel and energy prices remain several-fold lower than world levels, creating an incentive for inefficient energy consumption and the highest energy intensity in the world. And so, unlike Eastern European countries and many of the former Soviet republics, where the price of energy sources is already approaching world levels, the restructuring of the Russian economy is still far from complete.

What Russia should have done in past years was slowly devalue the exchange rate of the rouble, accumulating reserves even faster, and at the same time increase domestic prices for oil, gas, and electricity, compensating the producers for losses from the rising cost of energy with the benefits of stronger competitiveness resulting from the depreciating rouble rate. This could have increased the savings and investment rate, especially if supplemented by the expansion of budgetary financed investment into infrastructure. However, such a policy is not even on the drawing board for the moment.

In terms of pre-conditions for future growth, Russia has some obvious advantages as compared to other developing countries. The USSR ambitiously compared itself to the USA and was proud of its status of the second superpower aspiring to become the first superpower. Time changes the yardsticks for comparison; we live in an age of diminished expectations. Russia today has to compare itself to *other developing countries*. Russia is richer than Sub-Sahara Africa (SSA), South Asia (SA), and is roughly at par in terms of per capita income with Latin American (LA), the Middle East and North Africa (MENA), and East Asia (EA) countries. Life expectancy in Russia is lower than in LA, MENA, and EA countries and the distribution of income is often worse (except for LA countries), but levels of education, even though down from Soviet times, are still higher than in most developing countries, and recently institutional capacity has increased to virtually late-Soviet levels (higher than in LA and SSA, although not as high as in EA and MENA).

The time comparison may be less flattering for Russia. As one Russian journalist put it, what could Russia have been proud of in the nineteenth century? Great Russian literature and arts, Pushkin and Dostoyevsky, Repin and Chaikovsky. What should Russia have been ashamed of in the nineteenth century? Serfdom and the tsarist regime, the Pale of Settlement for Jews and poverty of the peasantry. What could Russia have been proud of in the twentieth century? The attempt to built a just society—the first state of the workers and peasants in the world, free education and health care, elimination of illiteracy and avant-garde arts, defeat of fascism and space achievements, Nobel prize winners and ballet. What should Russia of the twentieth century have been ashamed of? Stalin's purges and labour camps, the mass famine of 1932–33, authoritarianism and oppression of dissidents.

What should Russia be ashamed of in the twenty-first century? Corruption and bribery of state officials, oligarchic capitalism, deindustrialization of the economy and decline in R&D, income inequalities, deterioration of health and education, increase in mortality, clericalization of the society and cultural degradation. What can Russia be proud of in the twenty-first century? Nothing. It is a second-rate developing country, in no area is it number one. It is behind this or that nation in each and every area. And it does not even have the ambition to become number one. Or does it?

* * *

No matter what happens in the future, there are already important lessons to be learned by development economists from the comparison of the recent performances of China and Russia.

First, the institutional capacity of the state matters a lot and explains many of the differences in the long-term performances of countries. The acceleration of growth in China after the 1979 reforms is due not only, and not as much, to economic liberalization, as to the strong institutions created by the CPC in 1949–78. Without these strong state institutions liberalization would probably have produced the same effects as in Latin America in the 1980s or in Sub-Sahara Africa in the 1990s or even worse—as in the former USSR in the 1990s.

It is usually believed that institutions are endogenous, predetermined by past development trajectories, and cannot be easily changed by policymakers. However, many socialist governments in less-developed countries (Russia, China, Vietnam, Cuba, etc.) in a short period of time managed to decrease inequalities, create strong institutions (reduce crime and shadow economy), and build a system of provision of public goods for the masses (free education and health care and virtually free housing). These are precious achievements of developmental states that probably could be replicated elsewhere.

Second, mobilization of domestic savings is a *sine qua non* for development, there are virtually no examples of development based on foreign financing. If the domestic savings rate is high, there is usually the inflow of private capital from abroad as well, but not vice versa. Even more so, successful countries that mobilize domestic savings for investment usually have a current account surplus, i. e. they save more than they invest and they provide their domestic savings to other countries (East Asian countries/territories—Japan, South Korea, Taiwan, and later-ASEAN and China—provided their domestic savings to the USA). This is a price that competitive countries pay for their successful fast development, for the ability to export more than they import, to produce more than they consume, to supply not only their domestic market, but to capture an ever increasing share of the world market.

In fact, the USA enjoyed this kind of development for over 100 years—since the end of the Civil War (1865), and until the 1970s the USA had a mostly positive current account. The surplus was used to provide aid and credits to the rest of the world and to buy assets in foreign countries (foreign direct investment). Today, China and other countries that have positive current account and accumulate foreign exchange reserves pursue a similar policy, with the result that the so-called global imbalances persist. However, US and EU net international indebtedness is still low; Japan is a net creditor, so there is still some room for the Western countries to get into debt. This is desirable because it promotes the faster growth of developing countries and hence convergence in the levels of income between rich and poor countries.

Third, the optimal industrial policy is different at different stages of development, but for middle-income developing countries today the support of export-oriented medium and high-tech industries seems to be most promising. This support could be provided in the form of differentiated tariffs and taxes, subsidies, credits, government purchases, royalties and/or control over domestic prices for resources in resource rich countries, and so on, but the best universal instrument is undervaluation of the exchange rate of the national currency via accumulation of foreign exchange reserves. The advantage of this latter instrument is that it is non-selective and does not require the decisions of bureaucrats, hence it could be used even in countries where corruption is a problem. This instrument was used in the past by many East Asian countries, and is used today by China and many other developing countries that accumulate reserves rapidly.

The other side of the coin of such a policy is global imbalance, that is accumulation of external debts by the Western countries, but it was argued that the game is worth the candle and that developing countries have the moral right to proceed with this type of policy. In a sense, this policy is a more important development instrument than all the official development assistance provided by Western countries to the South.

Fourth, economic stimuli (liberalization) are definitely needed to promote development, but gradual reforms are preferable in most, if not all, cases. The rationale for such a preference is that the magnitude of restructuring that the economy can digest without a fall in total output and employment is limited, and is determined by the amount of national savings and investment. If there is not enough investment to create new jobs in industries replacing non-competitive industries going out of business, the speed of reforms (say elimination of protection of non-competitive industries) should be reduced. The general principle—do not kill non-competitive sectors before new jobs are created in competitive sectors—should always be observed.

Fifth, the contribution of the West to development should be not so much in the form of providing financial assistance to less-developed countries, but in adopting policies that promote growth in the South. Extensive research aimed at finding evidence that development aid contributes to better economic performance did not provide any tangible results. There is plenty of evidence of efficiency of aid at the micro level (building schools and hospitals and eliminating diseases and illiteracy) and no positive aggregate impact of aid at the macro level (higher growth rates). This became known from the 1980s as the 'micro–macro aid paradox', and it is believed that this paradox is still with us (Channing, Jones, and Tarp, 2010).

Rodrik (2012) describes two approaches to development: bottom-up and top-down. The former focuses directly on the poor, and on delivering services—for example, education, health care, and microcredit—to their communities. This tradition's motto could be, 'Development is accomplished one project at a time'. The other approach takes an economy-wide perspective. It emphasizes broad reforms that affect the overall economic environment, and thus focuses on areas such as international trade, finance, macroeconomics, and governance.

The first approach uses widely randomized controlled trials as an instrument that could allow the formulation of good policies—vaccinations and microcredit, additional teachers in schools, and mosquito bed nets dipped in insecticide—these and others are considered to be small projects that lead to big breakthroughs. But without reforms at the macro level it is often impossible to ensure the efficiency of micro projects (Reddy, 2013). If the assistance provided for particular investment projects merely crowds out government or private investment in other areas, the macro impact of the assistance will be zero.

As Rodrik (2012) writes, 'poverty is often best addressed not by helping the poor be better at what they already do, but by getting them to do something different'. This latter approach is precisely the one defended in this book: the global South can gain much more from economy-wide reforms aimed at promoting export-oriented growth based on domestic savings, than from meager official foreign assistance or even from all foreign financing. A benevolent Western attitude to these reforms would be more beneficial to catch-up development than a thousand specific development projects with the most noble goals.

In addition to 'accepting' global imbalances and the policy of accumulation of reserves by developing countries, the West could also 'accept' protectionist policies in the South, eliminate its own agricultural subsidies, share technology and knowledge in the framework of a less prohibitive intellectual property rights regime, lower the barriers for the migration of low skilled workers from the South while compensating developing countries for the 'brain drain', provide the financing for the energy-saving clean technologies that would allow developing countries to reach the same consumption standards as the West with lower use of energy and less emission of greenhouse gases, and so on.

The adoption of these growth friendly policies for the global South would mean radical reform of the international economic order. It will not happen automatically, even if the share of the South in the gross world product increases. It can only happen if the South unites in pushing for its needs.

References

Acemoglu, D. and Robinson, J. (2012). *Why Nations Fail. The Origins of Power, Prosperity, and Poverty*. Crown Publishers, New York.

Acemoglu, D., Simon J., and Robinson, J. (2001). The colonial origins of comparative development: an empirical investigation, *American Economic Review*, 91(5): 1369–401.

Acemoglu, D., Philippe A., and Zilibotti, F. (2002a). Distance to Frontier, Selection, and Economic Growth. (<http://http://www.discovery.ucl.ac.uk/17788/1/17788.pdf>) [Accessed 30 September 2013].

Acemoglu, D., Philippe A., and Zilibotti, F. (2002b). Vertical Integration and Distance to Frontier. August 2002 (<http://http://www.discovery.ucl.ac.uk/17787/1/17787.pdf>) [Accessed 30 September 2013].

Acemoglu, D., Robinson, J.A., and Verdier, T. (2012). Can't We All Be More Like Scandinavians? Asymmetric Growth and Institutions in an Interdependent World? Massachusetts Institute of Technology, Department of Economics. Working Paper Series, Working Paper 12–22 August 20, 2012. (<http://www.papers.ssrn.com/sol3/papers.cfm?abstract_id=2132939>) [Accessed 30 September 2013].

Allen, R.C. (2003). *Farm to Factory: A Reinterpretation of the Soviet Industrial Revolution*. Princeton University Press, Princeton.

Alonso, J.A. and Garcimatrin, C. (2013). The determinants of institutional quality. More on the debate. *Journal of International Development*, 25: 206–26.

Alvaredo, F., Atkinson, A.B., Piketty, T., and Saez, E. (2012). The World Top Incomes Database, <http://www.g-mond.parisschoolofeconomics.eu/topincomes>, April 25, 2012 [Accessed 30 September 2013].

Angeles, L. (2011). Institutions, Property Rights, and Economic Development in Historical Perspective. Sire Discussion Paper, SIRE-DP-2011-08, University of Glasgow.

Arndt, C., Jones, S., and Tarp, F. (2010). 'Aid, growth, and development: have we come full circle?,' *Journal of Globalization and Development*, Berkeley Electronic Press, vol. 1(2). DOI: 10.2202/1948-1837.1121.

Arrighi, G. (2007). *Adam Smith in Beijing: Lineages of the Twenty-first Century*. Verso, London.

Atkinson, A.B. and Søgaard, J.E.(2013). The long-run history of income inequality in Denmark: Top incomes from 1870 to 2010. EPRU Working Paper Series 2013-01. Economic Policy Research Unit Department of Economics University of Copenhagen.

Atkinson, A.B., Piketty, T., and Saez, E. (2011). Top incomes in the long run of history. *Journal of Economic Literature*, 49(1): 3–71.

References

Bardhan, P. (1993). Economics of development and the development of economics. *Journal of Economic Perspectives*, 7(2): 129–42.

Bergson, A. (1983). Technological progress. In: *The Soviet Economy Towards the Year 2000*, A. Bergson and H. Levine, George Allen and Unwin, London.

Bergsten, F.C., Gill, B., Lardy, N.R., and Mitchell, D.J. (2006). *China: The Balance Sheet. What the World Needs to Know Now about the Emerging Superpower.* Institute for International Economics and Center for Strategic and International Studies, Washington.

Bhalla, S.S. (2012). *Devaluing to Prosperity. Misaligned Currencies and Their Growth Consequences.* Peterson Institute for International Economics, Washington DC.

Bogoyavlensky, D. (2001). Mortality from external causes in Russia, *Demoscope*, 31–326, 29–30 (August). In Russian: Богоявленский Д. Смертность от внешних причин в России.

Boldrine, M. and Levine, D.K. (2007). *Against Intellectual Monopoly.* Cambridge University Press, New York.

Brenner, R. and Isett, C. (2002). England's divergence from China's Yangzi Delta: property relations, microeconomics, and patterns of development. *The Journal of Asian Studies*, 61(2): 609–62.

Bresser-Pereira, L.C. (2010). *Globalization and Competition.* Cambridge University Press, Cambridge.

Bresser-Pereira, L.C. (2012). Structuralist macroeconomics and the New Developmentalism. *Brazilian Journal of Political Economy*, 32(3): 347–66.

Bryant, J.M. (2006). The West and the rest revisited: debating capitalist origins, European colonialism, and the advent of modernity. *Canadian Journal of Sociology*, 31(4): 403–44.

Calvo, G., Reinhart, C., and Vegh, C. (1995). Targeting the real exchange rate: theory and evidence. *Journal of Development Economics*, 47: 97–133.

Campos, N.F. (1999). Back to the Future: The Growth prospects of Transition Economies Reconsidered. William Davidson Institute Working Paper No. 229, Ann Arbor, April 1999.

Castanheira, M. and Popov, V. (2001). Framework Paper on the Political Economy of Growth in Transition Countries. EERC Working Paper.

Chang, G.G. (2001). *The Coming Collapse of China.* Random House, New York.

Chang, H.-J. (2002). *Kicking Away the Ladder.* Anthem Press, London.

Chang, H.-J. (2007). State Owned Enterprise Reform. UN DESA Policy Note, 2007 (<http://www.esa.un.org/techcoop/documents/PN_SOEReformNote.pdf>) [Accessed 30 September 2013].

Chen, J., Hou, W., and Jin, S. (2008). The Effects of Population on Income Disparity in a Dual Society: Evidence from China. 2008 Chinese (UK) Economic Association Annual Conference at Cambridge, UK and the 2008 Hong Kong Economic Association Fifth Biennial Conference at Chengdu, China.

Chibber, V. (2005). The Good Empire—Should we pick up where the British left off?, *Boston Review*, February/March.

Cinnirella, F., Klemp, M.P.B., and Weisdorf, J. (2012). Malthus in the Bedroom: Birth Spacing as a Preventive Check Mechanism in Pre-Modern England. CEPR Discussion Paper No. 9116 <http://www.d.repec.org/n?u=RePEc:cpr:ceprdp:9116&r=his> [Accessed 30 September 2013].

Clark, G. (2007). *A Farewell to Alms: A Brief Economic History of the World*. Princeton University Press, Princeton.

Confucius. The Analects (*ca.* 500 BC) <http://www.classics.mit.edu/Confucius/analects. html>. [Accessed 16 September 2013].

Davies, James B., Sandstrom, S., Shorrocks, A., and Wolff, E.N. (2007). Estimating the Level and Distribution of Global Household Wealth. WIDER Research Paper No. 2007/77, November 2007.

De Melo, M., Denizer, C., and Gelb, A. (1996). Patterns of Transition From Plan to Market. *World Bank Economic Review*, 3: 397–424.

De Melo, M., Denizer, C., Gelb, A., and Tenev, S. (1997). *Circumstance and Choice: The Role of Initial Conditions and Policies in Transitions Economies*. The World Bank, Washington, DC.

Derluguian, G. (2013). Lessons of communism. In: *Does Capitalism Have a Future*, I. Wallerstein, R. Collins, M. Mann, G. Derluguian, and C. Calhoun, Oxford University Press, London.

Desai, P. (1976). The production function and technical change in postwar Soviet industry. *American Economic Review*, 60(3): 372–81.

Di Nino, V., Eichengreen, B., and Sbracia, M. (2011). Real Exchange Rates, Trade, and Growth: Italy 1861–2011. Quaderni di storia economica (Economic History Working Papers) 10, Bank of Italy, Economic Research and International Relations Area.

Diamond, J. (1997). *Guns, Germs and Steel: The Fate of Human Societies*. W.W. Norton, New York.

Djankov, S., Montalvo, J.G., and Reynal-Querol, M. (2006). Does foreign aid help? *Cato Journal*, 26(1): 1–28.

Dollar, D. (1992). Outward-oriented developing economies really do grow more rapidly: evidence from 95 LDCs, 1976–1985. *Economic Development and Cultural Change*, 40(3): 523–44.

Dornbush, R. and Edwards, S. (1989). Economic Populism Paradigm. NBER Working Paper No. 2986. Cambridge, Mass.

Dubrovsky, S. (1956). *Peasants' Movement in Russia in the 1905-07 Revolution*. Publishing House of the Academy of Sciences of the USSR, Moscow. In Russian: Дубровский С. М. Крестьянское движение в революции 1905–1907 гг. М.: изд. АН СССР, 1956.167 с.

Durant, W. (1980). *Caesar and Christ (The Story of Civilization. Vol. 3)*. Simon Schuster, New York.

Easterly, W. (1999). The lost decades: explaining developing countries stagnation 1980–1998. *Journal of Economic Growth*, 6(2): 135–157.

Easterly, W. (2001). *The Elusive Quest for Growth: Economists' Adventures and Misadventures in the Tropics*. MIT Press, Cambridge.

Easterly, W. and Fisher, S. 1995. The Soviet economic decline. *The World Bank Economic Review*, 9(3): 341–71.

EBRD (2005). *Transition Report 2005*. EBRD, London.

References

Eichengreen, B. and Sachs, J. (1985). Exchange rates and economic recovery in the 1930s. *Journal of Economic History*, 45: 925–46.

Eichengreen, B. and Gupta, P. (2012). The Real Exchange Rate and Export Growth: Are Services Different? MPRA Paper 43358, University Library of Munich, Germany.

Eisner, M. (2003). Long-term historical trends in violent crime. *Crime and Justice*, 30: 83–142.

Faltsman V. (1985). *Proizvodstvenniye Moschnosty. (Production Facilities)—Voprosy Economiki*, 1985, No. 3. In Russian: Фальцман В. Производственные мощности.—*Вопросы экономики*, 1985, № 3.

Faye, M.L., McArthur, J.W., Sachs, J. and Snow, T. (2004). The challenges facing landlocked developing countries, *Journal of Human Development*, 5(1): 31–68.

Feldman, G.A. (1964). On the theory of growth rates of national income. Translated in: N. Spulber, (ed.), *Foundations of Soviet Strategy for Economic Growth*. Indiana University Press, Bloomington.

Feinstein, C. H. (1981), Capital accumulation and the Industrial Revolution. In: *The Economic History of Britain Since 1700*, vol. 1, R. Floud and D. N. McCloskey (eds), Cambridge University Press, Cambridge, 1st edition, pp. 128–42.

Feldstein, M. and Horioka, C. (1980). Domestic saving and international capital Flows. *Economic Journal*, 90: 314–29. <http://www.jstor.org/stable/2231790?origin=crossref> [Accessed 30 September 2013].

Findlay, R. (2009). The Trade-Development Nexus in Theory and History. UNU-WIDER Annual Lecture, No. 13, October, 2009. <http://www.wider.unu.edu/publications/annual-lectures/en_GB/AL13/_print/> [Accessed 30 September 2013].

Fourie, J. and von Fintel, D. (2009). A History With Evidence: Income inequality in the Dutch Cape Colony. Department of Economics, Stellenbosch University, and Department of Economic and Social History, Utrecht University. Working Paper No. 184.

Frenkel, R. and Rapetti, M. (2008). Five years of competitive and stable real exchange rate in Argentina, 2002–2007. *International Review of Applied Economics*, 22(2): 215–26.

Galor, O. (1998). Economic Growth in the Very Long-Run. In: *New Palgrave Dictionary of Economics*—2nd edition, S. Duraluf and L. Blume, (eds), Palgrave, New York.

Galor, O. and Weil, D. (2000). Population, technology, and growth: from malthusian stagnation to the demographic transition and beyond. *American Economic Review*, 90(4): 806–28.

Gerschenkron, A. (1962). *Economic Backwardness in Historical Perspective, A Book of Essays*. Belknap Press of Harvard University Press, Cambridge MA.

Ghosh, J. (2007). Macroeconomic and Growth Policies. Background Note. UN DESA, New York, <http://www.esa.un.org/techcoop/documents/PN_MacroBackgroundNote.pdf> [Accessed 30 September 2103].

Gibbs, M. (2007). Trade Policy. Background Note. UN DESA, New York <http://www.esa.un.org/techcoop/documents/PN_TradePolicyNote.pdf> [Accessed 30 September 2013].

Gilboy, G.J. (2004). The myth behind China's miracle. *Foreign Affairs*, 83(4): 33–48.

Goldstein, M. and Lardy, N.R. (2009). *The Future of China's Exchange Rate Policy*. Policy Analyses in International Economics 87. Peterson Institute for International Economics, Washington DC.

Goldstone, J.A. (2007). Unraveling the mystery of economic growth. A review of Gregory Clark's 'A Farewell to Alms: A Brief Economic History of the World'. Princeton and Oxford: Princeton University Press. September, 2007. *World Economics*, 8(3), 207–25.

Goldstone, J.A. (2009). Unpublished comments on Popov, V. Why the west became rich before China and why China has been catching up with the West since 1949: Another Explanation of the 'Great Divergence' and 'Great Convergence' Stories. NES/CEFIR Working Paper No. 132, October 2009.

Gomulka, S. (1977). Slowdown in Soviet industrial growth, 1947–1985 reconsidered. *European Economic Review*, 10(1): 37–49.

Gottschalk, R. (2012). Innovative Development Finance: The Latin American Experience. UN-DESA Background Paper, 2012.

Gupta, B. and Ma, D. (2010). Europe in an Asian mirror: the great divergence. In: *The Cambridge Economic History of Modern Europe*, S. Broadberry and K. O'Rourke, (eds), Cambridge University Press, Cambridge, pp. 264–85.

Guriev, S. and Ickes, B. (2000). Microeconomic Aspects of Economic Growth in Eastern Europe and the Former Soviet Union, 1950–2000. Working Paper No. 348, November 2000, William Davidson Institute at the University of Michigan, <http://www.wdi.umich.edu/files/publications/workingpapers/wp348.pdf> [Accessed 30 September 2103].

Hahn, C. H. and Kim, J. (2000). Sources of East Asian Growth: Some Evidence from Cross- country Studies. A paper prepared for the Global Research Project 'Explaining Growth'. GDN, 2000. <http://www.depot.gdnet.org/gdnshare/pdf/300_Hahn-kim.pdf> [Accessed 30 September 2013].

Hausmann, R., Hwang, J., and Rodrik, D. (2006). What You Export Matters. NBER Working Paper, January 2006.

Heybey, B. and Murrell, P. (1999). The relationship between economic growth and the speed of liberalization during transition. *Journal of Policy Reform*, 3(2): 121–37.

Hellman, J., Jones, G., and Kaufmann, D. (2000) How profitable is buying the state officials in transition economies? *Transition: The Newsletter About Reforming Economies*, 11(April): 8–11.

Holmes, S. (1997). What Russia teaches us now. *The American Prospect*, No. 33: 30–39.

Huang, Y. and Khanna, T. (2003). Can India overtake China? *Foreign Policy*, 82(4): 74–81.

Hutton, W. (2007). *The Writing on the Wall: China and the West in the 21st Century*. Little, Brown, London.

Iacopetta, M. (2004). Dissemination of technology in market and planned economies. *Contributions to Macroeconomics*, 4: (1) Article 2 (<http://www.bepress.com/bejm/contributions/vol4/iss1/art2> [Accessed 30 September 2013]).

Ickes, B. and Ryterman, R. (1997). Entry Without Exit: Economic Selection Under Socialism. Department of Economics. The Pennsylvania State University. Mimeo.

References

Inglehart, R. and Christian Welzel (2005). *Modernization, Cultural Change, and Democracy: The Human Development Sequence*. Cambridge University Press, Cambridge Mass.

Intriligator, M.D. (1998). Democracy in reforming collapsed communist economies: blessing or curse? *Contemporary Economic Policy*, 16(2): 241–46.

Islam, R. and Montenegro, C.E. (2002). What Determines the Quality of Institutions? Policy Research Working Paper No. 2764. World Bank, January 2002.

Jomo, K.S. (1997). *Southeast Asia's Misunderstood Miracle: Industrial Policy and Economic Development in Thailand, Malaysia and Indonesia* (with others). Westview, Boulder.

Jomo, K.S. (1998). Economic Diversification and Primary Commodity Processing in the Second-tier Southeast Asian Newly Industrializing Countries (with Michael Rock). UNCTAD Discussion Paper No. 136, Geneva, June 1998.

Jomo, K.S. (2013). The best approach to economic development is pragmatism. In: *22 Ideas to Fix the World Conversations with the World's Foremost Thinkers*, P. Dutkiewicz and R. Sakwa (eds), New York University Press, New York.

Karamurzov, R. and Friedman, L. (2011a). Карамурзов Р.Б., Л.А. Фридман. Проблемы международных экономических сопоставлений (о некоторых спорных вопросах и расчетах).—*Россия XXI*, 2011, №3, с. 54–85.

Karamurzov, R. and Friedman, L. (2011b). Карамурзов Р.Б., Л.А. Фридман. Проблемы международных экономических сопоставлений (Китай, Россия и другие страны в геоэкономической картине мира).—*Россия XXI*, 2011, №4, с. 20–57.

Kaufmann, D., Kraay, A., and Mastruzzi, M. (2010). The Worldwide Governance Indicators: A Summary of Methodology, Data and Analytical Issues. World Bank Policy Research, Working paper 5430, The World Bank Development Research Group Macroeconomics and Growth Team, Washington, September 2010 <https://openknowledge.worldbank.org/bitstream/handle/10986/3913/WPS5430.pdf?sequence=12010> [Accessed 30 September 2013].

Khan, M.H. (2007). Governance, Economic Growth and Development since the 1960s. DESA Working Paper No. 54, August 2007. <http://www.un.org/esa/desa/papers/2007/wp54_2007.pdf> [Accessed 30 September 2013].

Khruschev, N. and Nixon, R. (1959). The Kitchen Debate, 1959, U.S. Embassy, Moscow, Soviet Union (<http://www.teachingamericanhistory.org/library/index.asp?document=176> [Accessed 30 September 2013]).

Kim, D.H. and Lin, S-C. (2009). Trade and growth at different stages of economic development. *Journal of Development Studies*, 45(8): 1211–24.

King, L., Stuckler, D., and McKee, M. (2009). Mass privatisation and the post-communist mortality crisis: a cross-national analysis. *The Lancet*. 373(9661): 399–407.

Klyamkyn, I. (1987). Which street leads to the temple?—*Noviy Mir*, 1987, No.11. In Russian: И. Клямкин. Какая улица ведет к храму?—*Новый мир*, 1987, № 11, с. 150–188.

Kolodko, G.W. (2004) *From Shock to Therapy. Political Economy of Postsocialist Transformation*. Oxford University Press for UNU-WIDER: New York.

Kosterina, A. (2007). Modelling of Non-optimal Investment Resources Usage and Consequent Output Decline in the Soviet Economy. New Economic School, Moscow, MA thesis.

Krueger, G. and Ciolko, M. (1998). Note on initial conditions and liberalization during transition. *Journal of Comparative Economics*, 26(4): 618–34.

Krugman, P. (1994). The myth of Asia's miracle. *Foreign Affairs*, 73(6): 62–78.

Krugman, P. (2009). Finance mythbusting, third world edition. November 10, 2009. Paul Krugman's blog: <http://www.krugman.blogs.nytimes.com/2009/11/09/finance-mythbusting-third-world-edition/> [Accessed 30 September 2013].

Kuznets, S. (1966). *Modern Economic Growth: Rate, Structure and Spread*. Yale University Press, New Haven.

Landes, D. (1998). *Wealth and Poverty of Nations. Why Are Some So Rich and Others So Poor?* W.W. Norton, New York.

Leontief, W. (1974). Sails and rudders, ship of state. In: *Capitalism, the Moving Target*, L. Silk (ed.), Quadrangle Books, New York, pp. 101–104.

Lewis, W.A. (1954). Economic development with unlimited supplies of labour. *The Manchester School*, 22(2): 139–91.

Litvak, B.G. (1967). *A Statistical Study of the Peasant Movement in Russia in the 19th Century*. Nauka Publishers, Moscow. In Russian: Опыт статистического изучения крестьянского движения в России XIX века. М., Наука, 1967, таблица 1. Opyt statisticheskogo izucheniia krestianskogo dvizheniia v Rossii XIX v. Moskva, Nauka.

Loayza, N., Schmidt-Hebbel, K., and Servén, L. (2000). What drives private saving across the world?' *The Review of Economics and Statistics*, MIT Press, vol. 82(2), pp. 165–81.

Lu, A. (1999). *China and the Global Economy Since 1840*. St. Martin's Press, New York.

Lu, K. (2012). The Chongqing model worked. *Foreign Policy*, August 8, 2012 <http://www.foreignpolicy.com/articles/2012/08/08/the_chongqing_model_worked?page=full> [Accessed 30 September 2013].

Maddison, A. (1992). A long run perspective in savings. *Scandinavian Journal of Economics*, 25(2): 649–98.

Maddison, A. (1995). *Monitoring the World Economy*. OECD, Paris.

Maddison, A. (1998). *Chinese Economic Performance in the Long-Run*. OECD, Paris.

Maddison, A. (2003). *The World Economy: Historical Statistics*, OECD, Paris.

Maddison, A. (2005). Explanatory Background Note on Historical Statistics. <http://www.ggdc.net/MADDISON/Historical_Statistics/BackgroundHistoricalStatistics_03-2010.pdf> [Accessed 30 September 2013].

Maddison, A. (2008). Statistics on World Population, GDP and Per Capita GDP, 1–2006 AD <http://www.ggdc.net/maddison/Historical_Statistics/horizontal-file_09-2008.xls> [Accessed 30 September 2013].

Maddison, A. (2010). Statistics on World Population, GDP and Per Capita GDP, 1–2008 AD <http://www.ggdc.net/MADDISON/oriindex.htm> [Accessed 30 September 2013].

Malafeev, A.N. (1964). *The History of Price Formation in the USSR 1917–63*. Mysl' Publishers, Moscow. In Russian: Малафеев А. Н. История ценообразования в СССР. 1917–1963 гг. Москва, Мысль.

Marx, K. (1843). *Contribution to the Critique of Hegel's Philosophy of Right*. In: *Marx-Engels Reader*, R. Tucker (ed.). Oxford University Press, London.

Mayer, J. and Wood, A. (2001). South Asia's exports in a comparative perspective. *Oxford Development Studies*, 29(1): 5–29.

Mel'yantsev, V. (2006). *East and West in the Second Millennium*. Moscow University Publisher, Moscow. In Russian: Мельянцев, В. А. Восток и Запад во втором тысячелетии: экономика, история и современность.— Москва, 1996—Изд-во Московского университета.

References

Milanovic, B. (2012). Does economic inequality set limits to EU expansion? Conference on Sovereign Insolvency, Opatija, November 2012.

Milanovic, B. (2013). All the Ginis database- <http://www.econ.worldbank.org/WBSITE/EXTERNAL/EXTDEC/EXTRESEARCH/0,contentMDK:22301380~pagePK:64214825~piPK:64214943~theSitePK:469382,00.html> [Accessed 30 September 2013].

Milanovic, B., Lindert, P.H., and Williamson, J.G. (2007). Measuring Ancient Inequality, World Bank Policy Research Working Paper; No. WPS 4412. (Published as: Pre-industrial inequality. *The Economic Journal*, 121(March): 255–72.)

Mironov, B.N. (1985). In search of hidden information: some issues in the socio-economic history of Russia in the eighteenth and nineteenth centuries. *Social Science History*, 9(4): 339–59.

Mironov, B.N. (2000). *The Social History of Imperial Russia, 1700–1917*. Westview Press, Boulder, vol. 2.

Modalsli, J. (2013). Inequality and Growth in the very Long Run: Inferring Inequality from Data on Social Groups. Discussion Papers No. 734. Statistics Norway Research Department, February 2013.

Mokyr, J. (2002). *The Gifts of Athena: Historical Origins of the Knowledge Economy*. Princeton University Press, Princeton.

Montes, M. and Popov, V. (2011). Bridging the gap: a new world economic order for development. In: *Aftermath. New Global Economic Order*, C. Calhoun and G. Derlyugian (ed.). NYU Press, New York.

Montes, M.F. (1997). Viet Nam: Transition as a Socialist Project in East Asia UNU-WIDER. Working Paper No. 136. June 1997.

Morris, I. (2013). *The Measure of Civilization. How Social Development Decides the Fate of Nations*. Princeton University Press, Princeton and Oxford.

Murphy, K.M., Shleifer, A., and Vishny, R.W. (1989). Industrialization and the big push. *The Journal of Political Economy*, 97: 1003–26.

Murphy, K.M., Shleifer, A., and Vishny, R.W. (1992). The transition to a market economy: pitfalls of partial reform. *Quarterly Journal of Economics*, 107(3): 889–906.

Narkhoz (Narodnoye Khosyaistvo SSSR), various years, Goskomstat.

Naughton, B. (1997) Economic reform in China. Macroeconomic and overall performance. In: *The System Transformation of the Transition Economies: Europe, Asia and North Korea*, D. Lee (ed.), Yonsei University Press, Seoul.

Nayyar, D. (2006). India's unfinished journey. Transforming growth into development. *Modern Asian Studies*, 40(3): 797–832.

Needham, J. (1954–2008). *Science and Civilisation in China*. Vol. 1–7, 1954–2008. (<http://www.en.wikipedia.org/wiki/Science_and_Civilisation_in_China> [Accessed 30 September 2013]).

New Developmentalism (2010). Ten Theses on New Developmentalism. São Paulo School of Economics of Getulio Vargas Foundation. Structuralist Development Macroeconomics Center, São Paulo, September 29, 2010 <http://www.tenthesesonnewdevelopmentalism.org/> [Accessed 30 September 2013].

NDS (2008). National Development Strategies. Policy Notes. UN, DESA, Washington, <https://unp.un.org/details.aspx?pid=17687> [Accessed 30 September 2013].

Nolan, P. (1995). *China's Rise, Russia's Fall: Politics, Economics and Planning in Transition from Stalinism*. St. Martin's Press, New York.

Nureyev, R. (1993). Asian mode of production as an economic system. In: *The Phenomenon of Oriental Despotism: Structure of Management and Power*. Moscow, Nauka Publishers, pp. 62–87. In Russian: Нуреев Р.М. АЗИАТСКИЙ СПОСОБ ПРОИЗВОДСТВА КАК ЭКОНОМИЧЕСКАЯ СИСТЕМА.—«Феномен восточного деспотизма: структура управления и власти», М.: Наука, 1993 год,с. 62–87.

Ocampo, J.A. (2013). The new order is being born, but the old order is still strong. In: *22 Ideas to Fix the World Conversations with the World's Foremost Thinkers*, P. Dutkiewicz and R. Sakwa (ed.), New York University Press, New York.

Ocampo, J.A., Jomo K.S., and Rob Vos (2007). Explaining growth divergences. In: *Growth Divergences. Explaining Differences in Economic Performance*, J.A. Ocampo (ed.), Orient Longman, Hyderabad.

Ofer, G. (1987). Soviet economic growth: 1928–85. *Journal of Economic Literature*, 25(4): 1767–833.

Ortiz, I. (2007). Social Policy Notes. UN DESA, New York. <http://www.esa.un.org/techcoop/documents/PN_SocialPolicyNote.pdf> [Accessed 30 September 2013].

Özyurt, S. (2013). Currency undervaluation and economic rebalancing towards services: Is China an exception? *China &World Economy*, 21(1): 47–63.

Peerenboom, R. (2007). *China Modernizes. Threat to the West or Model for the Rest?* Oxford University Press, London.

Pei, M. (2006). *China's Trapped Transition: The Limits of Developmental Autocracy*. Harvard University Press, Cambridge Mass.

People's Web (2003). Today in History: Mao Zedong Said: I Did 2 Things in My Life. 15 June 2003 (<http://www.www.people.com.cn/GB/tupian/1097/1914967.html> [Accessed 30 Septemeber 2013]). In Chinese.

Peterson, G. (1994). State literacy ideologies and the transformation of rural China. *The Australian Journal of Chinese Affairs*, 32: 95–120.

Phillips, K. (2002). *Wealth and Democracy: A Political History of the American Rich*. Broadway Books, New York.

Polterovich, V. (2001). Transplantation of economic institutions. *Economics of Contemporary Russia*, №3, (15) pp. 24–50. In Russian: [PDF, 303 К] Полтерович В.М. Трансплантация экономических институтов//*Экономическая наука современной России*. 2001. № 3 (15), с. 24–50.

Polterovich, V. and Popov, V. (2004) Accumulation of foreign exchange reserves and long term economic growth. In: *Slavic Eurasia's Integration into the World Economy*, S. Tabata and A. Iwashita (eds) Slavic Research Center, Hokkaido University, Sapporo (<http://www.www.nes.ru/%7Evpopov/documents/EXCHANGE%20RATE-GrowthDEC2002withcharts.pdf> [Accessed 30 September 2013]).

Polterovich, V. and Popov, V. (2005). Appropriate Economic Policies at Different Stages of Development. NES, 2005 <http://www.nes.ru/english/research/pdf/2005/PopovPolterovich.pdf> [Accessed 30 September 2013].

Polterovich, V. and Popov, V. (2006). Stages of Development, Economic Policies and New World Economic Order. Paper presented at the Seventh Annual Global Development Conference in St. Petersburg, Russia. January 2006. (<http://www.http-server.carleton.

ca/~vpopov/documents/NewWorldEconomicOrder.pdf> [Accessed 30 September 2013]).

Polterovich, V. and Popov, V. (2007). Democratization, quality of institutions and economic growth. In: *Political Institutions and Development. Failed Expectations and Renewed Hopes*, N. Dinello and V. Popov (ed.), Edward Elgar Publishing, Cheltenham.

Polterovich, V., Popov, V., and Tonis, A. (2007). Resource Abundance, Political Corruption, and Instability of Democracy. NES Working Paper No. WP2007/73 (<http://www.nes.ru/russian/research/pdf/2007/PolterPopovTonisIns.pdf> [Accessed 30 September 2013]).

Polterovich, V., Popov, V. and Tonis, A. (2008). Mechanisms of Resource Curse, Economic Policy and Growth. NES Working Paper No. WP/2008/082 (http://www.nes.ru/english/research/pdf/2008/Polterivich_Popov.pdf [Accessed 30 September 2103]).

Pomeranz, K. (2000). *The Great Divergence: Europe, China, and the Making of the Modern World Economy*. Princeton University Press, Princeton.

Pomeranz, K. (2008). Chinese development in long-run perspective. *Proceedings of the American Philosophical Society*, 152(1): 83–100.

Popov, V. (2000). Shock therapy versus gradualism: the end of the debate (explaining the magnitude of the transformational recession). *Comparative Economic Studies*, 42(1): 1–57 (<http://www.nes.ru/%7Evpopov/documents/TR-REC-full.pdf> [Accessed 30 September 2013]).

Popov, V. (2001). Reform strategies and economic performance of Russia's regions. *World Development*, 29(5): 865–86.

Popov, V. (2007a). China's rise, Russia's fall: Medium term perspective. *História e Economia Revista Interdisciplinar*, 3(1–2): 14–38. <http://www.bbs.edu.br/apresentacaoprofessor/01%20Vladimir%20Popov%20-%20China's%20Rise%20in%20the%20Medium%20Term%20Perspective.pdf [Accessed 30 September 2013]>.

Popov, V. (2007b). Shock therapy versus gradualism reconsidered: lessons from transition economies after 15 years of reforms. *Comparative Economic Studies*, 49(1): 1–31 (<http://www.nes.ru/%7Evpopov/documents/Shock%20vs%20grad%20reconsidered%20-15%20years%20after%20-article.pdf> [Accessed 30 September 2013]).

Popov, V. (2007c). Life cycle of the centrally planned economy: Why Soviet growth rates peaked in the 1950s. In: *Transition and Beyond*, S. Estrin, G.W. Kolodko, and M. Uvalic, (eds) Palgrave Macmillan, Basingstoke.

Popov, V. (2007d). Russia redux. *New Left Review*, 44(March–April): 37–44.

Popov, V. (2008). Lessons from the Transition Economies. Putting the Success Stories of the Postcommunist World into a Broader Perspective. UNU/WIDER Research Paper No. 2009/15.

Popov, V. (2009). Why the West Became Rich before China and Why China Has Been Catching Up with the West since 1949: Another Explanation of the 'Great Divergence' and 'Great Convergence' Stories. NES/CEFIR Working Paper No. 132, October 2009.

Popov, V. (2010a). The Long Road to Normalcy. Where Russia Now Stands. Working Paper No. 2010/13. February 2010.

Popov, V. (2010b). Global Imbalances: An Unconventional View. *IDEAs*, October 19. <http://www.networkideas.org/featart/oct2010/Global_Imbalances.pdf> [Accessed 30 September 2013].

Popov, V. (2010–11). Mortality Crisis in Russia Revisited: Evidence from Cross-Regional Comparison. MPRA Paper No. 21311, March 2010; CEFIR and NES Working Paper No. 157, January 2011.

Popov, V. (2011a). Do We Need to Protect Intellectual Property Rights? CEFIR and NES Working Paper, No. 161. February 2011.

Popov, V. (2011b). Developing New Measurements of State Institutional Capacity. PONARS Eurasia Policy Memo, No. 158, May 2011. <http://www.ponarseurasia.org/sites/default/files/policy-memos-pdf/pepm_158.pdf> [Accessed 30 September 2013].

Popov, V. (2011c). To devaluate or not to devalue? How East European countries responded to the outflow of capital in 1997–99 and in 2008–09. *Acta Oeconomica*, 61(3): 255–79.

Popov, V. and Shmelev, N. (1989). At the crossroads. So was there the alternative in 1929? *Studencheskiy Meridian*, No 1, 2 (pp. 25–61), 2 (pp. 13–66). In Russian: Попов В., Шмелев Н. На развилке дорог: Так была ли альтернатива в 1929 году?//Студенческий меридиан. 1989. №1 (с. 2–-61), 2 (с. 13–66).

Prasad, E., Rajan, R., and Subramanian, A. (2006). Foreign Capital and Economic Growth. Research Department, IMF, August 30.

Preobrazhensky, E. (1926). *The New Economics*. Oxford, Clarendon Press [1965].

Radelet, S. and Sachs, J. (1997). Asia's reemergence. *Foreign Affairs*, 76(6): 44–59.

Ramo, J. (2004). *The Beijing Consensus*. The Foreign Policy Centre, London.

Reddy, S. G., (2013), 'Randomise this! On poor economics,' *Review of Agrarian Studies*, 2(2): available at <http://www.ras.org.in/randomise_this_on_poor_economics> [Accessed 30 September 2013].

Reinert, E.S. (2007). *How Rich Countries Got Rich . . . And Why Poor Countries Stay Poor*. Constable, London.

Ridha, N., Plane, P., and Sekkat, K. (2011). Exchange Rate Undervaluation and Manufactured Exports: A Deliberate Strategy? Centre d'Etudes and de Recherches sur le Development Internationale (CERDI), Etudes et Documents, E 2011.25 Document de travail de la série Etudes et Documents E 2011.25. July 2011.

Rodriguez, F. (2007). Openness and growth: What have we learned? In: *Growth Divergences. Explaining Differences in Economic Performance*, J.A. Ocampo, Jomo K.S., and R. Vos. Orient Longman, Hyderabad.

Rodriguez, F. and Rodrik, D. (1999). Trade and Economic Growth: A Skeptic's Guide to the Cross-National Evidence. CEPR Discussion Paper No. 2143.

Rodrik, D. (2004a). 'Industrial Policy for the Twenty-First Century' Working Paper Series rwp04-047, Harvard University, John F. Kennedy School of Government <http://myweb.rollins.edu/tlairson/pek/rodrikindpolicy.pdf>

Rodrik, D. (2004b). Institutions and Economic Performance - Getting Institutions Right, CESifo DICE Report, Ifo Institute for Economic Research at the University of Munich, vol. 2(2), pp. 10–15.

Rodrik, D. (2006a). The social cost of foreign exchange reserves. *International Economic Journal*, 20(3): 253–66.

Rodrik, D. (2006b). What's So Special About China's Exports? Working Paper Series rwp06-001, Harvard University, John F. Kennedy School of Government. January 2006.

Rodrik, D. (2008). The Real Exchange Rate and Economic Growth, Brookings Papers on Economic Activity, 2008:2.

Rodrik, D. (2012). Doing Development Better. Project Syndicate, 14 May 2012. <http://www.project-syndicate.org/commentary/doing-development-better> [Accessed 30 September 2013].

Rodrik, D., Subramanian, A., and Trebbi, F. (2002). Institutions Rule: The Primacy of Institutions over Geography and Integration in Economic Development. October 2002 (<http://www.imf.org/external/pubs/ft/wp/2002/wp02189.pdf> [Accessed September 2013]).

Rodrik, D., Hausmann, R., and Velasco, A. (2005). Growth Diagnostics. 2005. (<http://www.hks.harvard.edu/fs/drodrik/Research%20papers/barcelonafinalmarch2005.pdf> [Accessed 30 Septemeber 2013]).

Rosenstein-Rodan, P.N. (1943). The problems of industrialisation of eastern and south-eastern Europe. *The Economic Journal*, 53(210/211): 202–11.

O'Rourke, K.H. and Williamson, J.G. (2002). From Malthus to Ohlin: Trade, Growth and Distribution Since 1500, NBER Working Papers No. 8955.

Sachs, J.D. (1989). Social Conflict and Populist Policies in Latin America. NBER Working Paper No. 2897. Cambridge, Mass.

Sachs, J.D. (1996). Resource Endowments and the Real Exchange Rate: A Comparison of Latin America and East Asia. Mimeo. Harvard Institute for International Development, Cambridge, Mass.

Sachs, J.D. (2003). Institutions matter, but not for everything. The role of geography and resource endowments in development shouldn't be underestimated. *Finance & Development*, 40(2): 38–41.

Sachs, J.D. and Warner, A.M. (1995). Natural Resource Abundance and Economic Growth. NBER Working Paper Series, Working Paper No. 5398. National Bureau of Economic Research, Cambridge, Mass.

Sachs, J.D. and Warner, A.M. (1997a). Natural Resource Abundance and Economic Growth. Revised version. Unpublished manuscript. Harvard Institute for International Development. Cambridge, Mass.

Sachs, J.D. and Warner, A.M. (1997b). Sources of slow growth in African economies. *Journal of African Economics*, 6(3): 335–80.

Sachs, J.D. and Warner, A.M. (1999). The big push, natural resource booms and growth. *Journal of Development Economics*, (59): 43–76.

Sachs, J.D. and Warner, A.M. (2001). Natural resources and economic development. The curse of natural resources. *European Economic Review*, 45(2001): 827–38.

Saito, O. (1996). Historical demography: achievements and prospects. *Population Studies*, 50(3): 537–53.

Saito, O. (2006). Pre-transition fertility in Asia: a comparative-historical approach. *Journal of International Economic Studies*, 20(2006): 1–17.

Saito, O. (2009). Income Growth and Inequality Over the Very Long Run: England, India and Japan Compared. Paper presented at The First International Symposium of Comparative Research on Major Regional Powers in Eurasia. July 10, 2009.

Schmidt-Hebbel, K. and Serven, L. (2000). Does income inequality raise aggregate saving? *Journal of Development Economics*, 61(2): 417–46.

Schneider, F. (2007). Shadow Economies and Corruption All Over the World: New Estimates for 145 Countries. *Economics*. Open access, open assessment e-journal, No. 20079 July 24, 2007.

Schroeder, G. (1995). Reflections on economic Sovietology. *Post-Soviet Affairs*, 11(3): 197–234.

Shandong (2009). Shandong Province data base [Shandong sheng shengqing ziliaoku]. <http://www.infobase.gov.cn/bin/mse.exe?seachword=&K=a&A=16&rec=42&run= 13 http://www.bbs.tiexue.net/post_1207004_1.html>.

Shleifer, A. and Treisman, D. (2004). A normal country. *Foreign Affairs*, 83(2): 20–38.

Shmelev, N. and Popov, V. (1989). *The Turning Point: Revitalizing the Soviet Economy*. New York, Doubleday.

Sng, T-H. and Moriguchi, C. (2012). Taxation and Public Goods Provision in China and Japan before 1850. Mimeo. May 18, 2012 (<https://editorialexpress.com/cgi-bin/conference/download.cgi?db_name=NASM2012&paper_id=751> [Accessed 30 September 2013]).

Sokoloff, K.L. and Engerman, S.L. (2000). History lessons: institutions, factor endowments, and paths of development in the new world. *The Journal of Economic Perspectives*, 14(3): 217–32.

Solow, R.M. (2007). 'Survival of the Richest'? Review of 'A Farewell to Alms: A Brief Economic History of the World' by Gregory Clark (Princeton University Press, Princeton). *New York Review of Books*, 54(18), November 22.

Soltow, L. (1989). *Distribution of Wealth and Income in the United States in 1798*. University of Pittsburg Press, Pittsburg, 1989.

Spiegel, S. (2007). Macroeconomic and Growth Policy. Policy Note. UN DESA, New York, <http://www.esa.un.org/techcoop/documents/PN_MacroGrowthPolicyNote. pdf> [Accessed 30 September 2013].

Spufford, F. (2010). *Red Plenty*. Faber and Faber Ltd, London.

Stalin, J. (1927). *Interview with Foreign Workers' Delegations. November 5, 1927*. Works, vol. 10, August–December, 1927. Foreign Languages Publishing House, Moscow, [1954].

Stalin, J.V. (1976). The tasks of economic executives. In: *Problems of Leninism*, J. V. Stalin, Foreign Languages Press, Peking, pp. 519–31. <http://www.marx2mao. com/Stalin/TEE31.html> [Accessed 30 September 2013].

Stiglitz, J. (1997). More Instruments and Broader Goals: Moving Toward the Post-Washington Consensus. WIDER Annual Lecture. WIDER/UNU, Helsinki.

Stiglitz, J. (2012). *The Price of Inequality: How Today's Divided Society Endangers our Future*. W.W. Norton & Co., New York.

Subramanian, A. (2011). *Eclipse: Living in the Shadow of China's Economic Dominance*. Peterson Institute for International Economics, Washington.

Taylor, A.M. (1996). International Capital Mobility in History: The Saving-Investment Relationship, NBER Working Paper, No. 5743.

Tetlock, P.E., Lebow, R.N., and Parker, G. (eds). *Unmaking of the West. 'What if?' Scenarios that Rewrite the World History*. The University of Michigan Press, Ann Arbour.

Toye, J. (1987). Development theory and experiences of development. Issues for the future. In: *Milestones and Turning Points in Development Thinking*, R. Jolly, Palgrave Macmillan, New York.

Toye, J. (2009). Development in an Interdependent World: Old Issues, New Directions? Background Paper for WESS 2010.

Turchin, P. (2005). *War and Peace and War: The Life Cycles of Imperial Nations*. Pi Press, New York.

Turchin, P. (2013). Return of the oppressed. *AEON*, 7 February 2013 (<http://www.aeonmagazine.com/living-together/peter-turchin-wealth-poverty/> [Accessed 30 September 2013]).

Turchin, P. and Nefedov, S. (2009). *Secular Cycles*. Princeton University Press, Princeton, NJ.

UNODC (2012). UNODC Homicide Statistics. <http://www.unodc.org/unodc/en/data-and-analysis/homicide.html> [Accessed 30 September 2013].

Valtukh, K. and Lavrovskyi B. (1986). 'Proizvodstvennyi Apparat Strany: Ispol'zovaniye i Rekonstruktsiya' (Production Facilities of a Country: Utilization and Reconstruction). *EKO*, 2: 17–32.

Wade, R. (2004). Is globalization reducing poverty and inequality? *World Development*, 32(4): 567–89.

Wen, G.J. (2008). Why was china trapped in an agrarian society—an economic geographical approach to the Needham puzzle. *Frontiers of Economics in China*, 6(4): 507–34.

WDI database (2010). World Bank, 2010.

Weitzman, M. (1970). Soviet postwar economic growth and capital-labor substitution. *American Economic Review*, 60(5): 676–92.

WHO (2004). WHO Health for All Database, 2004. <http://www.who.int/research/en/> [Accessed 30 September 2013].

Williamson, J.G. (2002). Winners and Losers over Two Centuries of Globalization. WIDER Annual Lecture 6. WIDER/UNU, Helsinki, November 2002.

Williamson, J.G. (2009). History Without Evidence: Latin American Inequality Since 1491. Georg-August-Universität Göttingen. Discussion Paper No. 3.

Wilkinson, R. and Pickett, K. (2010) *The Spirit Level. Why Greater Equality makes Societies Stronger*. Bloomsbury Press, New York.

WIPO (2009). World Intellectual Property Indicators. WIPO, Geneva.

Wong, R.B. (1997). *China Transformed: Historical Change and the Limits of the European Experience*. Cornell University Press, Ithaca.

World Bank (1996). *From Plan to Market. World Development Report*. Oxford University Press, New York.

World Bank (1997). *The State in A Changing World. World Development Report*. Oxford University Press, New York.

Wrigley, E.A. and Schofield, R.S. (1981). *The Population History of England, 1541–1871. A Reconstruction*. Edward Arnold, London.

Yang, D.L. (2006). Economic transformation and its political discontents in China: Authoritarianism, unequal growth, and the dilemmas of political development. *Annual Review of Political Science*, 9: 143–64.

Young, A. (1994). Lessons from the East Asian NICs: A contrarian view. *European Economic Review*, 38(4): 964–73.

Zakaria, F. The rise of illiberal democracies. *Foreign Affairs*, 76(6): 22–43.

Zayonchkovsky, P. (1968). *Abolition of Serfdom in Russia*. Prosvescheniye, Moscow. In Russian: Зайончковский П.А. (1963). Отмена крепостного права в России.—Москва, Просвещение.

Name Index

Name Index

Preobrazhensky, E. 120
Putin, Vladimir 158, 159

Radelet, S. 67
Rajan, R. 124
Ramo, J. 5
Reinhart, C. 131
Robinson, J. A. 14, 17, 18, 19
Rodrik, D. 19, 112, 117, 130, 163
Rosenstein-Rodan, P. N. 117, 120
Ryterman, R. 74

Sachs, J. 18, 67
Saito, O. 26
Sbracia, M. 129, 130
Schleifer, A. 155
Shleifer, A. 101, 120
Solow, R. M. 13–14
Soltow, L. 44

Spufford, F. 58
Stalin, Joseph 120, 121, 157, 161
Stiglitz, J. 54, 112
Subramanian, A. 124

Tolstoy, Leo 116
Treisman, D. 155
Turchin, P. 17, 44

Vegh, C. 131
Verdier, T. 19

Weitzman, M. 68
Wen, G. J. 16
Williamson, M. 53

Yang, D. L. 153

Zilibotti, F. 145

Subject Index